I0901044

LEGENDARY LOCALS

OF

FORT MYERS

FLORIDA

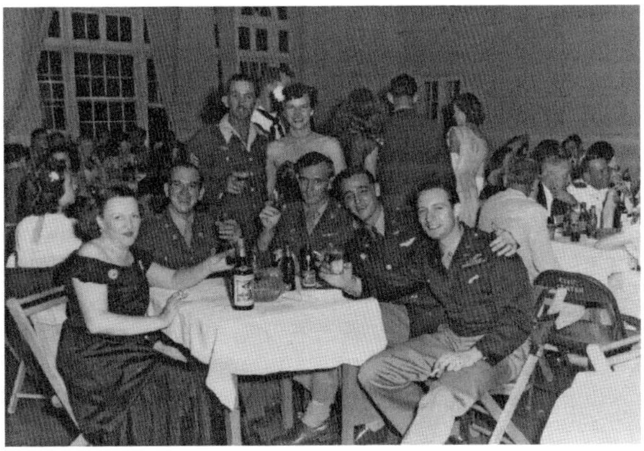

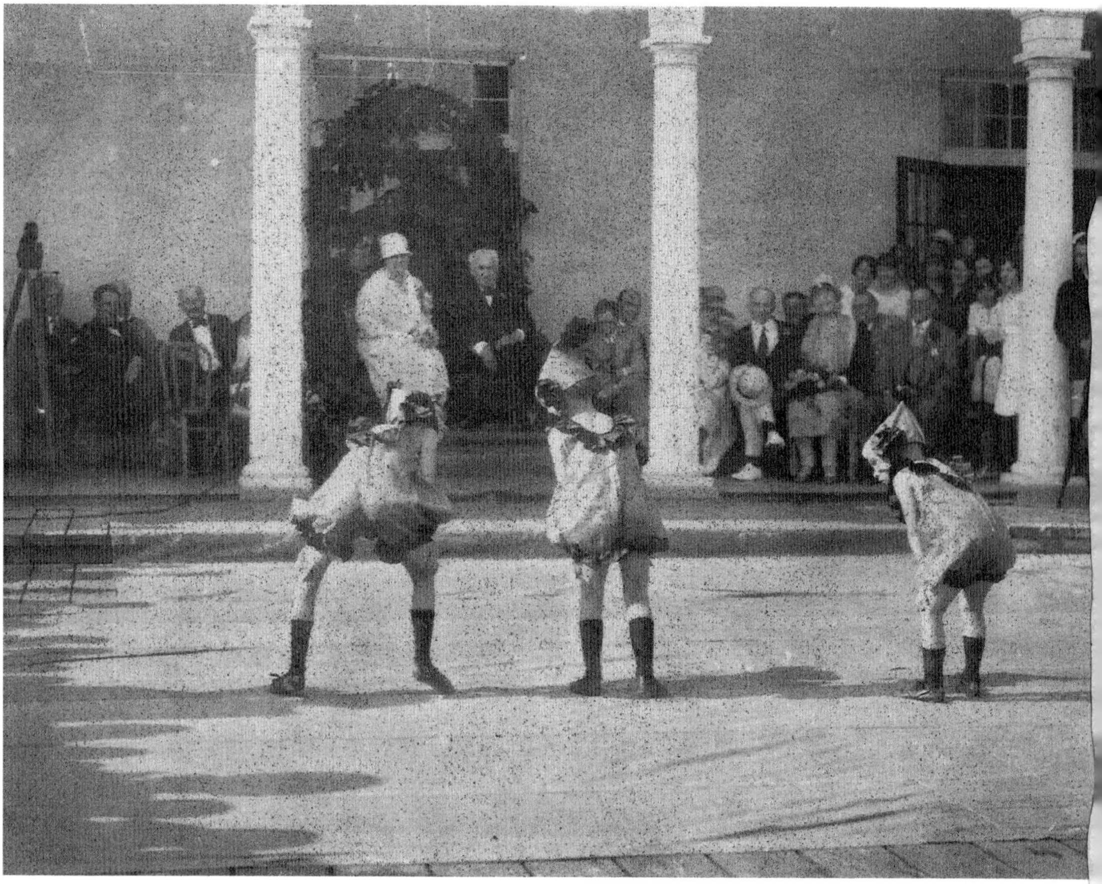

Page 1: Civic Center USO

Revelers gather at one of the many events held in the Civic Center's USO during the World War II years, when Buckingham Army Air Force Base and Page Field opened. This auditorium was part of the 1927 Moorish-style Pleasure Pier built on the downtown waterfront in 1927. In 1943, it was moved and rechristened the Hall of Fifty States. Countless servicemen fondly remembered Fort Myers. Many married local sweethearts or returned as tourists or seasonal residents, helping to propel the unprecedented post-World War II growth in the area. Seated are, left to right, Ruth and Bart Foley, Austin Evans, Harry Jennings, and Bill Gill; standing, Gus and Agnes Studstill. (Courtesy of AL.)

Page 2: Thomas A. and Mina Edison, Honored Residents

When local children performed for Thomas A. and Mina Edison and other distinguished guests, they could be sure of being captured on film, possibly for the newsreels. Such was the whirlwind of publicity and excitement that Fort Myers' most famous winter citizens brought with them from 1886 to 1931, the year the inventor died. This scene from around 1930 is the Pleasure Pier that extended over the Caloosahatchee River, where many celebrations, concerts, and public events took place. (Courtesy of SWFHS.)

LEGENDARY LOCALS

OF

FORT MYERS
FLORIDA

GERRI REAVES

LEGENDARY LOCALS

ISBN 978-1-4671-0018-2

Published by Legendary Locals, an imprint of Arcadia Publishing
Charleston, South Carolina

Printed in the United States of America

Library of Congress Control Number: 2011945287

For all general information, please contact Arcadia Publishing:
Telephone 843-853-2070
Fax 843-853-0044
E-mail sales@arcadiapublishing.com
For customer service and orders:
Toll-Free 1-888-313-2665

Visit us on the Internet at www.arcadiapublishing.com

Dedication

In memory of Sara Nell Hendry Gran

On the Cover: From left to right:

(TOP ROW) John Blalock, civil rights activist (Courtesy Mildred Blalock; see page 87), Billy Nalle, musician (Courtesy SWFHS; see page 49), Carolyn (Barden) Smith, aviatrix (Courtesy Rebecca Kinzie Holmes; see page 100), John Holzinger, educator (Courtesy Holzinger family; see page 93), Berne and Sidney Davis, community patrons (Courtesy SWFHS; see page 82).

(MIDDLE ROW) Marcus Jansen, artist (Courtesy author; see page 94), Mary Mildred (Hooker) Leffers, child model (Courtesy Jo Ann Beaumont; see page 37), Florence Fritz, mayor (Courtesy SWFHS; see page 28), Chief Billy Bowlegs, Seminole leader (Courtesy SAF; see page 38), Dr. Ella M. Piper, businesswoman and philanthropist (Courtesy SWFMH; see page 75).

(BOTTOM ROW) Julia (Allen) Hanson, civic leader and historian (Courtesy HFA; see page 91), Capt. Jack DeLysle, entrepreneur (Courtesy SWFHS; see page 60), Flossie Hill, pioneer businesswoman (Courtesy SWFHS; see page 117), Fort Myers baseball team (Courtesy SWFMH), Carol Newcomb-Jones, environmental activist (Courtesy author; see page 97).

CONTENTS

ACKNOWLEDGMENTS

Many people helped me get acquainted with the legendary locals who made Fort Myers a city I can't stop writing about. To anyone who contributed a photograph, "nominated" an individual for this project, or provided the kind of knowledge that only natives have, I am grateful.

Colleagues such as the late Sara Nell Hendry Gran, Doug Bartleson, Pete and Genevieve Bowen, Helen Farrell, and Pat Jungferman at the Southwest Florida Historical Society added immeasurably to my research. Special thanks to Ricki Howie for her discovery of aviatrix Carolyn Barden Smith.

Others deserving of appreciation are Yvonne Hill, Matt Johnson, and Harriet Winn-Smith. Eddie Howell and Cmdr. Kevin Boyd of American Legion Post 38 welcomed me to the Legion's fascinating history room.

Special thanks to those who shared materials from private archives: Woody Hanson, Alvin Lederer, Larry Wiggins, Paula Hendry, Margaret Garner, and Barbara Brown.

For their willingness to talk or correspond endlessly about the people and history of Fort Myers, I thank: Mildred Blalock, Charlie Powell, Donald Sawyer, Tom "Tinker" Stewart, Kathryn Wilbur, Suzanne Sutton, Jerry Haberle, Rebecca Kinzie Holmes, Carolyn Ford, Connie Holzinger, Greg Biolchini, Marjorie E. Wyatt, Pierre Thiffault, Laurence J. Lesh Jr., and Paula Lesh Baldwin.

The following people provided vital material or guided me to it: A.J. Bassett, Rae Ann Wessel, Cathy Hilley, Kevin McCarthy, Maureen Bashaw, Jared Beck, Larry Milberry, Dale Williams, Andy Tetlow, Jo Ann Beaumont, Lt. Jeffrey Bernice of the Fort Myers Police Department, Lydia Black, and Sue Bennett Grimes.

Many thanks to Arcadia editor Tiffany Frary for her speed-of-light responses, cheerful assistance, and expertise.

Many of the images in this volume appear courtesy of the Southwest Florida Historical Society (SWFHS), the Southwest Florida Museum of History (SWFMH), the American Legion Post 38 (AL), the State Archives of Florida (SAF), the Hanson Family Archives (HFA), and the Lee County Black History Society (LCBHS).

INTRODUCTION

Having completed an award-winning Utility and Streetscaping Improvements Project in January 2010, Fort Myers preserves its past and embraces its future. As always, the subtropical climate, the sand and sea, and the land's uncommon beauty lure new visitors and sustain its citizens. The City of Palms remains a pioneer city, albeit a modern one, with towering luxury condos and interstate highways, because it is imbued with a sense of possibility, of opportunity.

The city's origin lies in the establishment of Fort Harvie in 1841 during the Second Seminole War. Active for only several months, it was reactivated in 1850 and renamed Fort Myers when hostilities with the Seminoles erupted again. Gen. David E. Twiggs honored his daughter Marion's future husband, Col. Abraham C. Myers, when he rechristened the outpost "Myers." Curiously, Myers never saw the fort that bore his name.

The old fort site was largely in ruins when reactivated, and it took more than a year to erect sturdy buildings that didn't have palm-thatch roofs. With funds and a mandate from Washington, DC, an impressive fort emerged by the end of the 1850s. The fort's footprint evolved into the city of Fort Myers, with paths and boundaries foretelling today's streets. A large parade ground dominated the riverfront outpost, and a 1,000-foot railway pier terminated with a wharf, roughly marking the trajectory of today's Hendry Street, the center of the business district.

Capt. Francis A. Hendry, the "Father of Fort Myers," saw the fort in 1853, later writing that it was a "veritable oasis in the desert," and remarking on the state-of-the-art facilities. After the Seminole Wars concluded with Chief Billy Bowlegs departing from that very wharf to exile in western Indian Territory, the fort was inactive until late in the Civil War, when it became a Union outpost.

No sooner had the Civil War ended than settlers from around the globe wound their way to the fort, which offered ready accommodations and resources. Fort Myers' first families arrived, Manuel A. Gonzalez from Madrid, Spain, and Joseph Vivas, native of Belize, soon followed by the Powells and Clays. Gonzalez was familiar with the fort, having delivered mail and supplies up and down the southwest Florida coast since the 1850s.

An international group of settlers trickled in, among them Dr. William and Julia Allen Hanson and the Travers brothers from England, the Kinzie brothers from Germany, Carl Roberts from Sweden, as

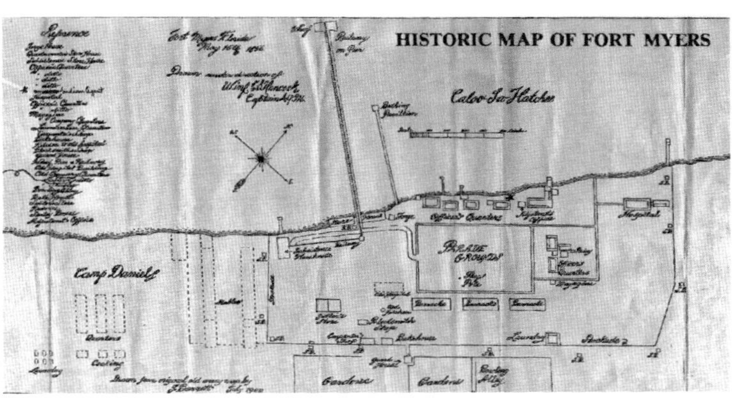

US Army's Fort Myers, 1856
Capt. Winfield Scott Hancock drew this map of the US Army's Fort Myers in 1856, a year after he was posted there. (Courtesy of SWFHS.)

well as citizens from across the United States. In August 1885, 45 men voted to incorporate the town, which soon had its own newspaper and celebrity winter homesteader, Thomas A. Edison.

The influential large Hendry clan established itself in almost every aspect of life—from business and politics to religion and public service—most significantly in what became one of the area's biggest industries, cattle. Immediately after the Civil War, Captain Hendry, along with other cattle barons such as William Towles and Jake Summerlin, made fortunes shipping cattle to Cuba from Punta Rassa, now the site of the Sanibel Harbor Resort.

Go-getter Harvie E. Heitman could not propel the town fast enough into the future with his never-ending building and boosterism. Wealthy and generous visitors, enchanted with the out-of-the-way river town, adopted it as a winter or permanent home; some, like Dr. Franklin Miles, even started a second career. Benefactors such as Ambrose and Tootie McGregor contributed immeasurably to the economic, social, and cultural life of Fort Myers.

Local women like mother and daughter entrepreneurs Mary Florence and Flossie Hill labored not only in the home, but ran businesses, championed education, and leveraged political influence. Through community organizations, women like Olive Stout and Julia Allen Hanson made sure that the town's cultural, intellectual, and spiritual lives were not left behind in the pursuit of economic development.

From the beginning, tourism flourished, driven in part by the discovery of tarpon fishing, along with fishing and agriculture. The arrival of the Atlantic Coast Line Railroad in 1904 put the young town in high gear. Fruit and fish packed in ice could now be shipped to northern markets and tourists could stream into town.

The 1910s boomed in Fort Myers chiefly due to the influx and influence of wealthy northern investors and developers such as John Morgan Dean and Peter Tonnelier. By the 1920s, the City of Palms vied with other Florida cities to be the premier tropical destination. Highly profitable agricultural and horticultural industries, particularly citrus, were showcased along with game-fishing in the Gulf and world-class golf courses.

The completion of the Tamiami Trail in 1928 made selling the city to motorists even easier. With the start of World War II, Fort Myers was forever changed by the establishment of two military bases, Buckingham Field and Page Field. The postwar population and economic boom lasted until the 1960s, when, like cities across the nation, Fort Myers experienced the social upheaval of desegregation and the decline of a vibrant downtown as the age of malls and sprawl took over. Now the revitalized downtown is restored to its classic boom-time 1920s appearance, with vintage brick streets and the predominance of a Mediterranean Revivalist architectural style.

The legendary locals who have peopled its past and shaped its future, be they celebrities, scoundrels, or saints, mirror the lives of us all. Those legends went about their lives having moments of insight, success, creativity, and despair. Some characters in this volume may not seem marked for the history books, but they are nevertheless extraordinary. They bring alive the texture of Fort Myers' past and present and remind us of the dignity of getting through a day or a difficulty, and of the value of service to others, to a cause, or even to the private imagination.

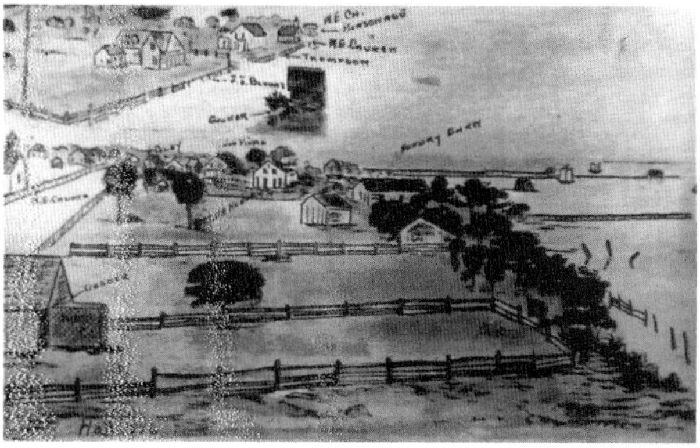

Fort Myers, 1886

The eastward view from the vicinity of today's Fowler Street shows some of the first riverfront homesteads, including those of Capt. Francis A. Hendry, Jehu J. Blount, and Joseph Vivas. The town's first religious institution, the Methodist Episcopal Church, is visible in the enlarged cut-out (upper center). (Courtesy of SWFHS.)

CHAPTER ONE

Pioneers

The intrepid people who took it upon themselves to build a town from the leftovers of a military outpost brought remarkable talent, endurance, and work ethic. What a miracle it must have seemed to Manuel S. Gonzalez, for example. He began by virtually camping out in fort ruins in 1866 as a boy and died in 1935 as the town reeled from the aftermath of the Hurricane of 1926, the collapse of the 1920s boom, and the Great Depression. Whether by boat, oxcart, or on horseback, pioneers arrived with willing hands. With Dr. William Hanson's medical skills, Mary Florence Hill's hotelier wizardry, Pink White's determination that black children would have a schoolhouse, and Harvie E. Heitman's unfailing business instincts, they had a lot going for them. They saw there was a job to do and got to it.

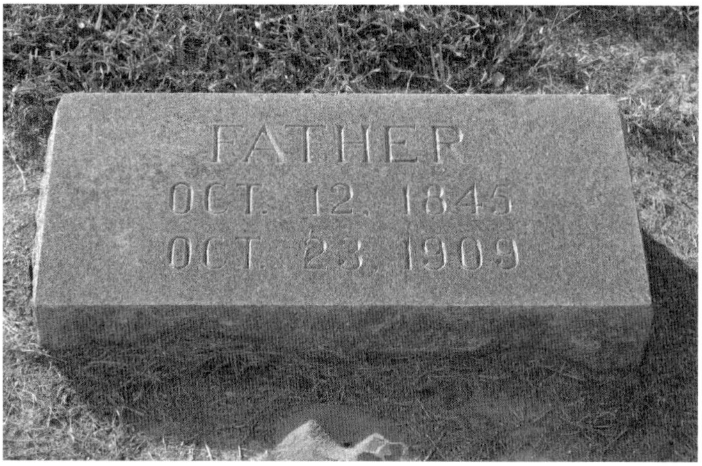

Joseph Vivas
The inscription "Father" marks Vivas' grave in the Fort Myers Cemetery. He and bride Christiana are among Fort Myers' very first settlers. They arrived on the shores of the abandoned US Army fort in 1866. A master carpenter and contractor, Vivas built the first bridges over Billy's Creek and Whiskey Creek, and a new wharf at the foot of Hendry Street. He died in 1909. (Photograph by the author.)

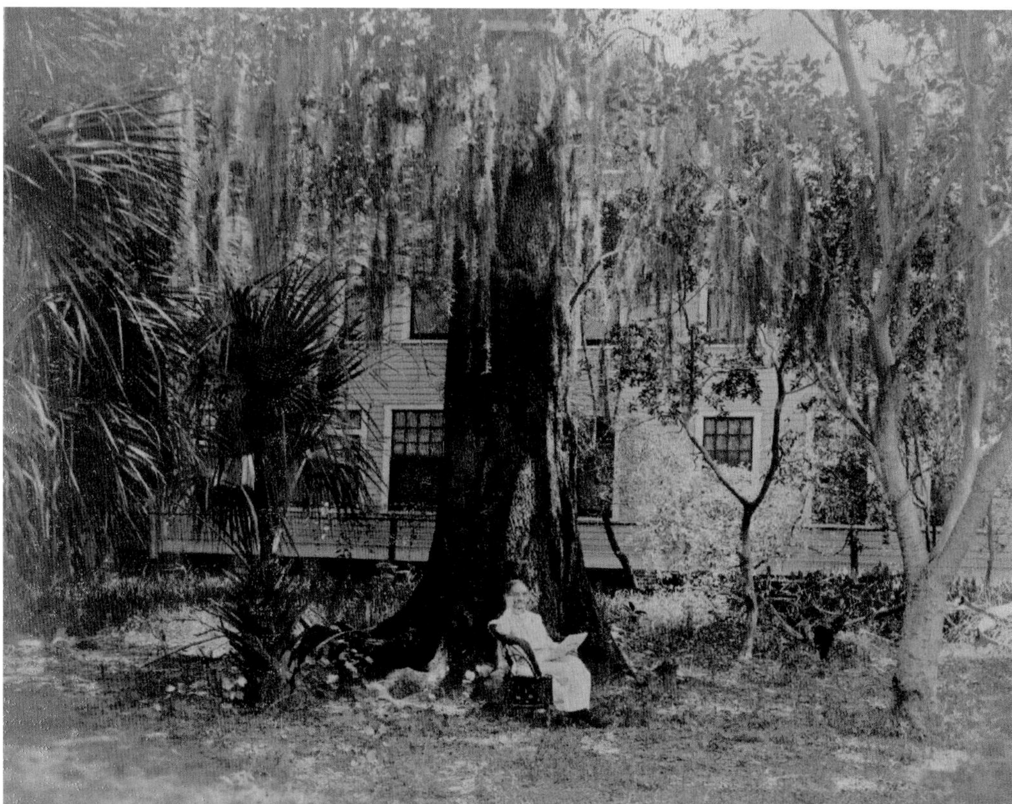

Christiana Stirrup Vivas
Fifteen-year-old Christiana Stirrup met and married Joseph Vivas in Key West in March 1866. The honeymooners sailed up the coast and set up housekeeping at the US Army's abandoned Fort Myers. With them were Manuel A. and Evalina Gonzalez and son, and John A. Weatherford, Evalina's brother. Stirrup was an orphan of English descent and a ward of the Gonzalezes. She died in 1930, not long after this photograph was taken, at her riverfront homestead. (Courtesy of SWFHS.)

Maj. James Evans

Evans is at the heart of one of Fort Myers' most puzzling real estate stories. In 1873, the native Virginian was given the title to 139.45 acres that encompassed the old US Army fort and all of future downtown Fort Myers for $174.32. However, only a few years after claiming the land, he gave away almost all of it. Evans had been in Florida as early as 1842 on a government survey crew. After surveying the Caloosahatchee region, he settled in Fort Myers in 1859 to grow tropical fruit and plants, planning to obtain the land through the Homestead Act of 1862. The outbreak of the Civil War intervened, however, and he returned to Virginia, subsequently serving in the Confederate Army and attaining the rank of major. Evans returned to Fort Myers in 1873 to find at least 10 other settlers squatting on his land. He followed through with the undisputed homestead claim, but deeded the interim settlers the land for little or nothing and platted the town to conform to the established property boundaries. Perhaps what mattered most to Evans was that Fort Myers was already a thriving community. The pioneer town embraced him, and he served the newly incorporated city in a variety of capacities, including seven years on the town council and eight years as county tax assessor. In 1878, he donated an acre of land for the first school, built at Second and Jackson Streets, where the Gwynne Institute stands today. In 1885, Evans also gave land for the Protestant Episcopal Church. He died in 1901. (Courtesy of SWFMH.)

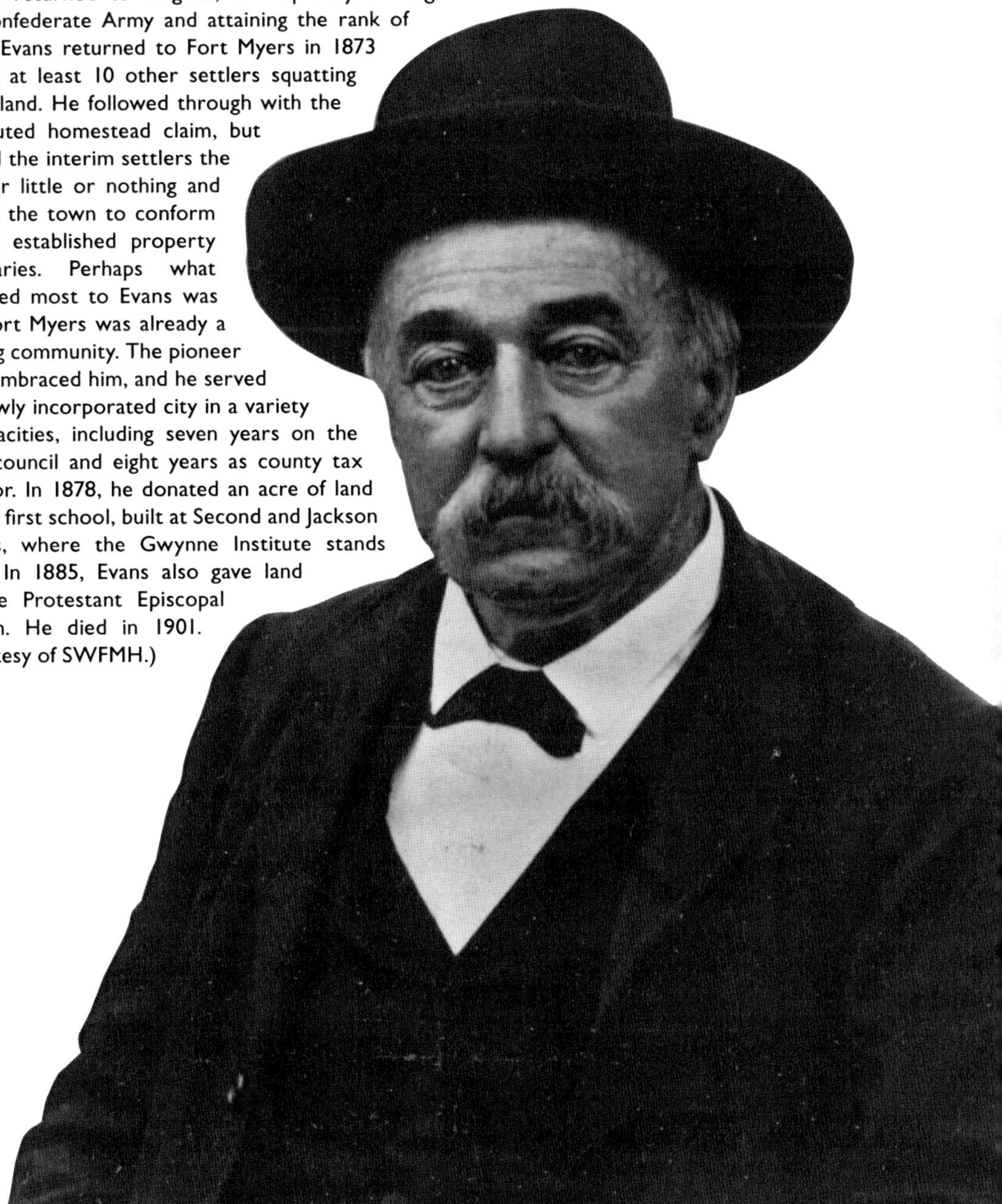

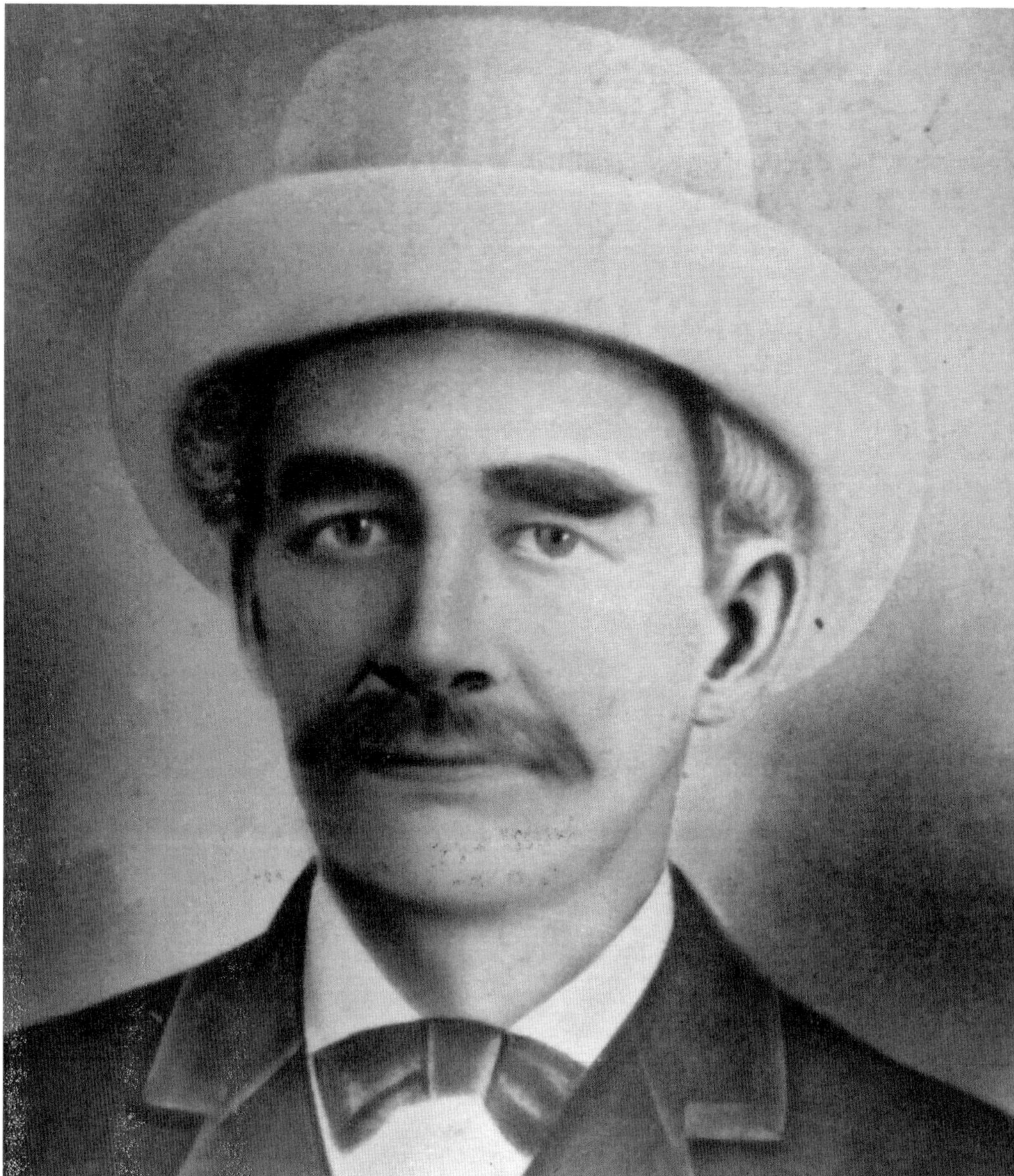

Manuel A. Gonzalez

Gonzalez, a native of Madrid, Spain, and an expert seaman, was a founding settler of Fort Myers. He knew the southwest Florida coast well because in the 1850s he had delivered mail and goods by boat between Tampa and Fort Myers. In 1861, he married Evalina Weatherford, a native of the Bahamas. In 1866, he, son Manuel S., and his brother-in-law, John Weatherford, made an investigative trip to the abandoned fort. Father and son remained in their rough homestead in the former officers' quarters, while the others returned to Key West for family members. Gonzalez was a master carpenter, and many of his homes stand today. He received the first land grant in Fort Myers and ran what was possibly the first store in the area, where he traded with the Seminole Miccosukee Indians. He died in 1902. (Courtesy of SWFHS.)

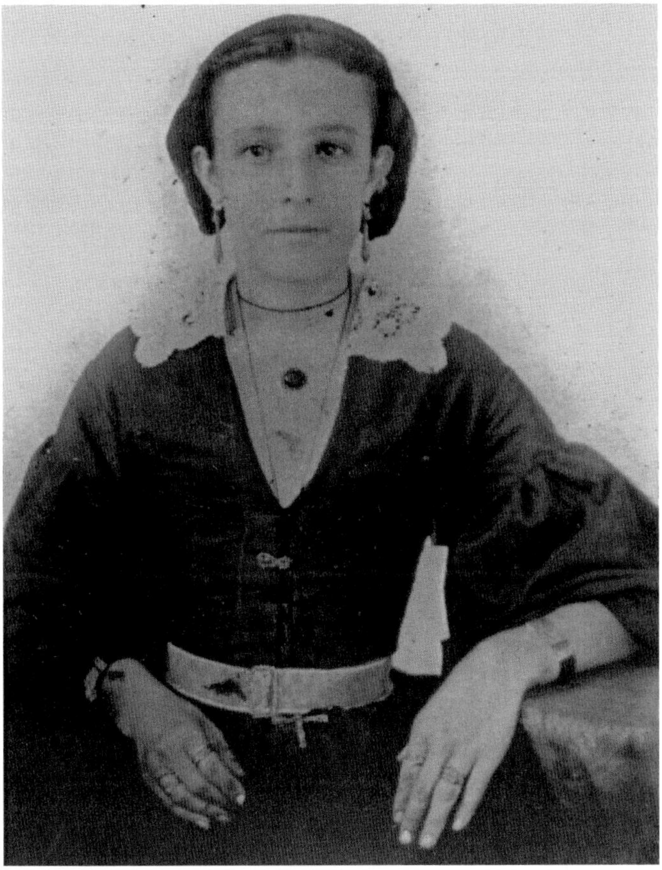

Evalina (Weatherford) Gonzalez
When the first pioneers arrived at the site of the US Army's Fort Myers in 1866, no public school system existed. After her husband obtained textbooks from Cuba, Gonzalez started the settlement's first school in her home. Classes began in fall 1868 with only four pupils, two Gonzalez children and the children of two neighbors. (Courtesy of HFA.)

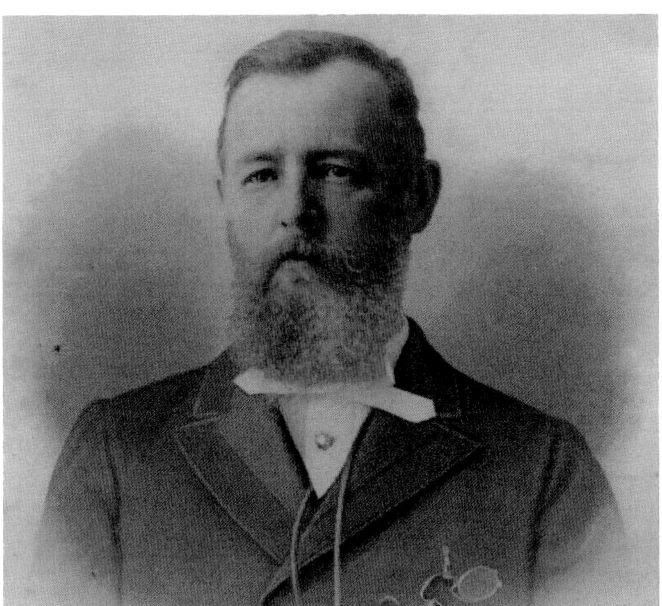

Dr. William Hanson
Along with other humanitarians such as Dr. Jacob E. and Clara Brecht, Hanson worked with the Seminoles, whose traditional life was threatened as settlers fenced off or cultivated the land. A native of England, Hanson was a fellow in the University of Edinburgh's College of Physicians and Surgeons before he settled in Fort Myers via Key West in 1884. He practiced medicine until he died in 1911. (Courtesy of HFA.)

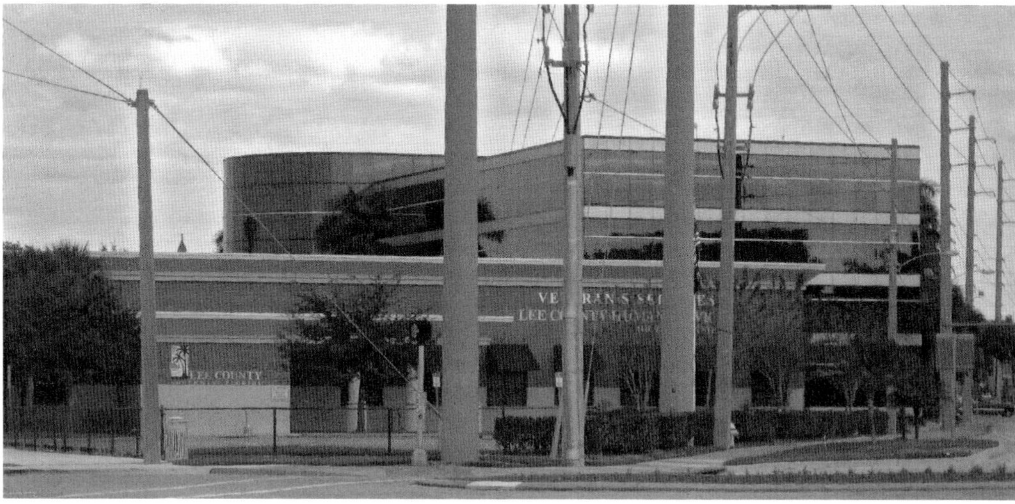

Pink White

Born into slavery in the 1850s in Georgia, White came to Fort Myers in 1886. White immediately gained a reputation as an enterprising member of the black community. He was appointed trustee for the "temporary school district" for colored children in 1888, arranged for Trinity Methodist Episcopal Church to be rented for a colored school (former site above), and was appointed supervisor of the school in 1894. He died in 1913. (Photograph by the author.)

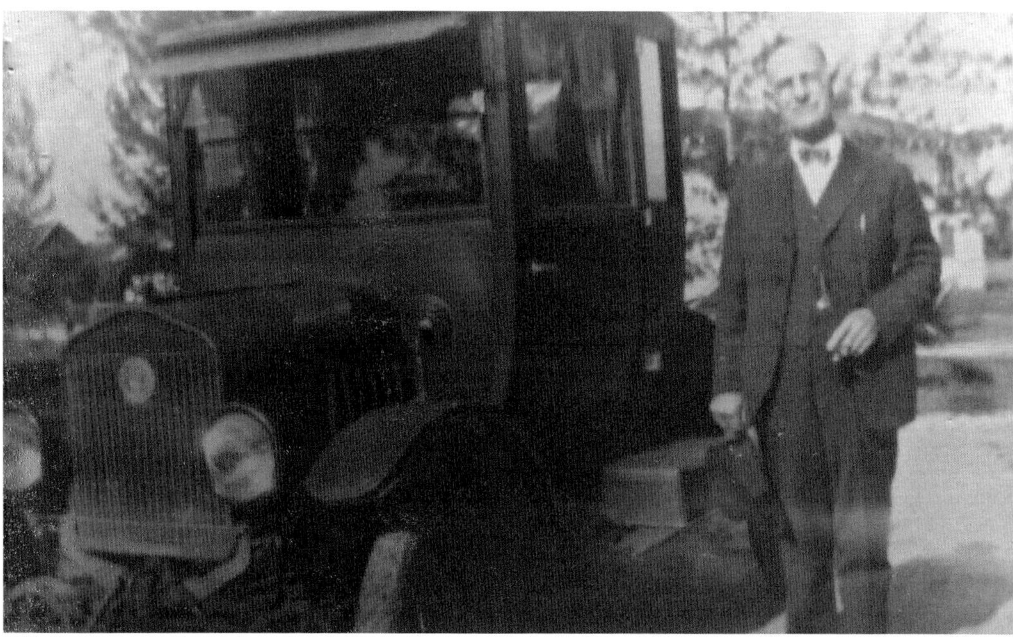

Dr. W.B. Winkler

At the turn of the 20th century when Fort Myers was still a cowboy town, Winkler rode on horseback to visit his far-flung patients, delivering more babies than any other pioneer doctor in the area. He was on staff at Lee Memorial Hospital from its start. He also farmed on Whiskey Creek and built the first hotel on Fort Myers Beach in 1912. He died in 1933. (Courtesy of SWFMH.)

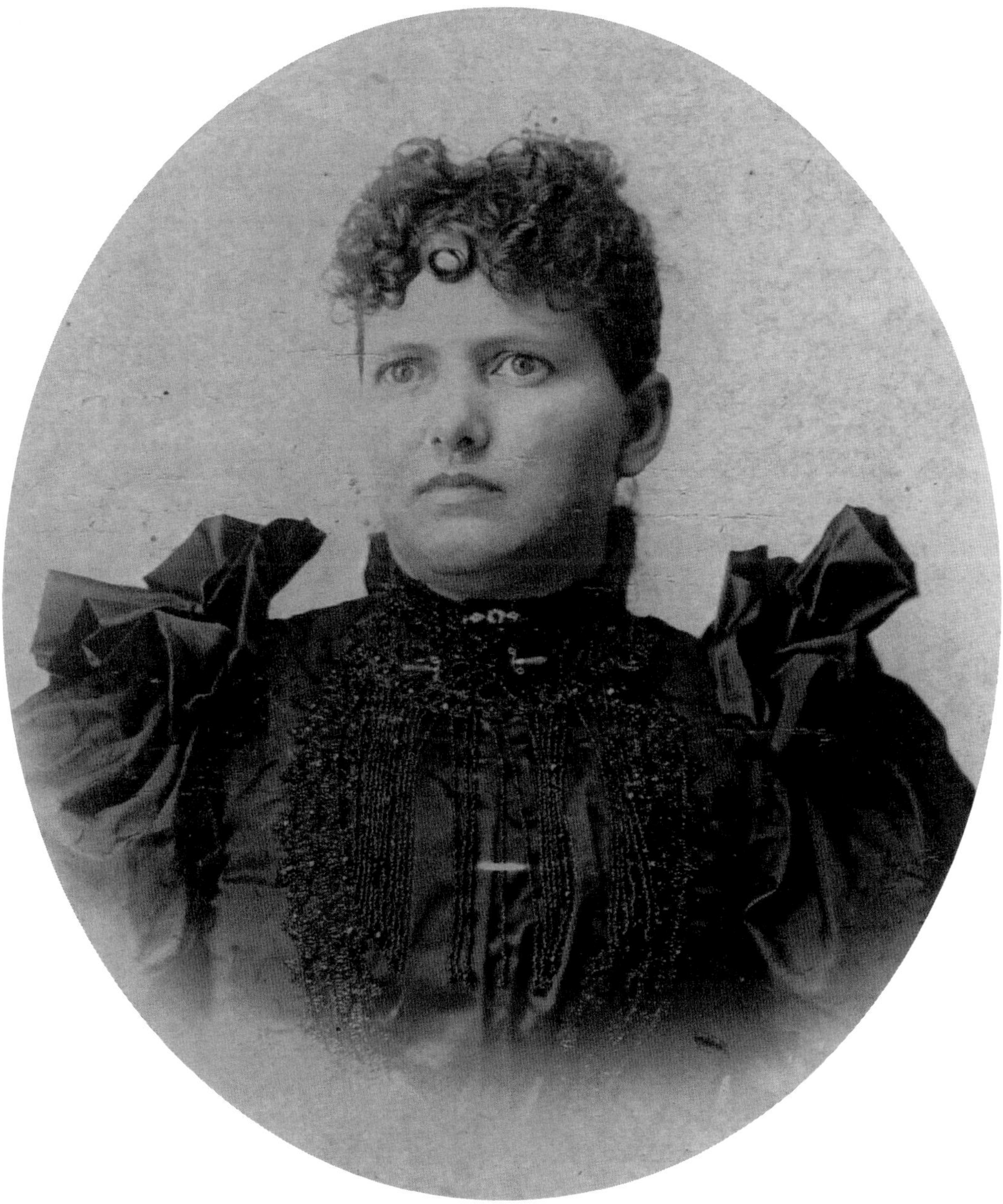

Julia Isabel (Frierson) Hendry
The year she was crowned Miss Tampa, 1874, Julia Isabel Frierson became engaged to James Edward Hendry Sr., son of Capt. Francis A. Hendry. They set the wedding date for June 14, 1875. But James, who was working on the frontier in his father's cattle business, missed the wedding due to severe weather and couldn't send her word. Her wedding dress and trousseau were ready, but the next day, still no James. Keeping the faith and refreshing the church flowers, she was rewarded on the third day with Jimmy's arrival. They were married on June 17. The newlyweds, along with his parents, moved to Fort Myers. In 1904, Julia had the honor of driving in the last spike to complete the Atlantic Coast Line Railroad's arrival in Fort Myers. (Courtesy of Larry Wiggins.)

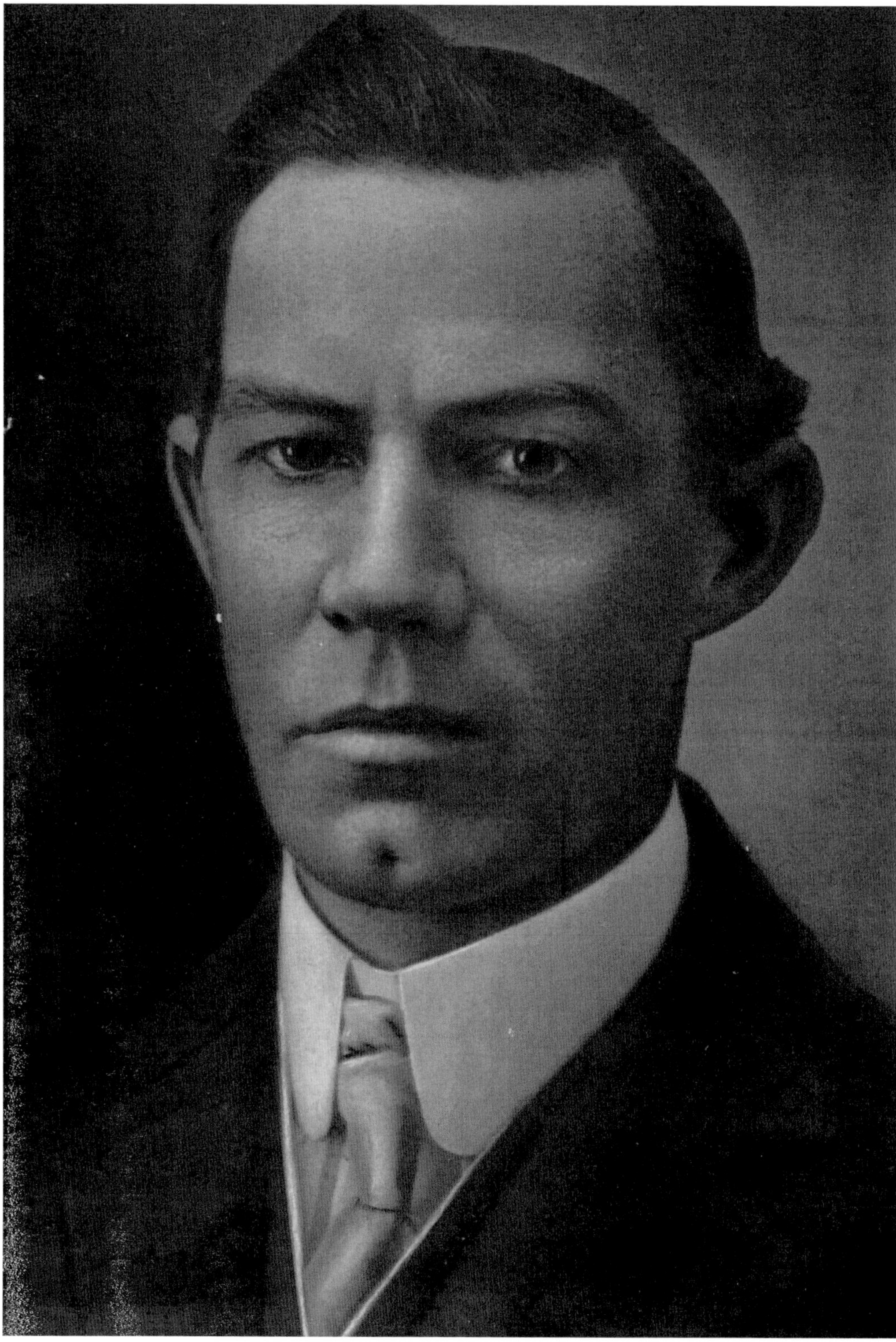

Harvie E. Heitman (LEFT)
A North Carolinian, Heitman came to Fort Myers in 1888 at the age of 16 to work in his great-uncle's store. A natural-born businessman, he often embarked on a new venture even before the current one was brought to completion. Heitman was one of early Fort Myers' major movers and shakers. He owned or maintained leadership roles in countless business, civic, and social concerns. In 1898, he built his own general store, the first brick structure in the town, and never stopped building and boosting the town until he died at age 49 in 1922. He constructed almost an entire city block that is still the historical heart of downtown, including the Bradford Hotel in 1905, backed financially by "Tootie" McGregor, and the Theatre Arcade with his brother Gilmer. He managed the local business affairs of Thomas A. Edison for years, and in 1914, he led the unsuccessful opposition to the construction of a new county courthouse championed by William "Wild Bill" Towles. Several leading citizens, including Heitman, joined forces to found Fort Myers' first home-owned bank in 1906, which evolved into the Bank of Fort Myers. The feud between Heitman's bank and the rival First National Bank of Fort Myers headed by Walter G. Langford is legendary. (Courtesy of SWFHS, Alvin Lederer Collection.)

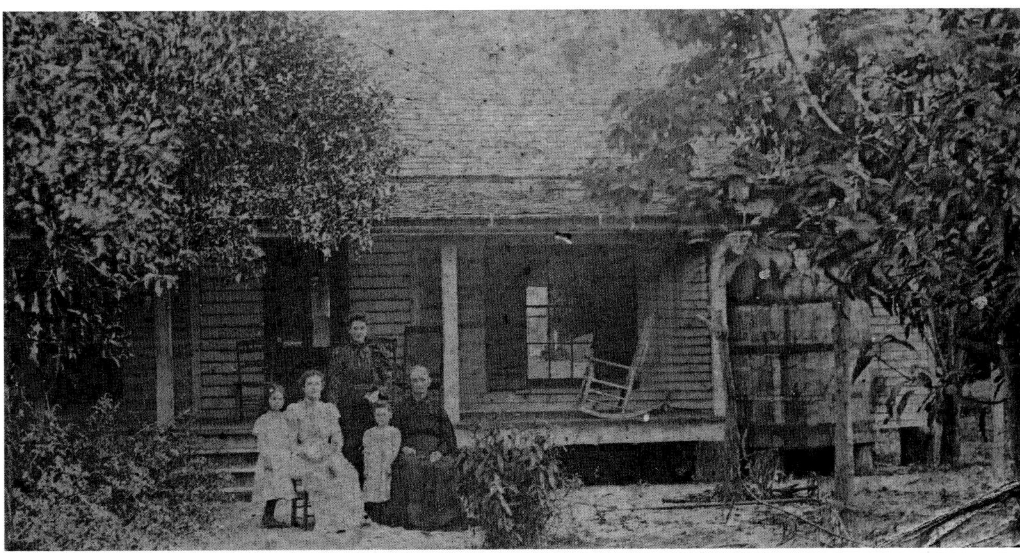

Jane Hendry
Hendry knew the emotional toll an isolated pioneer life could exact. In 1866, she married Charles W. Hendry, a cousin of Capt. Francis A. Hendry and W. Marion Hendry. After joining his cousins in the cattle business in 1872, he settled Jane and their four children in a log cabin near the Hendry grazing grounds south of the Caloosahatchee near Immokalee. In May 1873, Charles was on the trail, leaving Jane to cope with six-year-old Esther Ann, who was critically ill with fever. The nearest white neighbors were 30 miles away in Fort Myers, so she received help from a passing Seminole man who was able to track down her husband and give him the urgent news. The father rushed home and was there for his child's death later that night. After the child's burial the next day under a pine tree, the grieving mother began packing, insisting that she would not spend another night in the wilderness, far from neighbors and comfort. The Hendry men saw the futility of trying to convince her otherwise and began to help her load the household contents onto two oxcarts. The family traveled for four days before reaching Fort Myers. In 1893, while living in Key West, Charles died. Jane returned to Fort Myers and built a house on First Street. In the late 1890s photograph taken at that home, she sits (right) with, from left to right, (seated) granddaughter Amazon "Ammie" Tooke, daughter Alice McCann, granddaughter Josephine, and (standing) Claudia (Baxter) Stroup. She died in 1908, having known the sorrow of an isolated life in the wilderness as well as the comfort of town life. (Courtesy of SWFHS.)

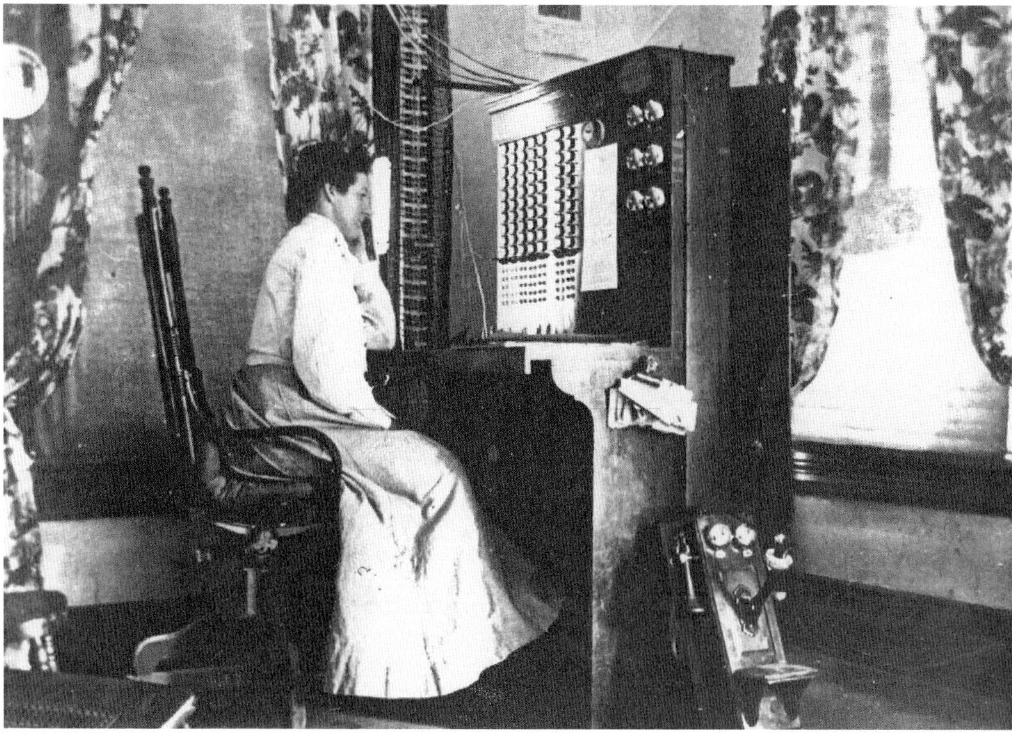

Alice (Hendry) McCann

McCann, Fort Myers' first telephone-switchboard operator, sat down to route calls for the Lee County Telephone Company in February 1900. Working the day shift, she helped to bring Fort Myers into a new century, as she operated a six-circuit exchange above Heitman's general store. When Sunday telephone service was added in 1903, she was entertained by the conversations of courting lovers. (Courtesy of SWFHS.)

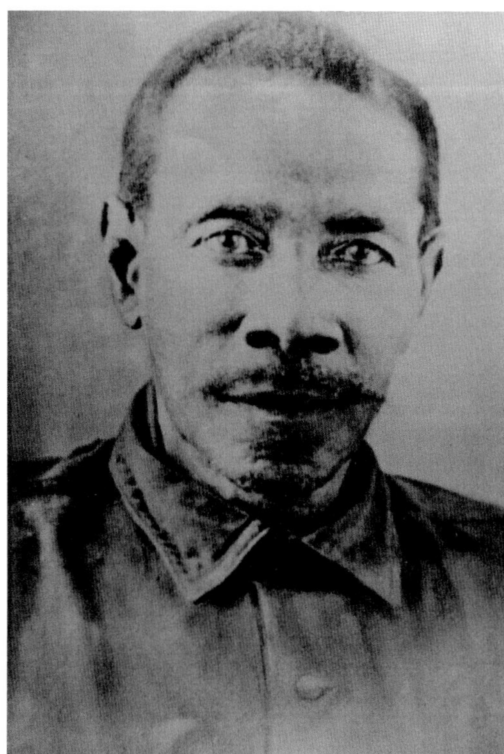

Nelson Tillis

Fort Myers' first black settler was a farmer and fishing guide, counting Thomas A. Edison among his clients. Tillis arrived in Fort Myers on Christmas Day 1867 with Capt. Peter Nelson, William S. Clay, and John Powell. He and wife Zilpha Ellen Summerall had 11 surviving children, for whom he hired a tutor from Key West and built a schoolhouse on his property near the Edison home. After departing for the Bahamas about 1910, he was never heard from again. (Courtesy of SWFMH.)

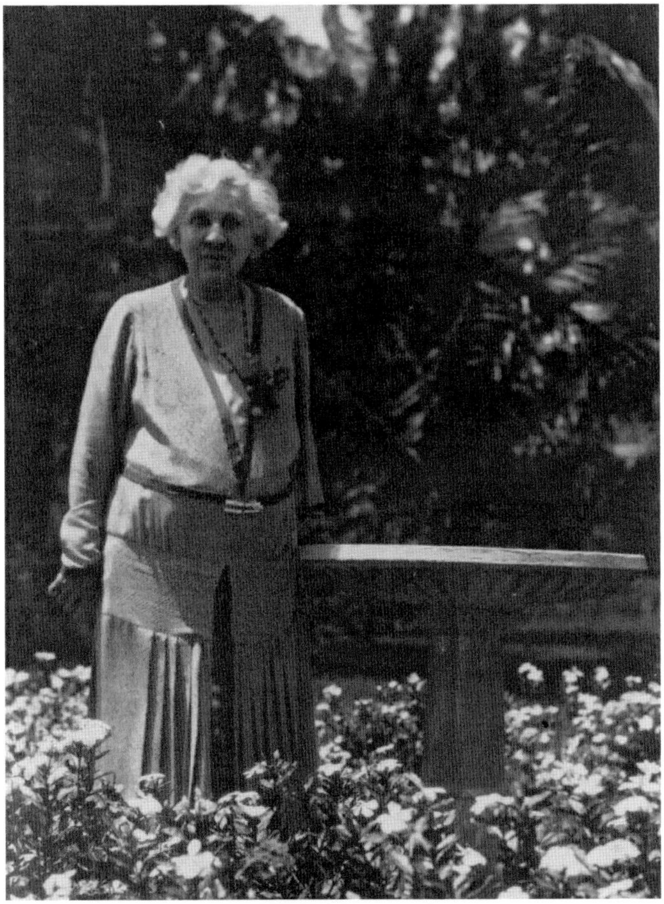

Mary Florence Hill
Widow Mary Florence Hill, came to Fort Myers in the early 1880s for health reasons, bringing her two young daughters, Annie and Flossie, with her. She bought a boardinghouse in 1889, named it Hill House, and ran it successfully until selling it in 1918. Known as "Mother Hill," she was active in civic affairs and loved by the community. (Courtesy of SWFHS.)

Annie Hill
Hill's 1909 obituary stated that "her death has cast a gloom over the entire city." Even a long summer trip with her mother to northern climes had not helped her lingering illness. In her last hours, she sat outside before being carried to bed. She then gave instructions on how she wished to be dressed and how to dispose of her possessions and quietly died. (Photograph by the author.)

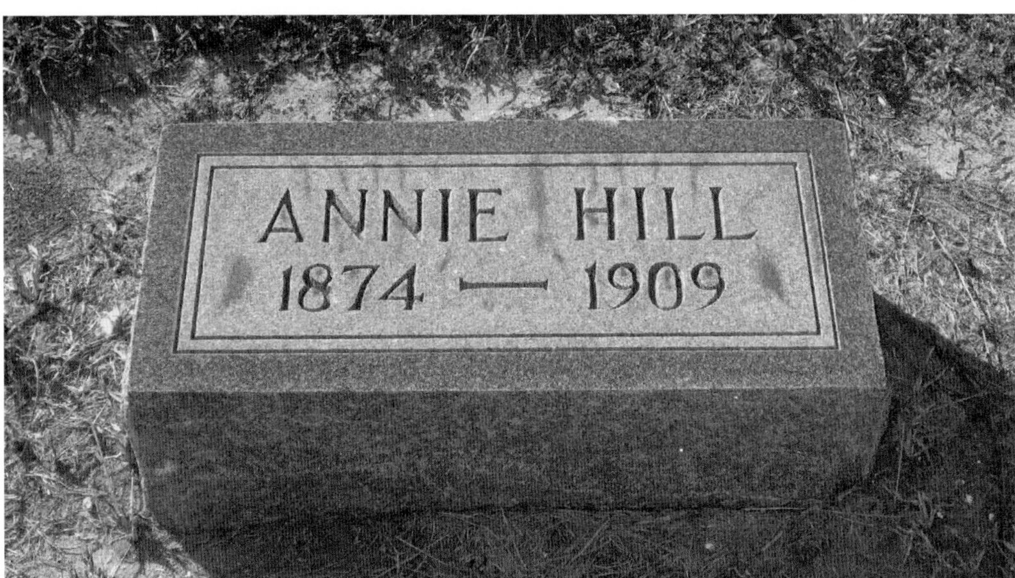

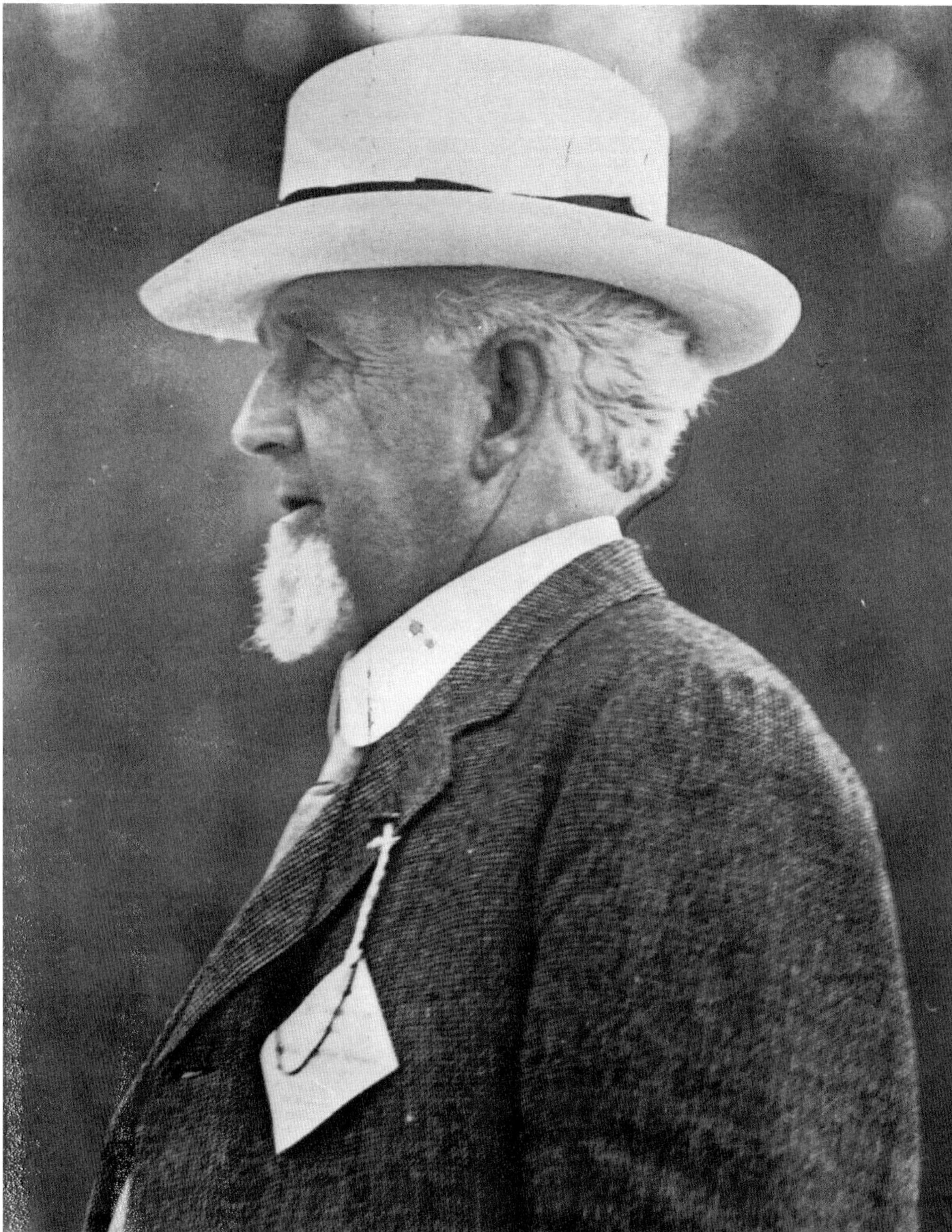

Capt. Francis A. Hendry
The "Father of Fort Myers," Hendry first glimpsed Fort Myers in 1853 while acting as a guide for the Army. Instrumental in city incorporation and creating and naming Lee County, he served as town councilman, state senator, one of the first county commissioners, and as a six-term state representative. His legacy lives in the names Hendry Street and Hendry County. He made a big success of shipping cattle to Cuban markets from Punta Rassa. (Courtesy of SWFHS.)

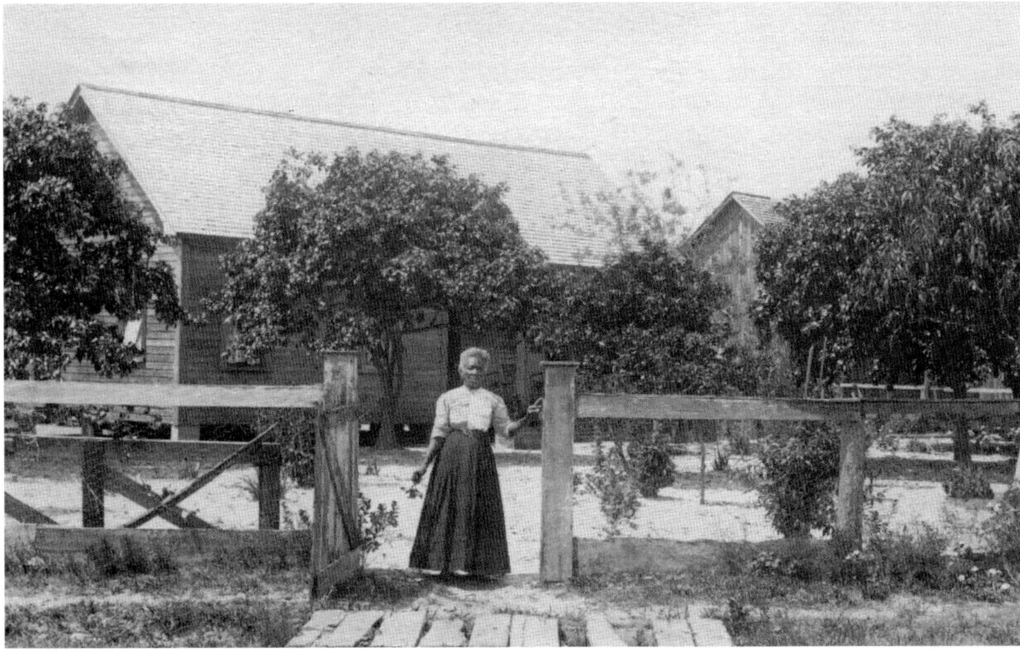

Sarah Williams
In 1915, Williams decided to give a Christmas tree party at her home for 15 little "colored" girls in the black community of Safety Hill. The annual celebration grew to embrace hundreds and continues today. After moving to Fort Myers around 1899, she became an owner of considerable property and a successful businesswoman. When she died in 1926, only days before Christmas, her daughter, Dr. Ella M. Piper, continued the party founded in true Christmas spirit. (Courtesy of SWFMH.)

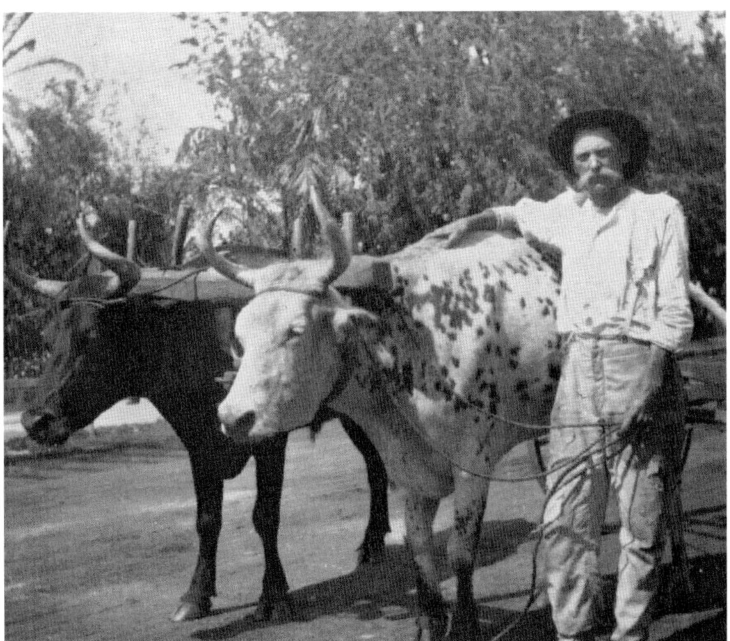

Bill Brown
Born into a well-to-do family in England, Brown left home at age 17. Apprenticing on a ship laying transatlantic cable in 1870, he jumped ship in Havana, Cuba, and made his way to Punta Rassa. At his Everglades trading post, he dealt exclusively with the Seminoles and was a supplier of bird plumes to the millinery industry, a profitable trade that killed millions of egrets, herons, flamingos, roseate spoonbills, and other species. He died in 1927. (Courtesy of SWFHS.)

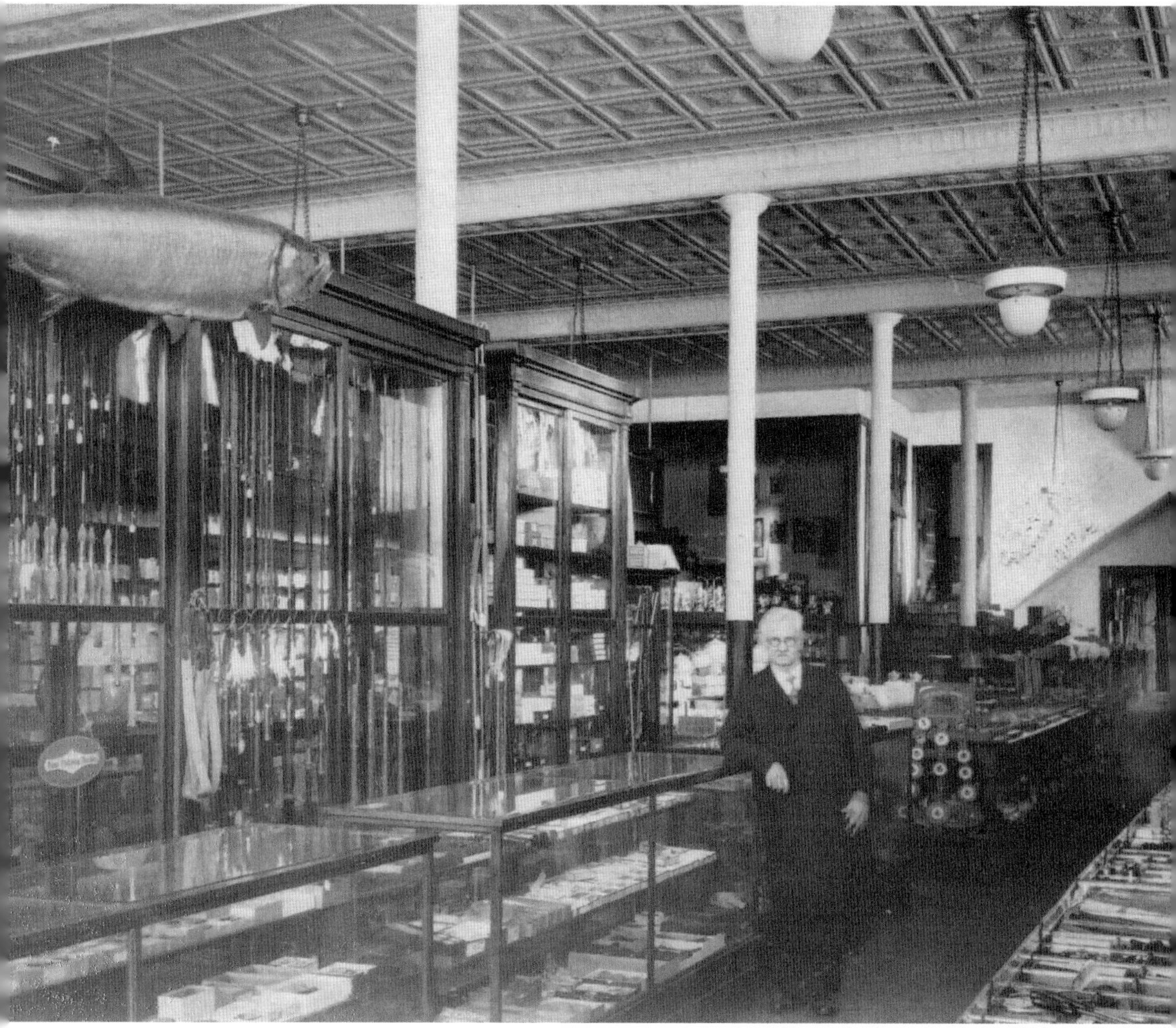

Edward L. Evans

Evans was one of the best impromptu public-relations officials Fort Myers ever had. In 1885, Thomas A. Edison visited Roan's Store, which Evans managed, while on a sightseeing tour. The inventor was always on the lookout for bamboo because of its use as an incandescent light filament. Evans offered to show him bamboo growing at Billy's Creek and used the time to convince Edison to establish a winter home in Fort Myers. The next day, Edison bought the 13 acres that became his winter estate, and a close friendship began. Evans was a longtime business partner of Harvie E. Heitman and managed the Heitman-Evans Company for years. Internationally known as a designer of fishing tackle, his seasonal fishing friends included celebrities such as writer Zane Grey. (Courtesy of SWFHS.)

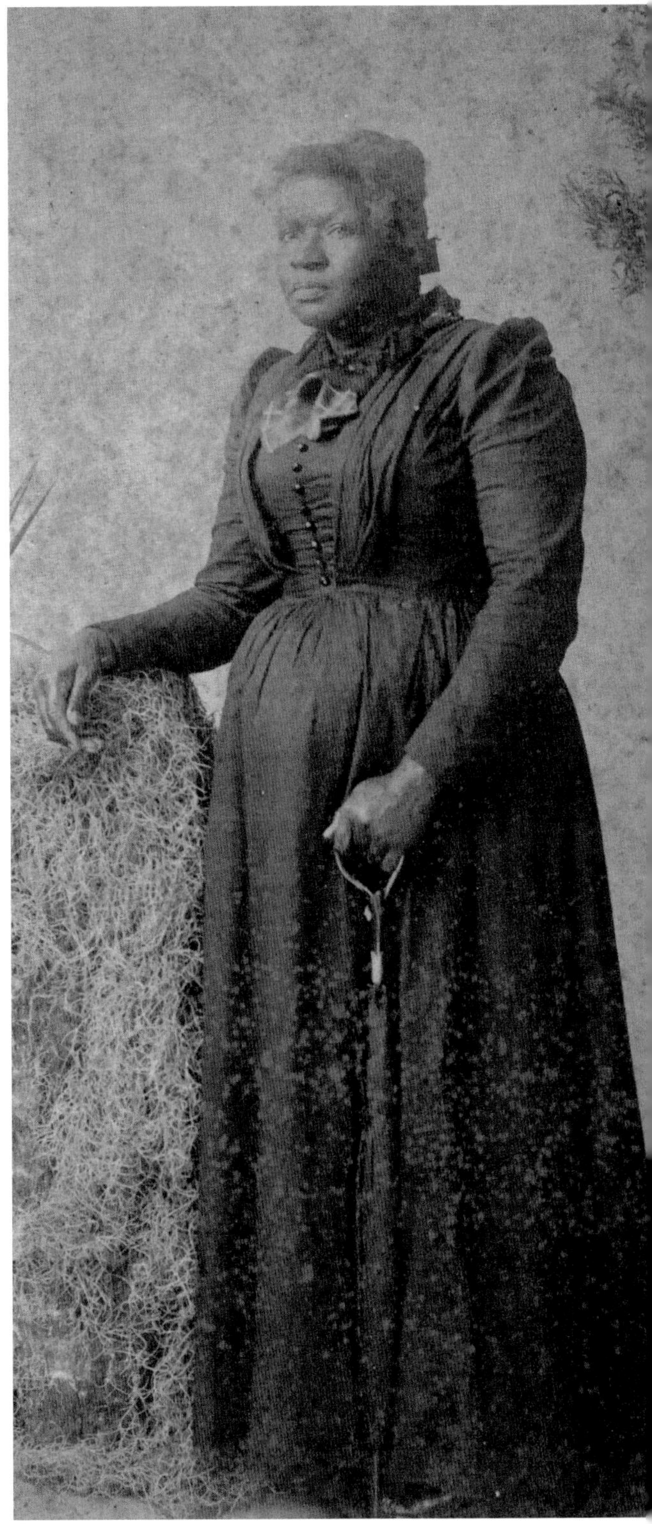

Aunt Clairie Henderson
Henderson was a slave given to Georgia Church upon her marriage to Jasper Henderson. "Aunt Clairie" remained in service as a personal maid for the Hendersons after the abolishment of slavery. Her son, Aaron Henderson, later worked for the successful son of that family, Robert A. Henderson Sr., in his general store. (Courtesy of SWFHS.)

Nick Armeda
When Thomas A. Edison sailed up the Caloosahatchee River in 1886, 16-year-old Nick Armeda was onboard the *Jeannette* as a cabin boy. He became a captain whose knowledge of the region's waters was legendary. Among his sailing ventures was delivering cattle from Punta Rassa to Cuba during the heyday of the cattle industry. During World War II, he applied his expertise as commander of a naval mine sweeper. Pictured with his wife, Josephine (left) and Josephine Bordenave, he died in 1955. (Courtesy of June Santini Johnson.)

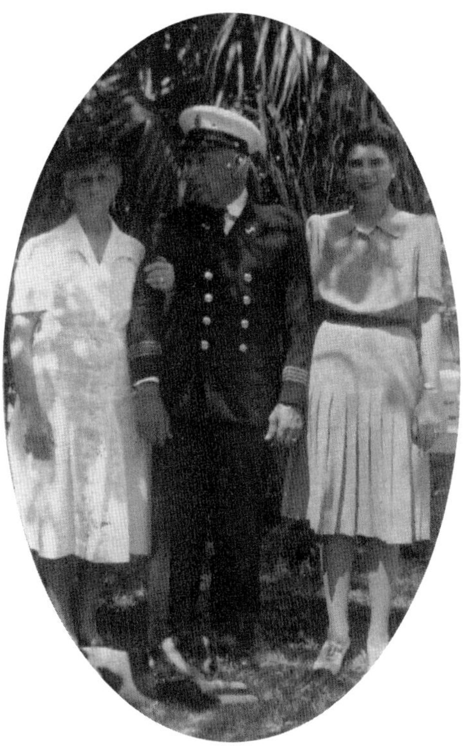

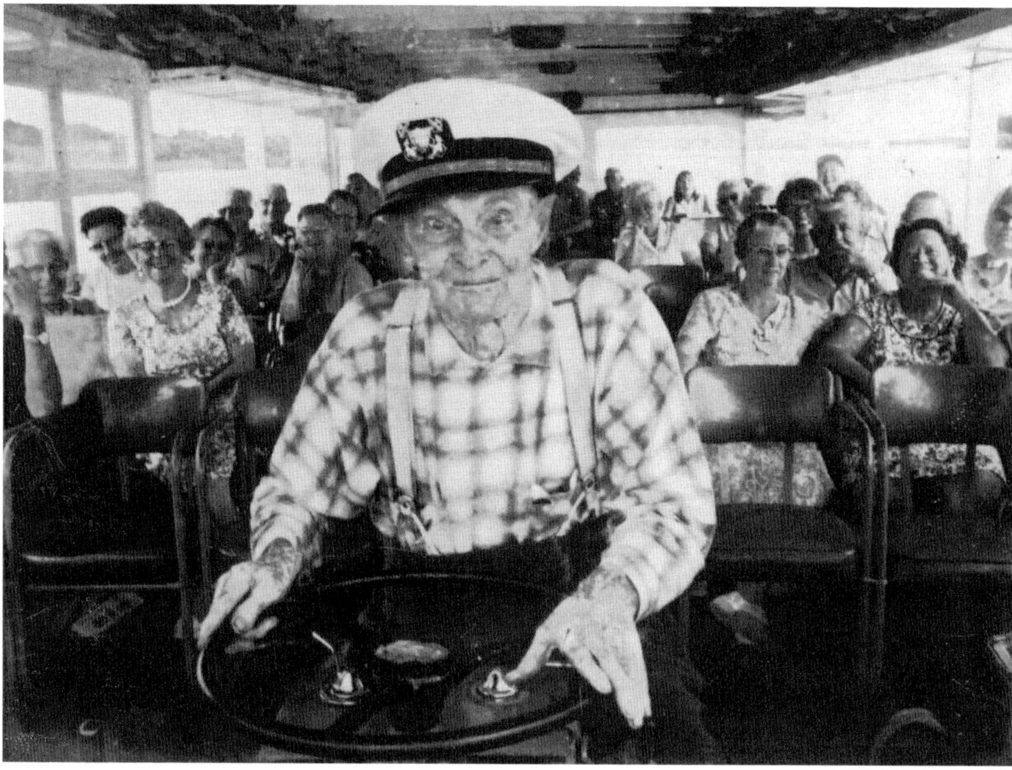

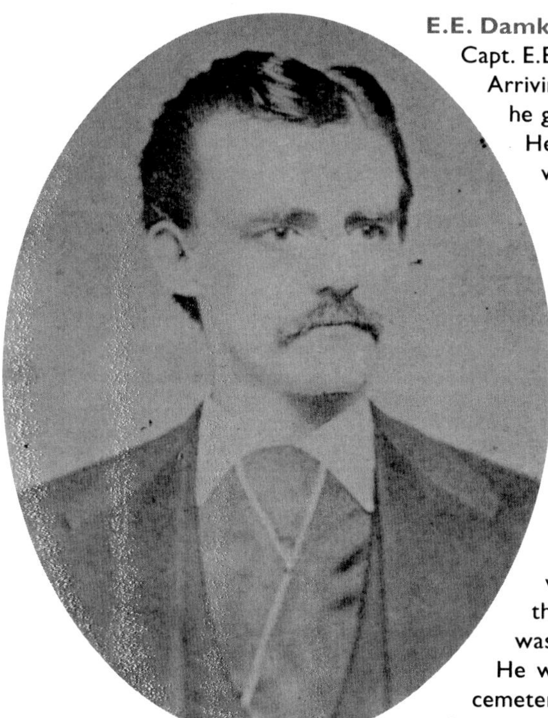

E.E. Damkohler

Capt. E.E. Damkohler's life reads like an adventure novel. Arriving in southwest Florida with his family in 1882, he grew up in Estero's Koreshan Unity community. He mined Alaska's gold rush, traveled the seas with the Merchant Marine, and worked almost 40 years as a fishing guide and coconut planter. He was an authority on local history, authored *Estero, Florida, 1882: Memoirs of the First Settler,* and could spin a good tale. He died in 1969 at age 90. (Courtesy of SWHS.)

Charles Hyde Stebbins

Stebbins was voted town clerk and treasurer in August 1885 when 45 electors incorporated Fort Myers. He died in 1888 at age 46 from a wound incurred years earlier while fighting for the Confederates in the Battle at Fort Myers. It was the southernmost attack of the Civil War. He was the first person buried in the Fort Myers cemetery. He and Ida Blount married in 1886 and had a daughter, Mary Hart Stebbins. (Courtesy of SAF.)

CHAPTER TWO

Unforgettable Characters

What is a town without the unpredictable characters, the ones who soar to fame or infamy, endure the unendurable, touch the human heart, are indifferent to controversy, or are otherwise simply phenomena unto themselves? The small city of Fort Myers has been blessed with more than its share of heroes who went beyond the usual measure of wartime sacrifice, exemplified by Rabe O. Wilkison and Charles D. Page. Other unforgettable characters, like Edgar Watson and Capt. Winfield Scott Hancock, belong to national history. Occasionally, trying circumstances test a principle, and such was the case with nurse LaVeta Allen, who spontaneously decided that the rules of her job made it not worth keeping. Politicians like larger-than-life William Towles were both respected and feared for their audacity—and repeatedly elected. For a life filled with public service or controversy, or a life sacrificed, these locals are remembered. For their eccentricity, charm, beauty, or contrariness, they live on.

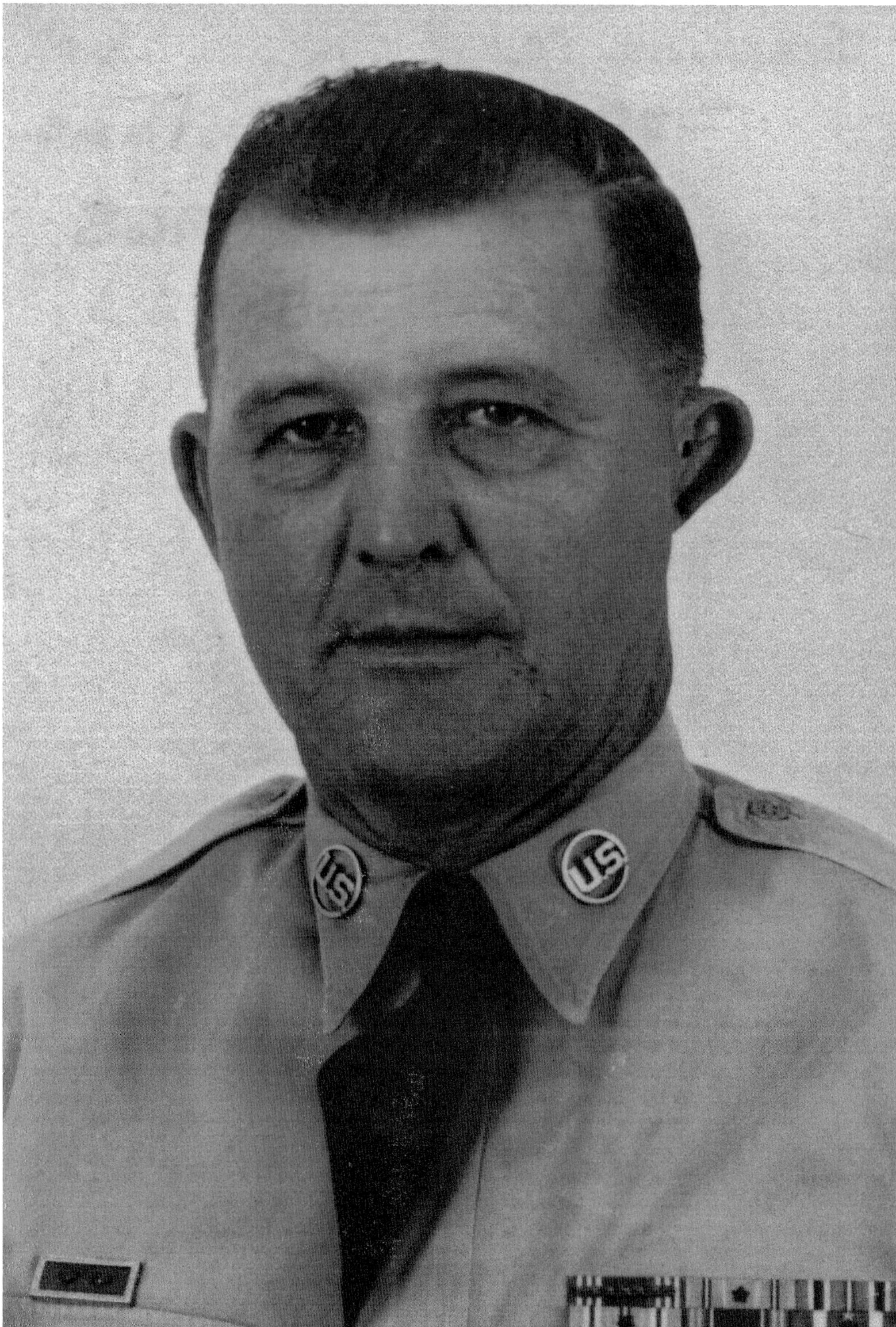

Charles D. Page (LEFT)
In late 1943 or early 1944, the parents of Pfc. Charles D. Page were told to rush to the Edison Theatre because a family friend had seen their son in a weekly newsreel. The Pages knew he had been captured by the Japanese in the Philippines, but nothing else. Taken prisoner in April 1942, Page had endured the 70-mile Bataan Death March. In a 1986 interview he said: "The weak and the sick were bayoneted where they fell. Every once in a while, a man would just go crazy and run screaming into the jungle. He'd get shot to death." Page retired from the US Air Force in 1965 as a senior master sergeant. For his next career he chose something close to home, working in mosquito control in North Fort Myers. (Courtesy of SWFMH.)

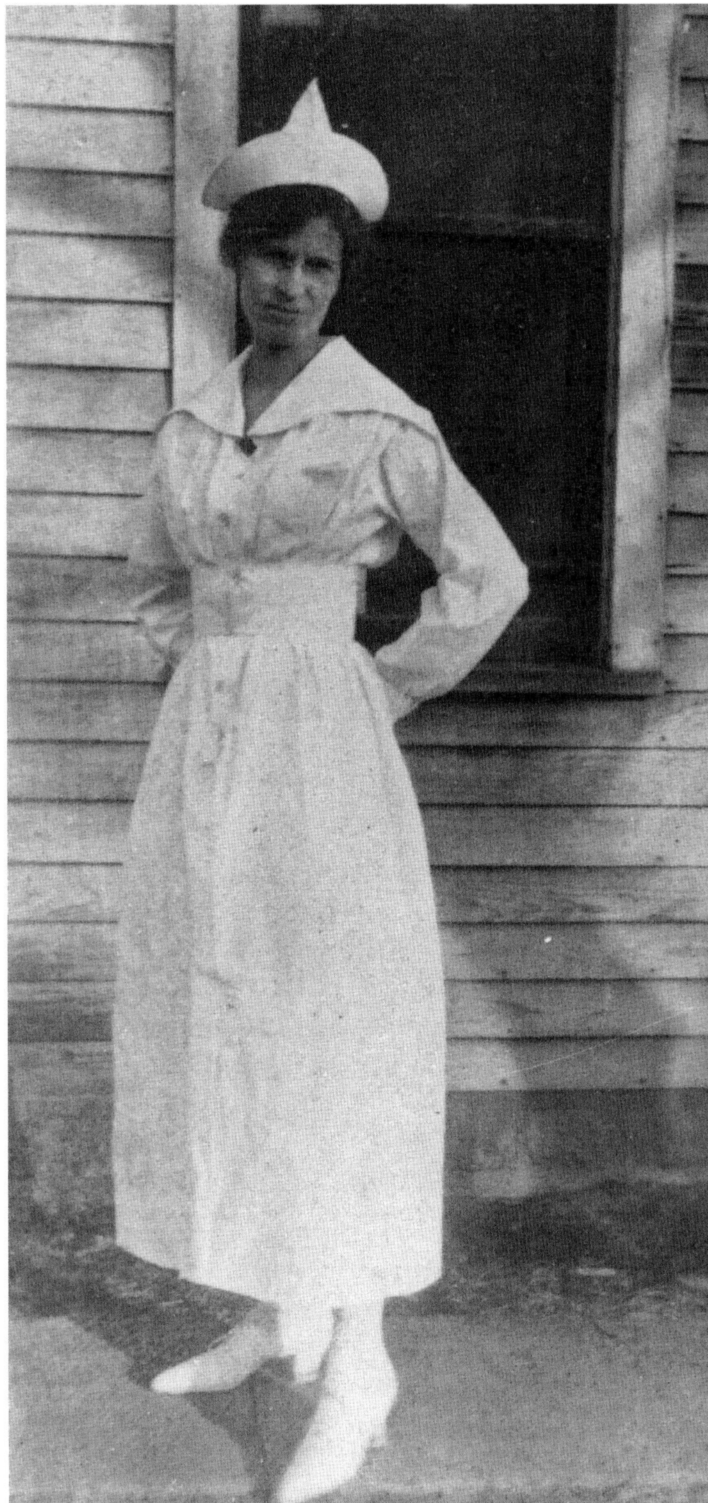

LaVeta Allen
Allen had a long career as a registered nurse, but a short one as superintendent at Lee Memorial Hospital. During her second year there, a critically ill black patient of Dr. M.F. Johnson was in convulsions and needed an immediate cesarean section. In the early 1920s, racial segregation prohibited blacks from receiving hospital care, even in an emergency. The idea of performing this serious operation in the patient's home was obviously out of the question for Allen. She told the physician to bring her to the hospital and was fired for that decision. She died in 1971 at the age of 80. (Courtesy of SWFMH.)

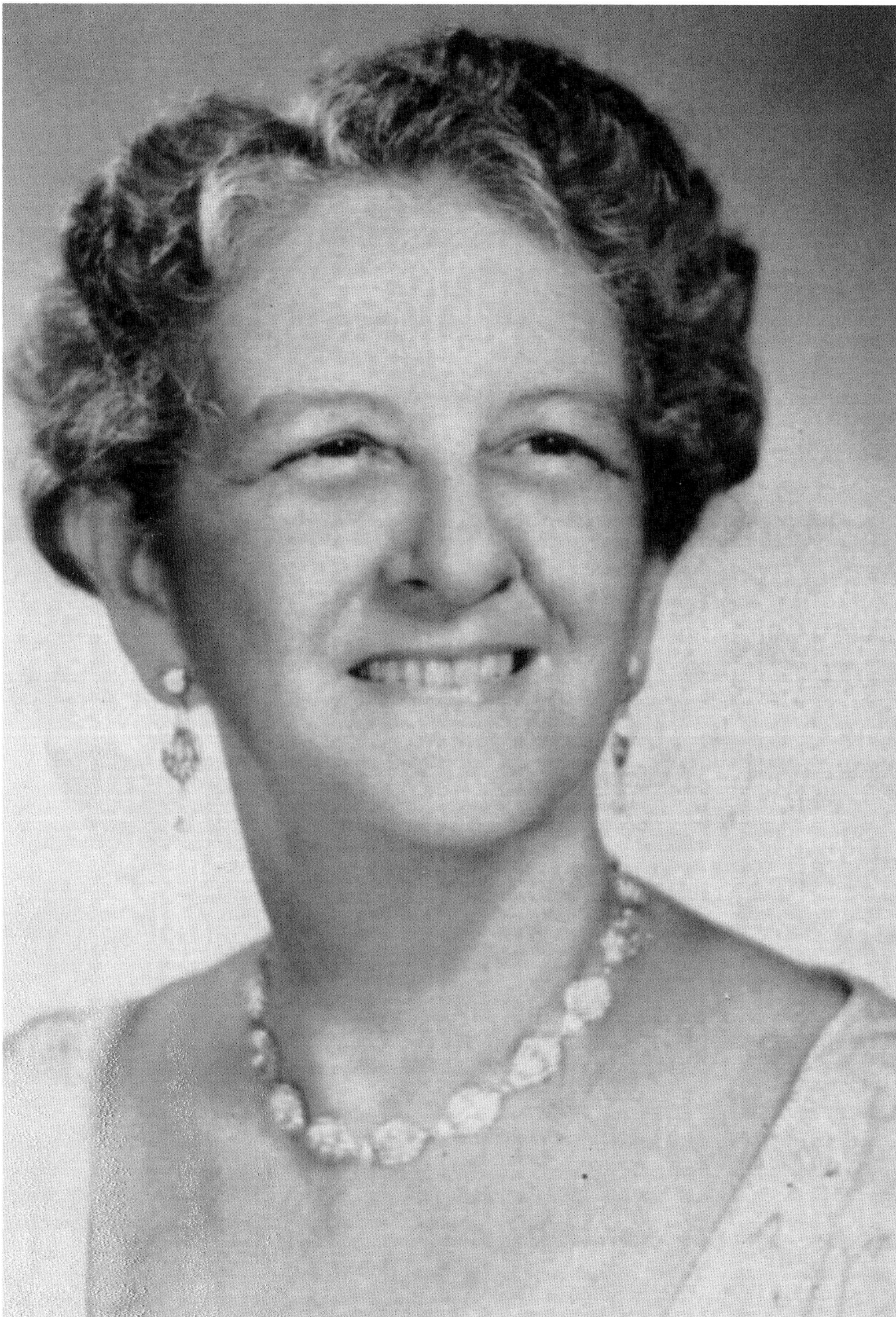

Florence Fritz (LEFT)
Fort Myers' first woman mayor had a stormy term that began in 1949 and ended in 1950 with a recall. Fritz first visited Fort Myers in the 1920s and settled there permanently in 1935. She represented southwest Florida for six years on the Florida State Welfare Board. During World War II, she served as executive secretary of the Red Cross at Buckingham Army Air Force Base and the Coast Guard bases. In 1944, she started publishing *Hello, Stranger!*, a weekly guide informing military personnel, tourists, and residents about what was going on in the Fort Myers area. Fritz went on to a substantial writing career, publishing articles and books such as *Unknown Florida* and *I Covered the Everglades*. She also was president of the Southwest Florida Historical Society. (Courtesy of SWFMH.)

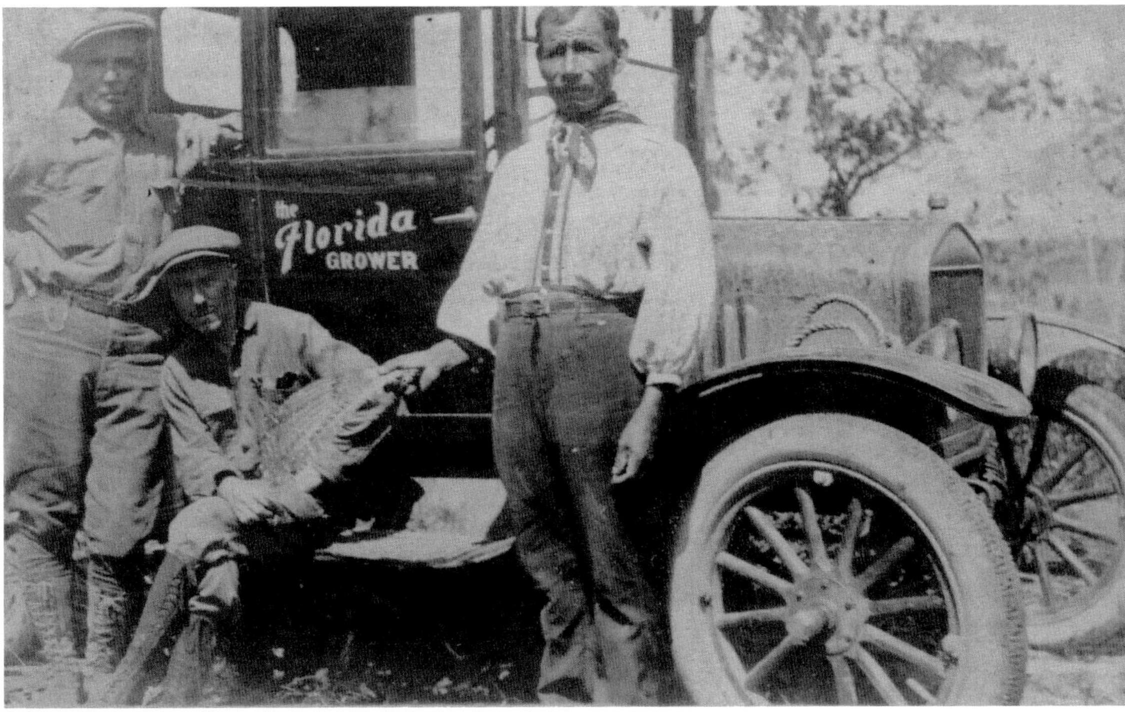

Billy Conapatchee
An encounter between a Seminole Indian boy and Capt. Francis A. Hendry in the late 1870s led to a cultural experiment. Cattleman Hendry, who had good relations with the Seminoles, proposed that young Billy Conapatchee live in his Fort Myers home and attend the school he was starting, which would be taught by a teacher brought from England. Permission was granted, and the boy became the first Seminole to attend the white man's school. He attended the school for three years and became one of the Hendry family. Fellow students gave him the nickname Billy Corn Patch. However, the Seminole authorities became skeptical about the boy learning white man's ways and sent word for him to return. Hendry intervened and insisted that Conapatchee must make the choice himself. He stayed, with the result that a divided Seminole council banned him from his tribe forever and even proposed his execution. But it was decided that the tribe might benefit from knowledge of white culture. Conapatchee would be allowed to return, but forbidden to teach any other tribe members—including his own children—to read or write. Devoted to Captain Hendry, he walked 60 miles from the Everglades to visit his father-figure and mentor when he was dying. He was the interpreter in 1880 when Dr. Clay McCauly reported on the Seminoles to the Secretary of Indian Affairs. In 1923, Conapatchee, right, with two unidentified men, would be one of the Indian guides to forge the final grueling section of the Tamiami Trail. (Courtesy of SWFHS.)

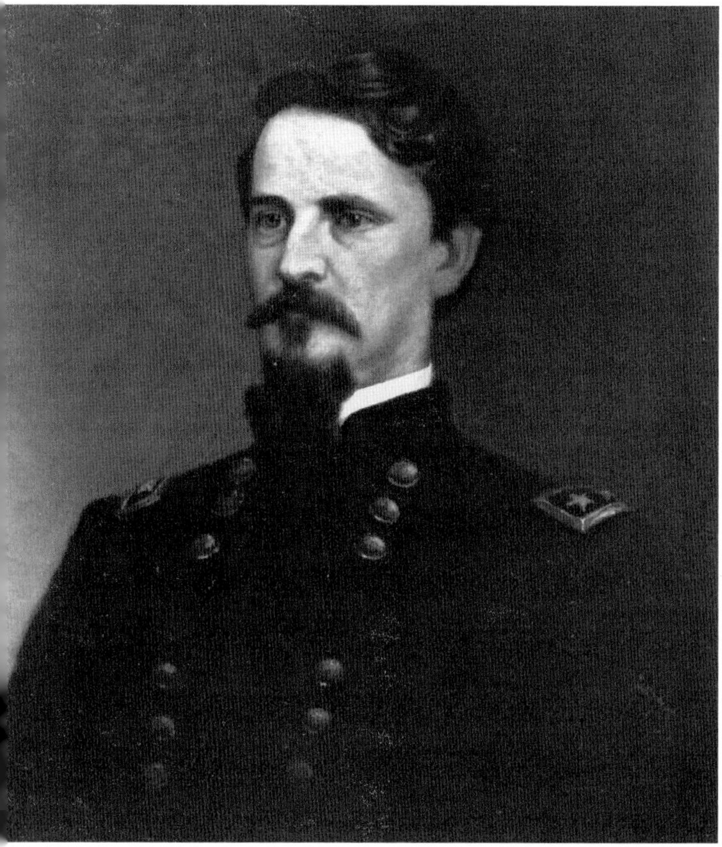

Capt. Winfield Scott Hancock
Scott was appointed quartermaster of Fort Myers in 1854. In 1857, a daughter was born to him and his wife Almira and is considered the first white child born in Fort Myers. The West Point graduate and Mexican War hero went on to national fame, becoming a prominent Union general in the Civil War and a Democratic nominee for US president in 1880. (Courtesy of SWFMH.)

Queenie Adams
Called the "kitchen genius" of the Thomas Edison home, Adams worked for the famous family for 11 years. When dying from a heart ailment in 1937 at the Edisons' New Jersey home, she longed to return to her native Fort Myers. The Seaboard Air Line rerouted a train for her and she died at home amid friends and family. Below is the Edison home where she worked her magic when Fort Myers' first family was in residence. (Photograph by the author.)

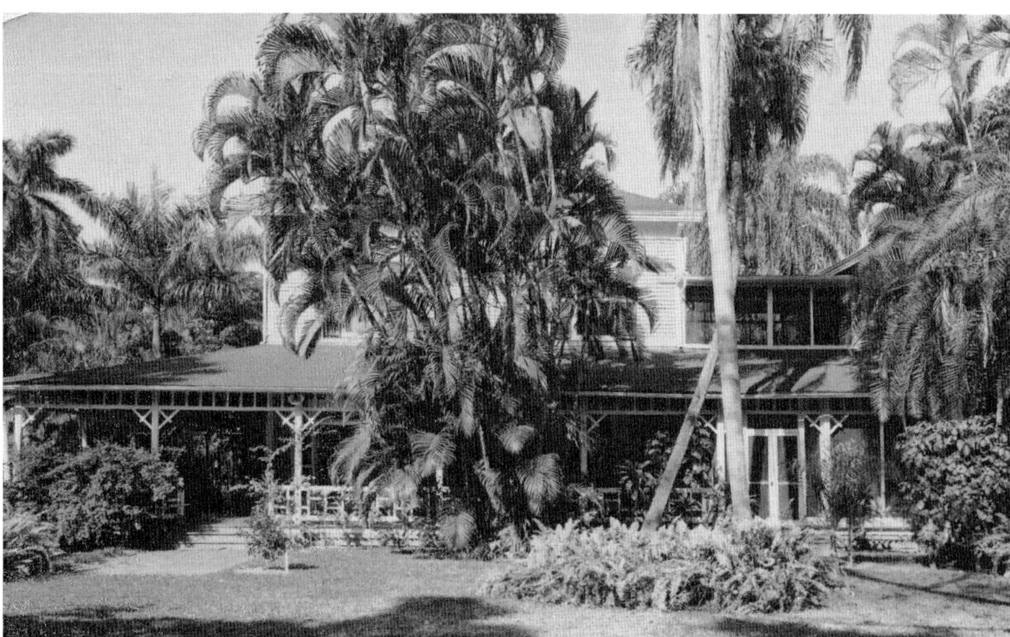

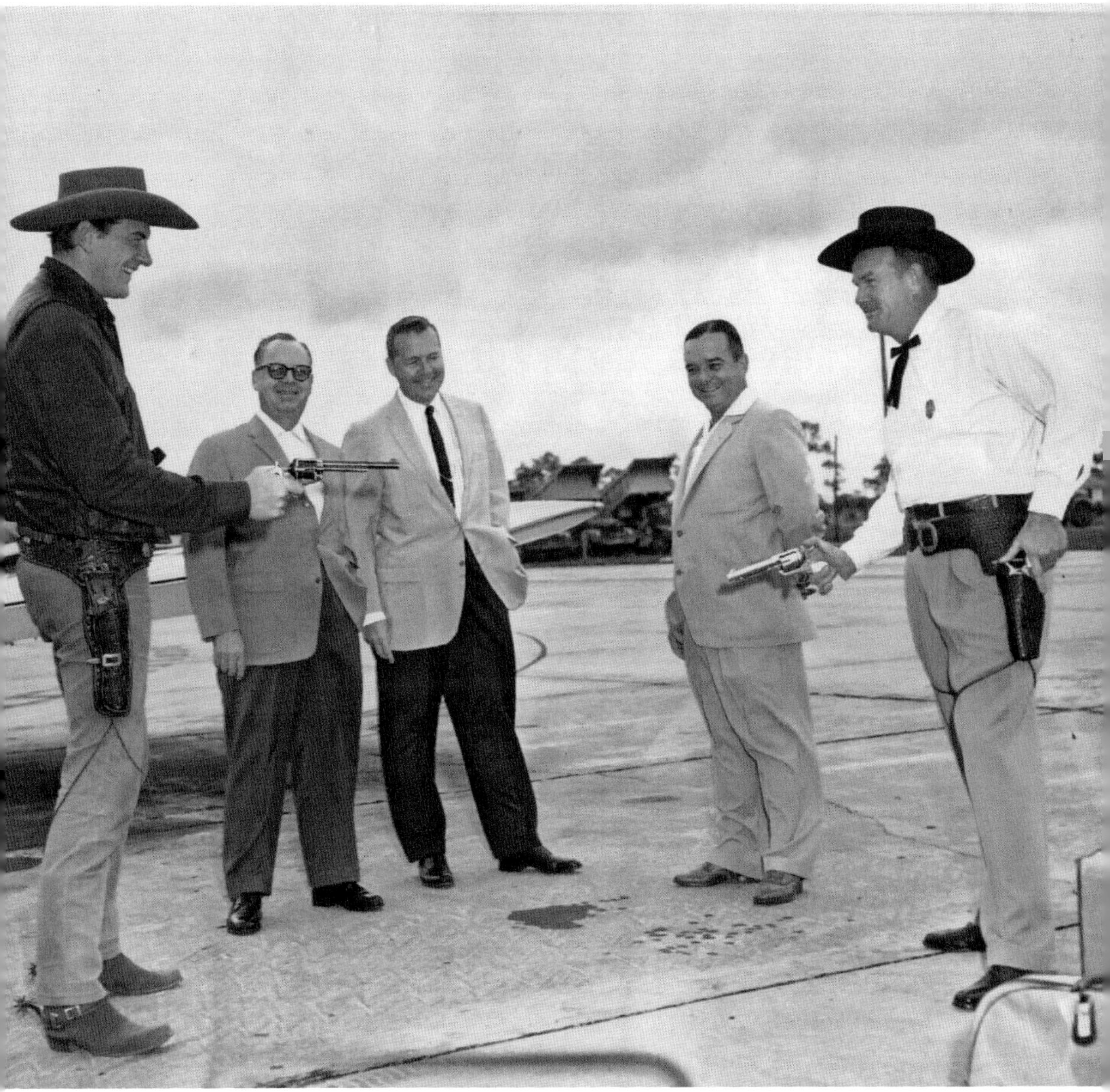

Snag Thompson

Born in 1917, Thompson served as Lee sheriff for a total of six consecutive terms for a total of 24 years. He embarked upon a career in law enforcement as a charter member of the Florida Highway Patrol in 1940 and was elected sheriff in 1948. In the 1956 photograph, Thompson (right) greets television star James Arness of *Gunsmoke* (left), along with, from left to right, Win Ellis, unidentified, and Mayor Heard Edwards. An elementary teacher gave Snag his nickname because of his chipped front tooth. It came in handy in both his athletic pursuits in high school and as sheriff, in headlines such as "Thompson snags a fly" and "Thompson snags a criminal." He is remembered for truly striving to keep the peace—always with good humor—and for remembering the names and faces of the community. (Courtesy of SWFMH.)

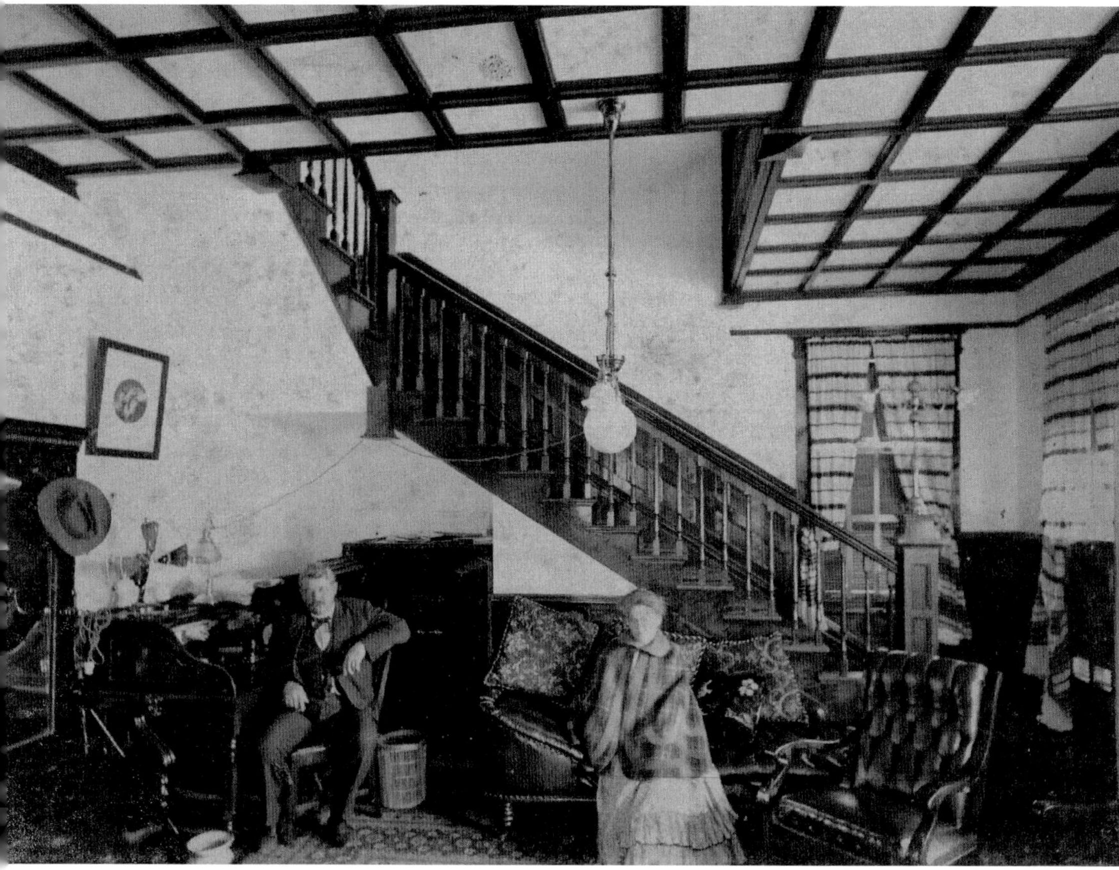

William Towles

Pictured with wife Willie Boyd Towles, William Towles was already a successful merchant and cattleman when he settled in Fort Myers in 1884 as a 32-year-old widower. William Towles, or Wild Bill, was a force to reckon with, especially during his tenure as county-commission chair. In October 1914, his patience ran out with commissioners opposing his plans for a modern courthouse, among them Harvie E. Heitman. When the opposition left town on the train to Arcadia to obtain a court injunction against demolishing the existing courthouse, Towles ordered it destroyed. The audacious process continued throughout the early morning hours. Legend has it that Towles stood guard with a shotgun to ensure that in the morning a new building would be necessary. The Lee County Courthouse that Towles fought for is listed on the National Register of Historic Places. (Courtesy of SWFHS.)

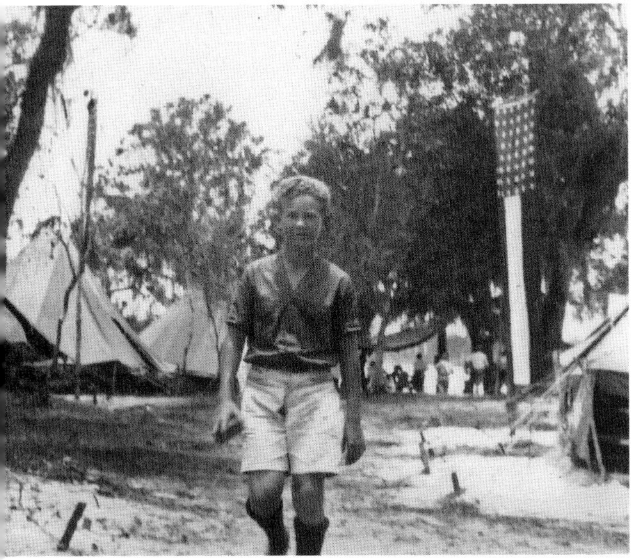

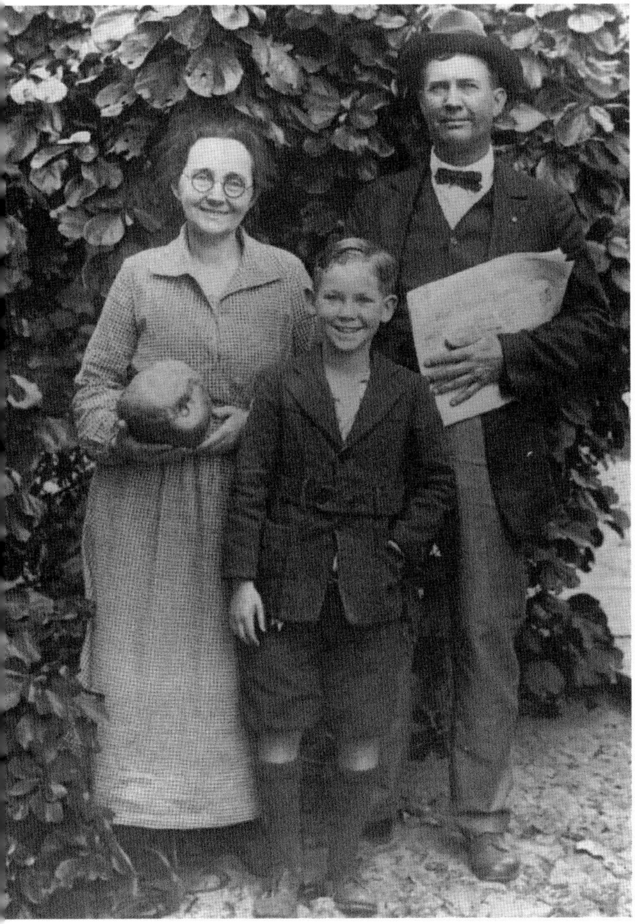

Thomas Goolsby

In July 1928, the death of 15-year-old Thomas Goolsby elicited such an outpouring of affection and community spirit that residents built a memorial in his honor in the city park. He was a popular young man, had a summer job as an usher at the Arcade Theatre, and was a member of Boy Scout Troop number 1 in the local Royal Palm Council. He is pictured at the council's Camp Ropaco in 1928. During the 1927 Christmas holiday, he was one of 125 scouts and their leaders who visited Cuba, where President Gerardo Machado presented him with the highest honor a scout can receive, the eagle badge. Goolsby's family listened to that ceremony via radio broadcast. That following summer, the scout's four-day illness was first diagnosed as ptomaine poisoning, but later identified as spinal meningitis. Upon his death, the Civitan Club organized a drive to build a memorial to Goolsby that would be used as a Boy Scout headquarters. It took only weeks for sufficient funds to pour in. Local contractors donated the construction materials and volunteers provided the labor. The memorial was torn down in 1973 to make way for the police station, but local scouts recall the plaque and portrait that memorialized young Goolsby. Below, he is pictured with his parents, Charles H. and Sarah Jane (Matthews) Goolsby. (Both photographs courtesy of Tom Stewart.)

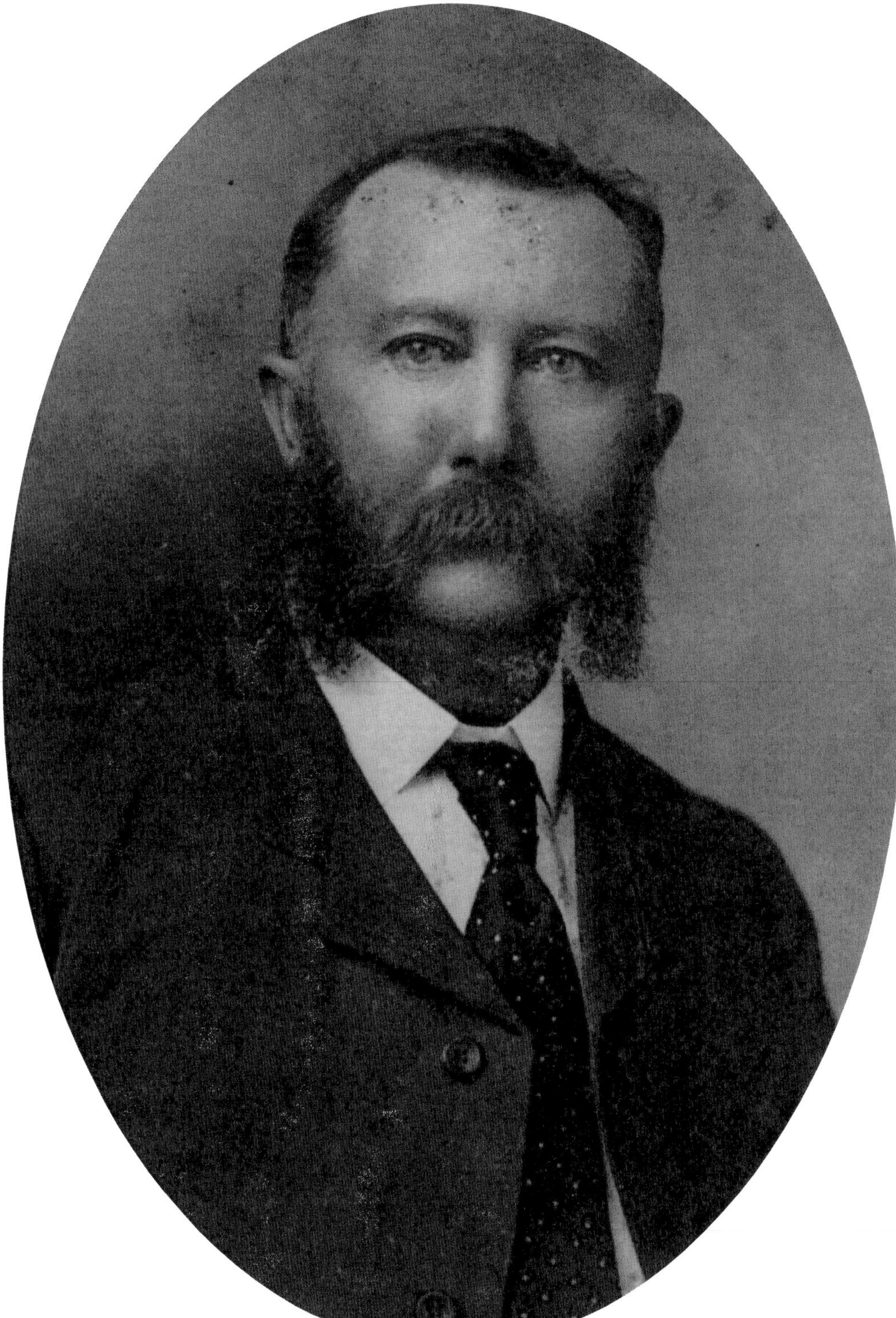

Edgar A. Watson (LEFT)
The entire truth of how the infamous Edgar A. Watson came to be executed on October 24, 1910, in the forbidding Ten Thousand Islands is clouded by mystery and conjecture. More than a century later, his killing by a group of armed vigilantes at Smallwood's store in remote Chokoloskee fascinates. His story inspired Peter Matthiessen's Watson series of novels, *Killing Mr. Watson*, *Lost Man's River*, *Bone by Bone*, and *Shadow Country*, which won the National Book Award in 2009. Watson was rumored to have killed bandit queen Belle Starr years before his arrival in Florida, but was acquitted due to insufficient evidence. Perhaps it was that rumor that fed the belief that he killed several workers on his homestead on Chatham's Bend to avoid paying them. Watson was a hardworking, enterprising farmer with political and commercial vision. He had established a successful cane syrup business in what in the early-20th century was part of Lee County. He was also known for a tendency to anger and alienate his neighbors. He frequently visited his wife and children in Fort Myers when traveling to Tampa and Sarasota on business. His daughter, Carrie, was married to prominent banker Walter G. Langford. Was Watson a serial murderer? Or was he the victim of rumors fed by fear or jealousy over his entrepreneurial and financial success? Watson was buried on Rabbit Key but was later disinterred and buried in the Fort Myers Cemetery. (Courtesy of SWFHS, Alvin Lederer Collection.)

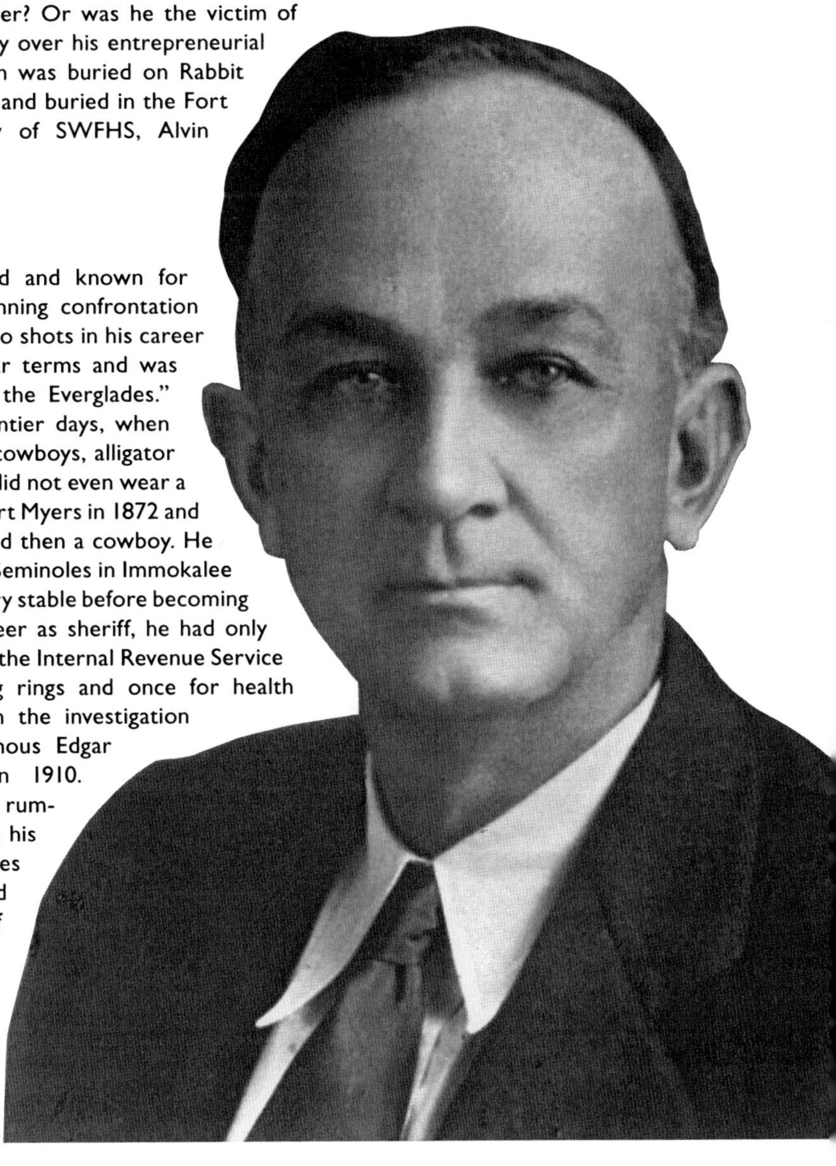

Sheriff Frank B. Tippins
Tippins was highly respected and known for winning with peace and shunning confrontation and violence. He fired only two shots in his career of eight consecutive four-year terms and was known as "the law west of the Everglades." In the pre–World War I frontier days, when he had to handle cattlemen, cowboys, alligator hunters, and adventurers, he did not even wear a gun or badge. He moved to Fort Myers in 1872 and worked as a printer's devil and then a cowboy. He taught at a federal school for Seminoles in Immokalee and then ran a Fort Myers livery stable before becoming a lawman. In his 32-year career as sheriff, he had only two breaks, once to work for the Internal Revenue Service on breaking up moonshining rings and once for health reasons. He was involved in the investigation of the murder of the infamous Edgar Watson in Chokoloskee in 1910. Whether he was bringing in rum-runners from the Bahamas in his own boat or bringing in fugitives from the wild Ten Thousand Islands, which were part of Lee County in the early days, he operated with cool confidence and authority. He then served as deputy US marshal in Tampa and Miami. He died in 1948. (Courtesy of SWFHS.)

Mammy Jane Hendry
Mammy Jane was given as a slave to William Marion Hendry and his bride in 1865. The only black member in the white Methodist church and noted for her church work, she was buried in the family cemetery in 1905. Pictured are, from left to right (first row, William Marion Hendry, Julia A. Hendry, Susan C. (Wall) Hendry, Lydia C. Hendry, and Mammy Jane Hendry; (second row) Henry A. Hendry, Mary S. Hendry, and William W. Hendry. (Courtesy of Paula Hendry.)

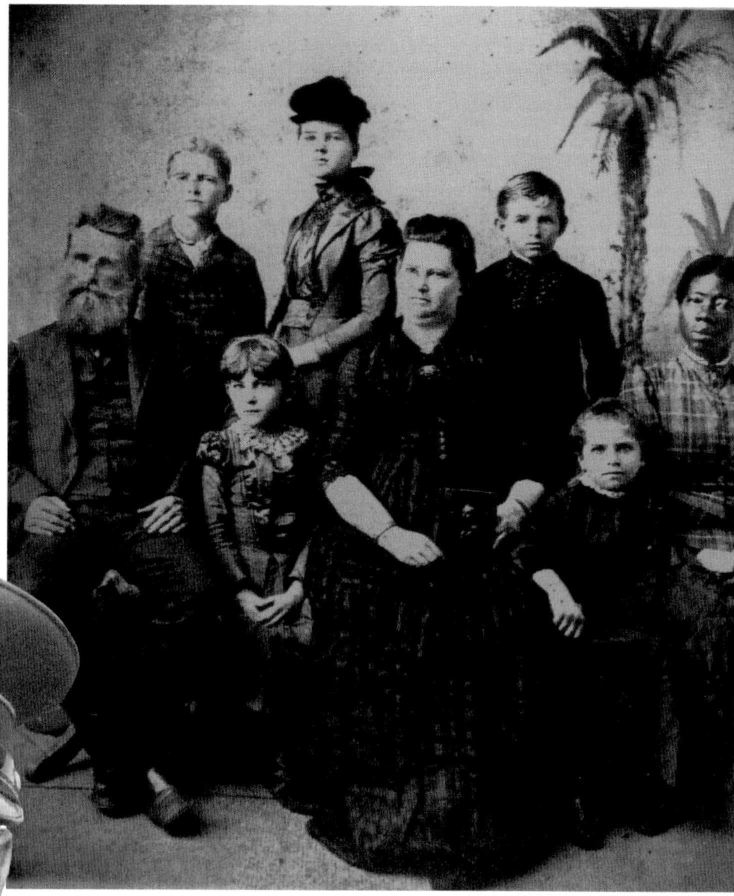

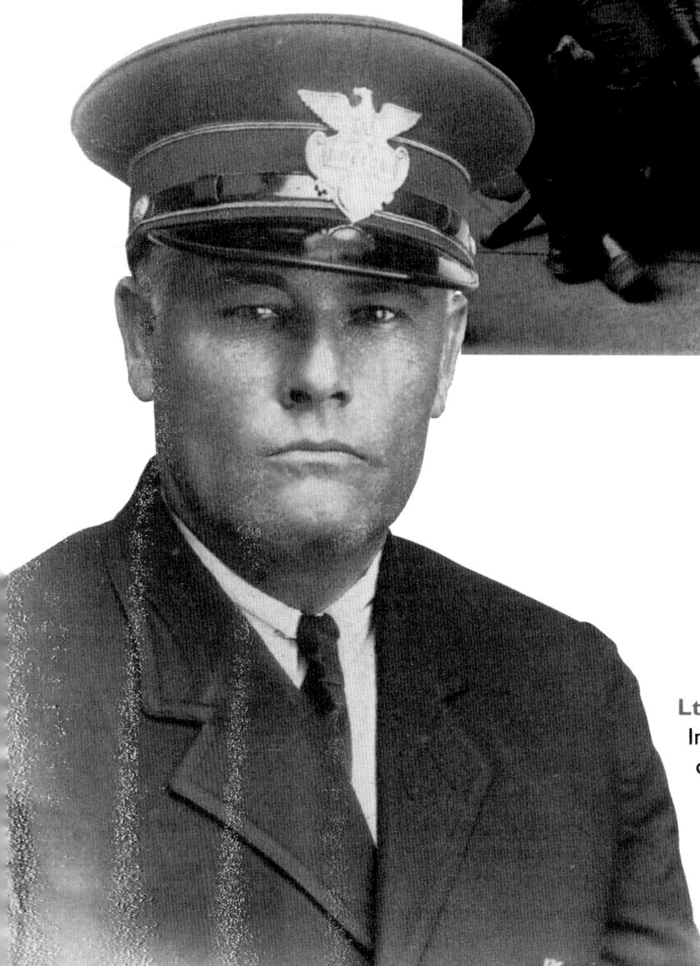

Lt. Matthew Hisler
In January 1930, Hisler was the first officer of the Fort Myers Police Department to be killed in the line of duty when he responded to a call and was shot in the head with a shotgun. The 56-year-old fallen officer was buried with full police honors, dressed in the new uniform that officers were to adopt that month. (Courtesy of Fort Myers Police Department.)

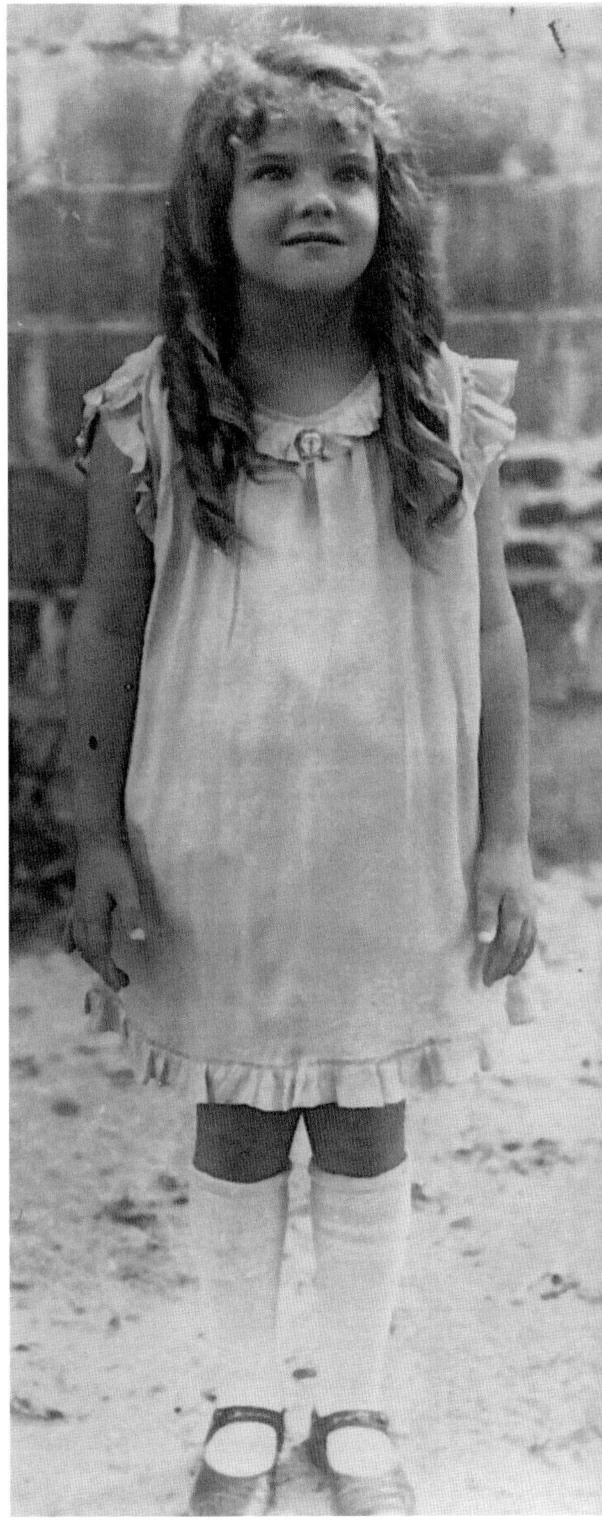

Mary Mildred (Hooker) Leffers
It was 1927, and booming Fort Myers was caught up in the excitement of the new opulent Moorish-style pleasure pier in the city park. An artist named Smith painted seven *Alice in Wonderland*–themed murals (below) for the palace. As a model for Alice, he chose a local child, Mary Mildred Hooker, who was about six years old at the time she posed for the paintings she inspired. When she grew up, the charming "Alice" graduated from Fort Myers High School in 1939, where she played on the basketball team. She was devoted to her family, church, and Fort Myers, where she lived all her life until 1992, when she moved to Lakeland, Florida, where she still resides, (Courtesy of Jo Anne Beaumont.)

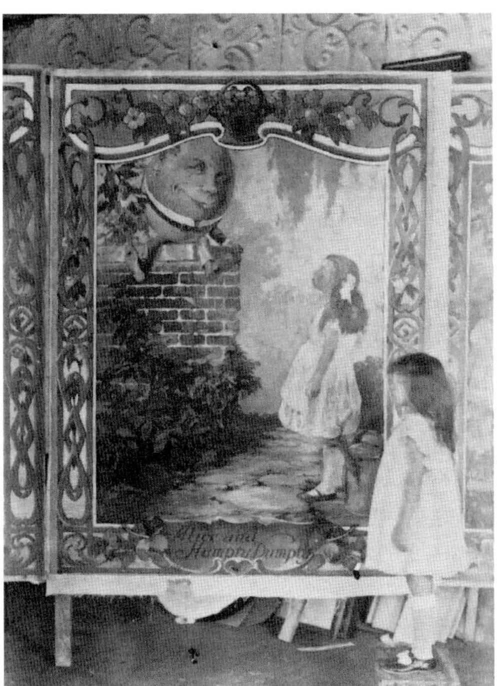

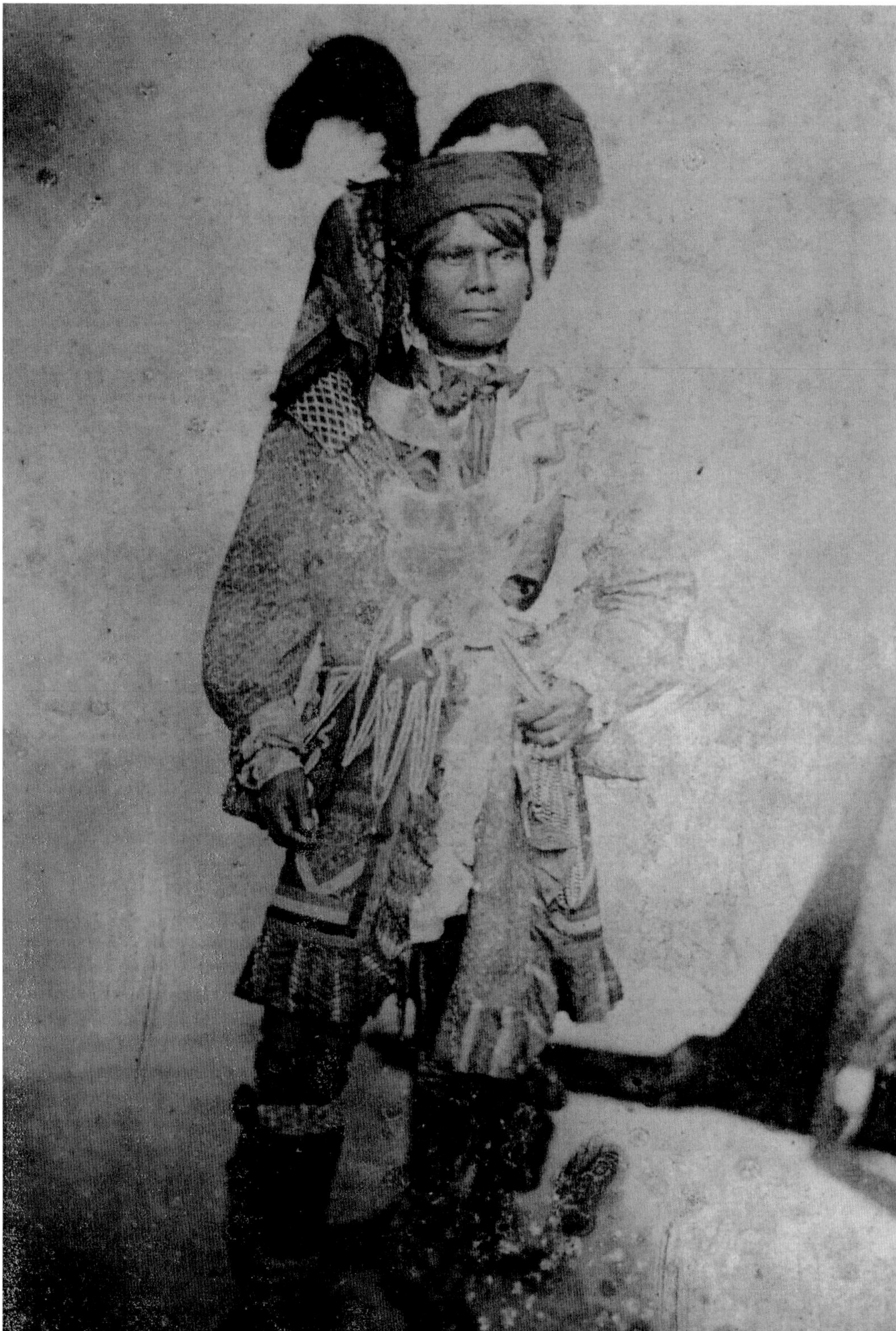

Chief Billy Bowlegs (LEFT)

In 1858, Seminole chief Billy Bowlegs and about 125 of his people camped by a small creek preparing to accept exile to Indian Territory in Oklahoma. Bowlegs had been one of several Seminole leaders during the Second and Third Seminole Wars. It was this departure, however, that effectively ended the third and last war after years of failed negotiations and intermittent fighting. On March 27, he accepted the terms negotiated at Fort Myers, including a $5,000 cash gift, $2,500 in claims for stolen cattle, $1,000 per warrior, $100 per woman and child, and payment for all animals and property in their possession. On May 4, the Seminoles walked to the fort's wharf and were loaded onto the steamer *Grey Cloud* and deported. Three days later, at Egmont Key, 41 more Seminoles boarded the boat for the long journey across the Gulf of Mexico to New Orleans. The Seminoles then traveled up the Mississippi and Arkansas Rivers to Fort Gibson, and then by land to Wewoka, Oklahoma. An estimated 300 Seminoles refused to leave Florida and remain undefeated to this day. Two theories of the chief's death exist, that he aided the Confederacy during the Civil War, dying during the fall of 1863 or winter of 1864, or that he died of fever soon after exile. (Courtesy of SAF.)

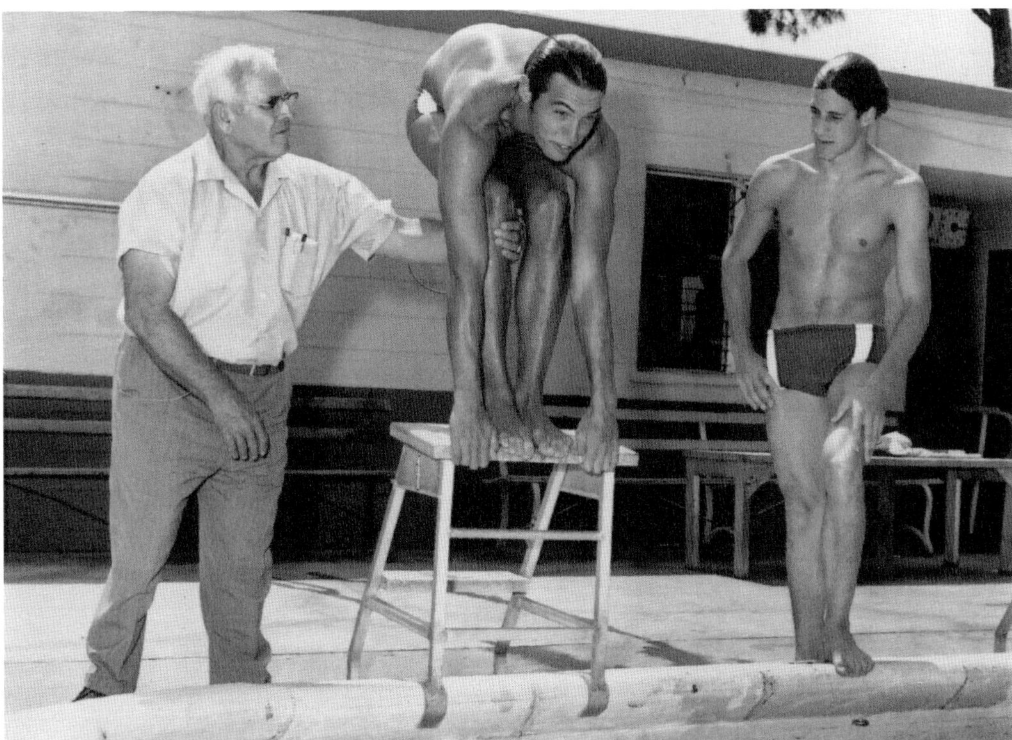

Coach Wes Nott

An estimated 8,000 children remember Coach Nott for helping them to achieve their best both in and out of the water by emphasizing hard work and good sportsmanship. In his native Ann Arbor, Michigan, he was state diving champion and lettered four years on his college swimming team. He also overcame the difficulties associated with having polio when he was 18 months old, which left him with a limp for the rest of his life. He joined the staff of Fort Myers High School as an assistant football coach in 1945, soon proving himself one of the best swim coaches in Florida. He retired in 1974. A pool on Cleveland Avenue was named in his honor, and a public monument to him by sculptor Don Wilkins is on that site. He died in 1984 at age 78. (Courtesy of Nott family.)

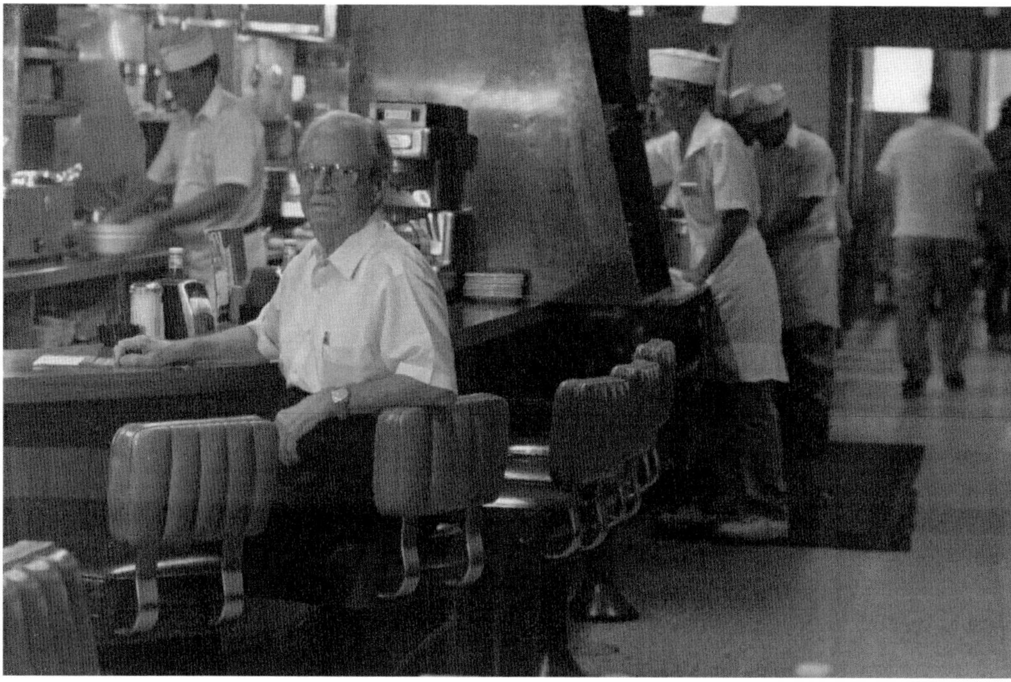

Win Ellis

Ellis is pictured in 1989 on the 40th anniversary of the opening of the Snack House, one of the most popular restaurants Fort Myers ever had. A tireless downtown booster and active in community organizations, he was a Fort Myers Chamber of Commerce president. He served on the committee that recruited the Pittsburgh Pirates to hold spring training in Fort Myers during the 1950s. Ellis closed his business in May 1993 after 44 years. He died in 2002. (Courtesy of SWFMH.)

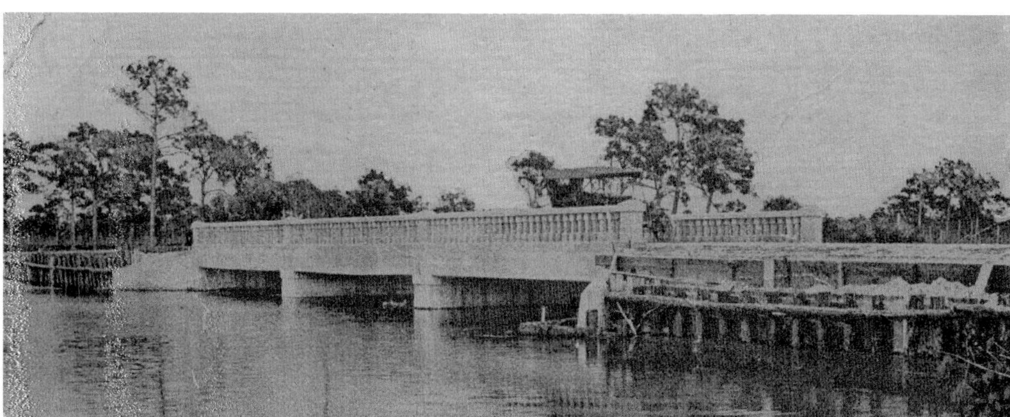

Bill Clay

Settling in Fort Myers in 1867, Clay became one of the region's most notorious moonshiners. He operated a still on a creek that was on a route for cowboys and Seminole Indians and appropriately named Wynomi to Indians and Whiskey Creek to whites. Clay had numerous arrests, but was never convicted, one time because the evidence mysteriously disappeared. He ran a blind tiger in a downtown shack, a pioneer-era type of speakeasy. The former Confederate soldier died in 1906. (Courtesy of SWFHS.)

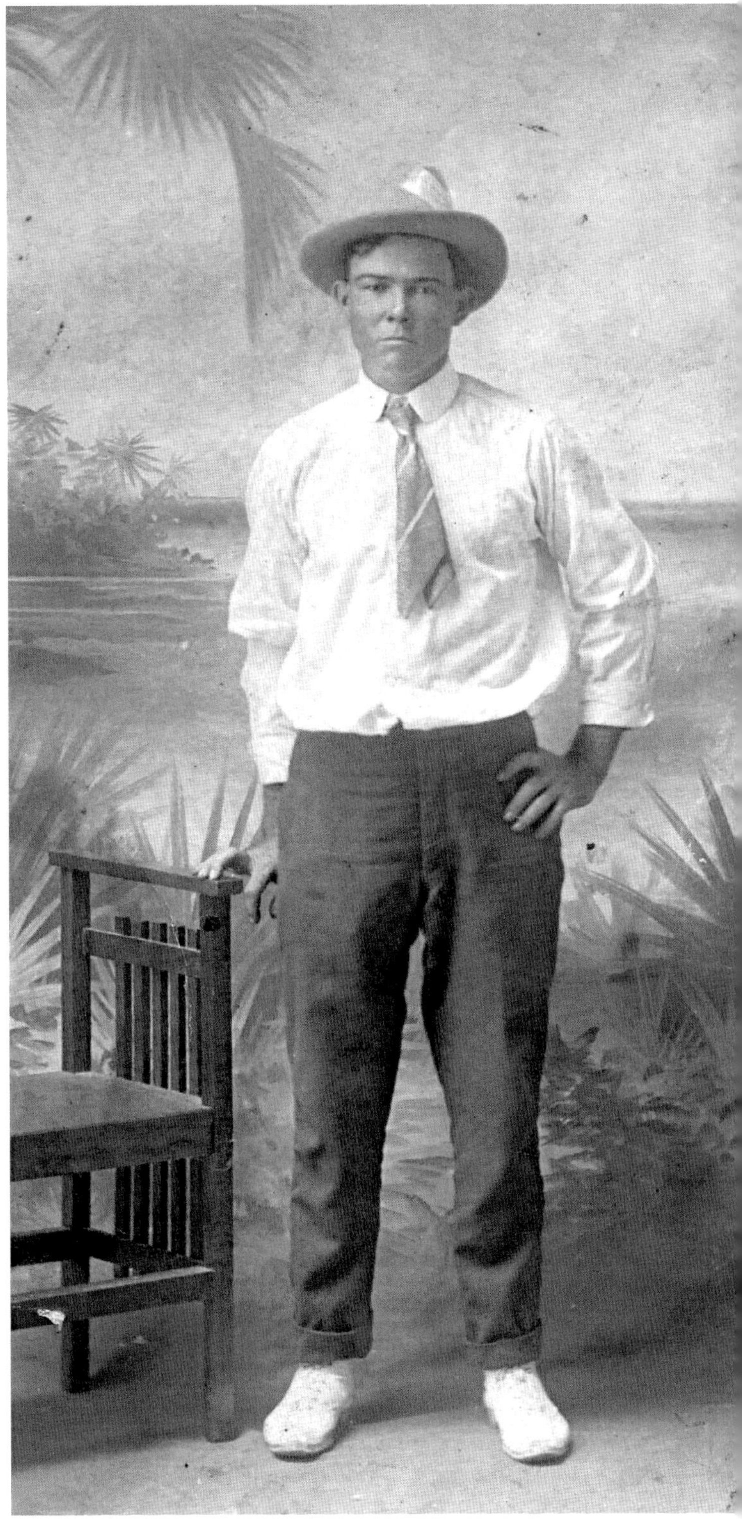

Rabe O. Wilkison
Not long before he went to war, Wilkison visited the Rembrandt Studio in downtown Fort Myers and posed for this postcard photograph. He had been notified that he was classified A-1 for immediate military service, so on June 26, 1918, the 22-year-old reported to the Lee County Draft Board in Fort Myers. Three months later, he would be dead. At the time of his enlistment, he reportedly said to Judge Nathan Stout: "I don't want to get into this thing, but now that I am to go I intend to give the Germans all that there is in me." Born in Immokalee, the young man was known for his courage and friendly disposition. He was sent to Camp Jackson, South Carolina, and given dog tag number 3,281,988. On August 5, he departed for Europe, one of almost two million American doughboys sent to France. That was a month of fierce fighting on the front. He volunteered for a mission so hazardous that no one was compelled to take it. His captain told the men, "The chances are a hundred to one that you will not live to tell the story." They were told to consider their decision carefully and give an answer at morning roll call. Wilkison made an immediate decision to accept the dangerous service. A fellow soldier tried to talk him out of it, but the next day he was transferred for the mission. Private Wilkison died in the battle at St. Mihiel on September 16, 1918, less than two months before Armistice Day would have brought him safely home. He is buried in the St. Mihiel American Cemetery, Thiacourt-Meurthe-et-Moselle, France. In 1963, he was posthumously awarded the Purple Heart. American Legion Post 38 in downtown Fort Myers is named for him. (Courtesy of AL.)

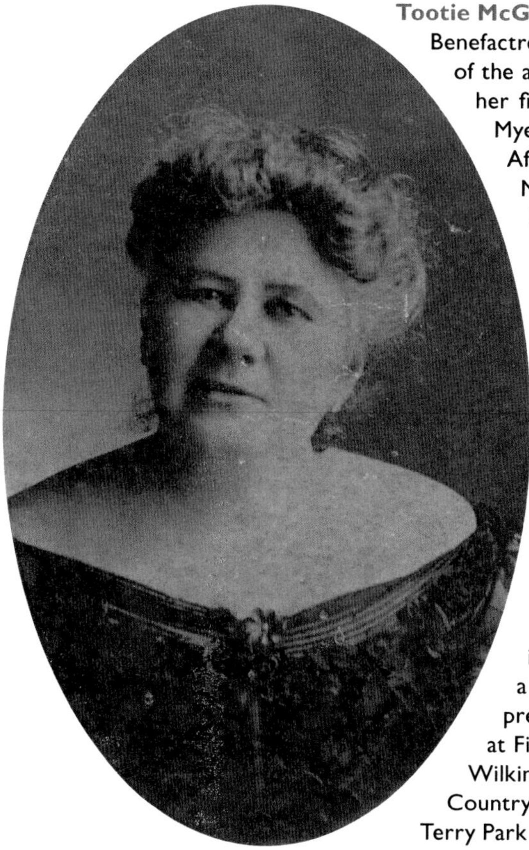

Tootie McGregor Terry

Benefactress and investor Tootie McGregor Terry was one of the area's most influential seasonal residents. She and her first husband, Ambrose McGregor, came to Fort Myers in 1891 for the health of their son, Bradford. After her husband and son died, she married Dr. M.O. Terry in 1905, whom she had known when he was a young medical student and she was Miss Barber, the judge's daughter. She financed Harvie E. Heitman in building the Bradford Hotel in 1905, and in 1912, offered to finance the paving of the road from Whiskey Creek to Punta Rassa in return for its being named McGregor Boulevard to honor her first husband. She died that year, but Dr. Terry completed the project. (Courtesy of SWFHS.)

Dr. M.O. Terry

Like his wife Tootie, Dr. M.O. Terry, pictured (below) with Thomas A. Edison, pushed for improvements, such as a riverfront boulevard and a golf and yacht club. After she died in 1912, he presented a memorial fountain to the town. It stood at Five Points until the early 1960s. Restored by Don Wilkins in the 1980s, it now resides at the Fort Myers Country Club. Terry donated the 40 acres now known as Terry Park to the county. (Courtesy of SWFHS.)

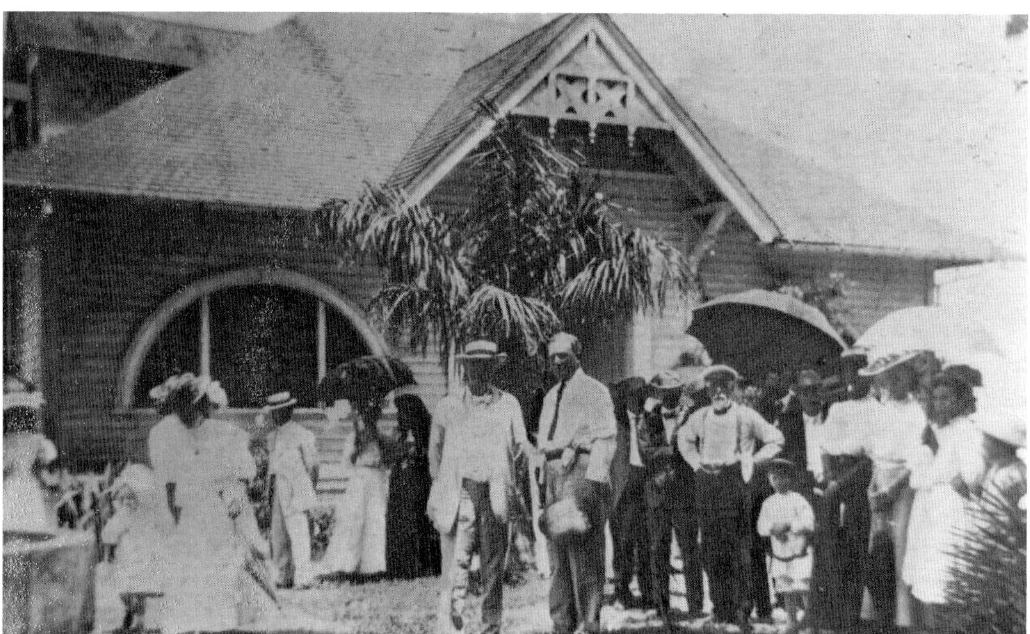

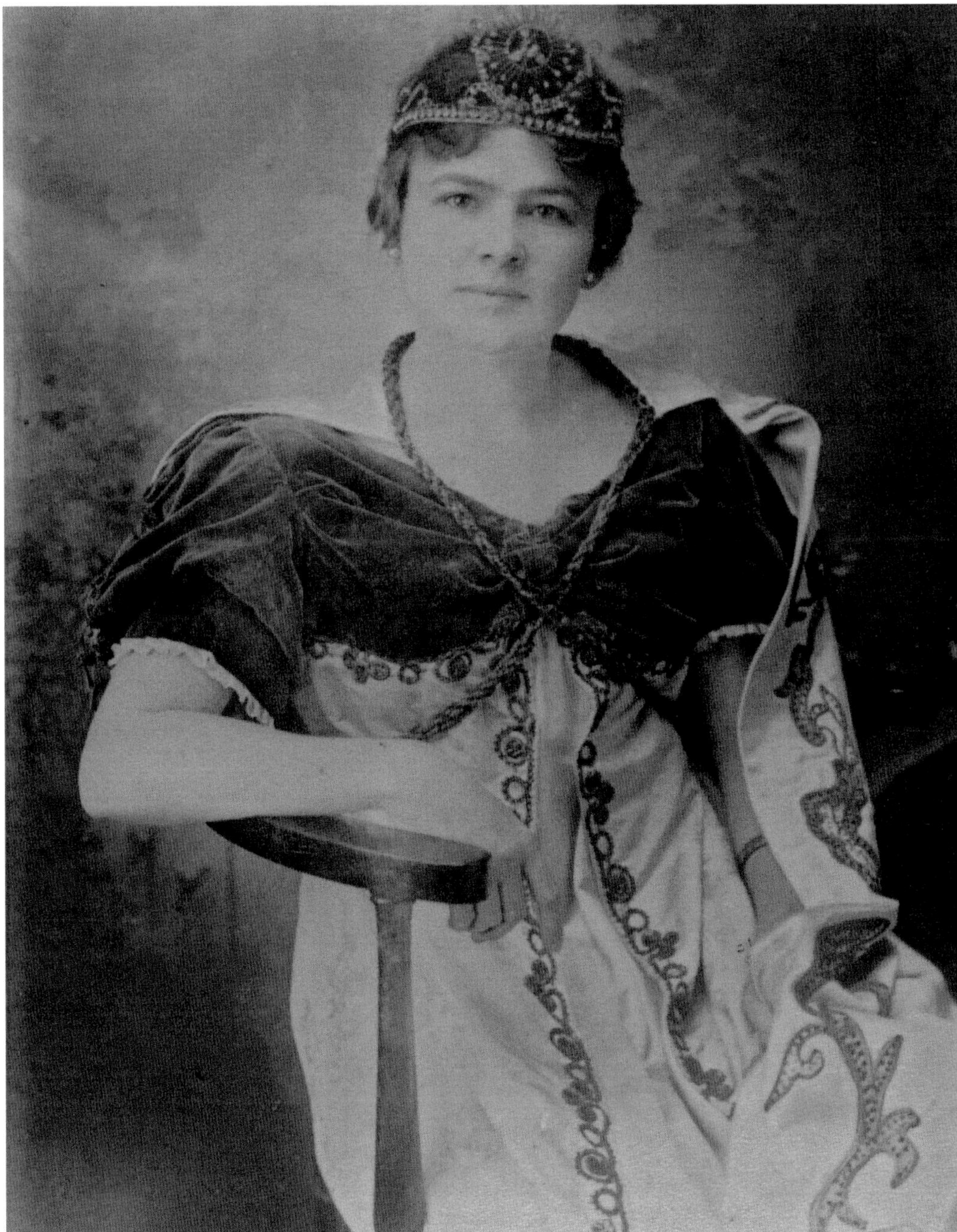

Lillian (Gilliam) Pursley

In 1917, Lillian Gilliam was crowned Princess Florida in La Conquista de Florida, the three-day forerunner to today's Edison Pageant of Light, complete with royalty, parades, and Indian, Spanish, and American Days. The secret ballot results heightened the suspense until the night's culminating moment when Gilliam removed her mask to reveal herself as Princess Florida. The event was suspended due to World War I and never revived. (Courtesy of SWFHS.)

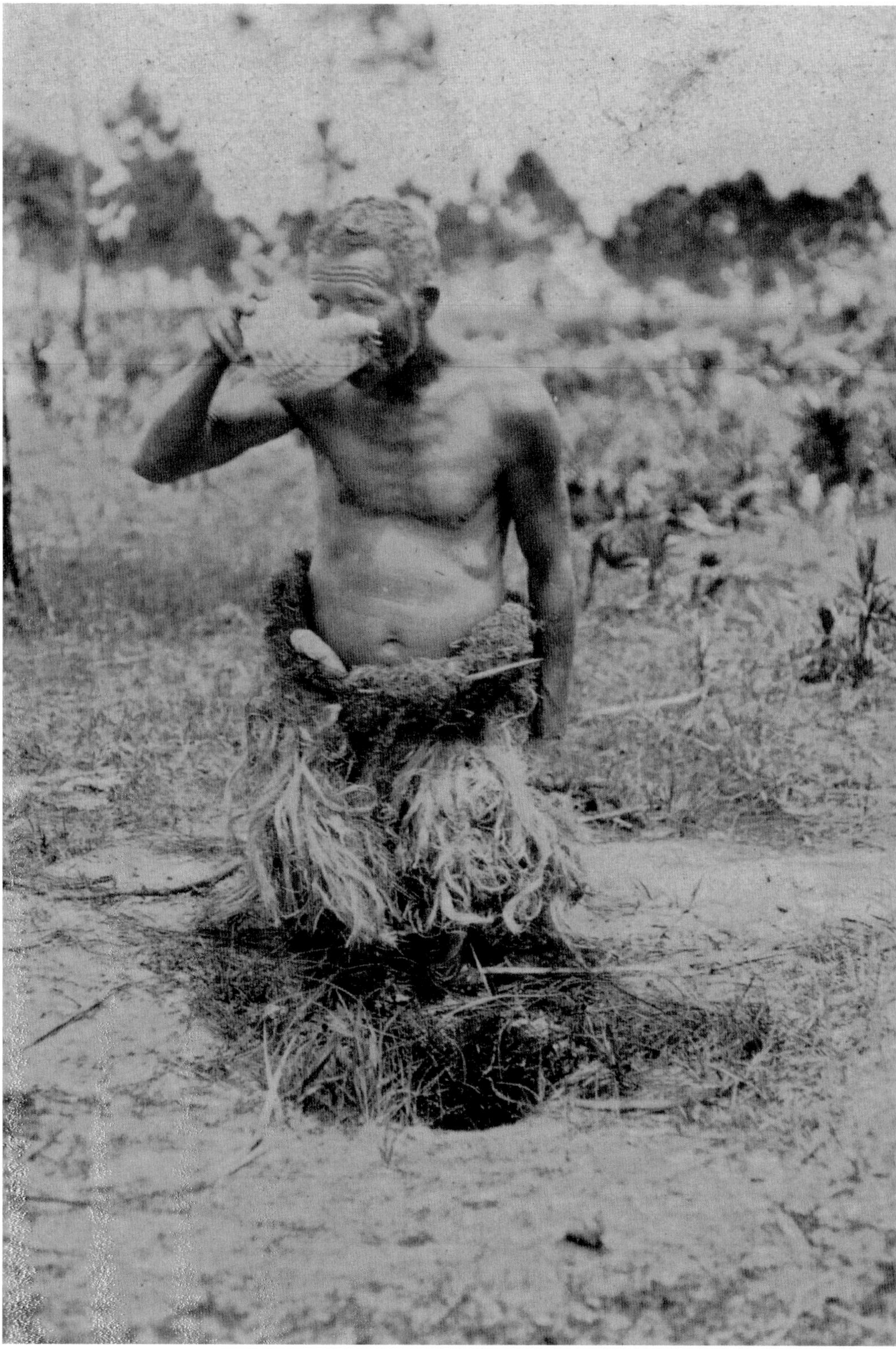

"Wild Bill" Belvin (LEFT)

In 1930, a self-ordained Methodist minister, hog farmer, and boiler maker went into the wild wearing only a bathing suit and armed only with an extra pair of false teeth and eyeglasses. It was a Depression-era stunt dreamed up by the *Tropical News* to promote southwest Florida as a place of easy living. Questions remain about whether Wild Bill Belvin was paid. He planned to live in a Seminole Indian–style palm-frond hut; dine on seafood, swamp cabbage, fruits and berries, and small game; and chronicle his adventure on bark paper with natural-dye ink. He reappeared in town one year later, tanned and several pounds heavier, and was arrested by Sheriff Tippins for stealing pelican eggs. Citizens raised $500 bail, and the next day Belvin had two speaking engagements. He died in 1963 at age 86. His grave was rediscovered in the Fort Myers Cemetery in 2003. (Courtesy of SWFHS.)

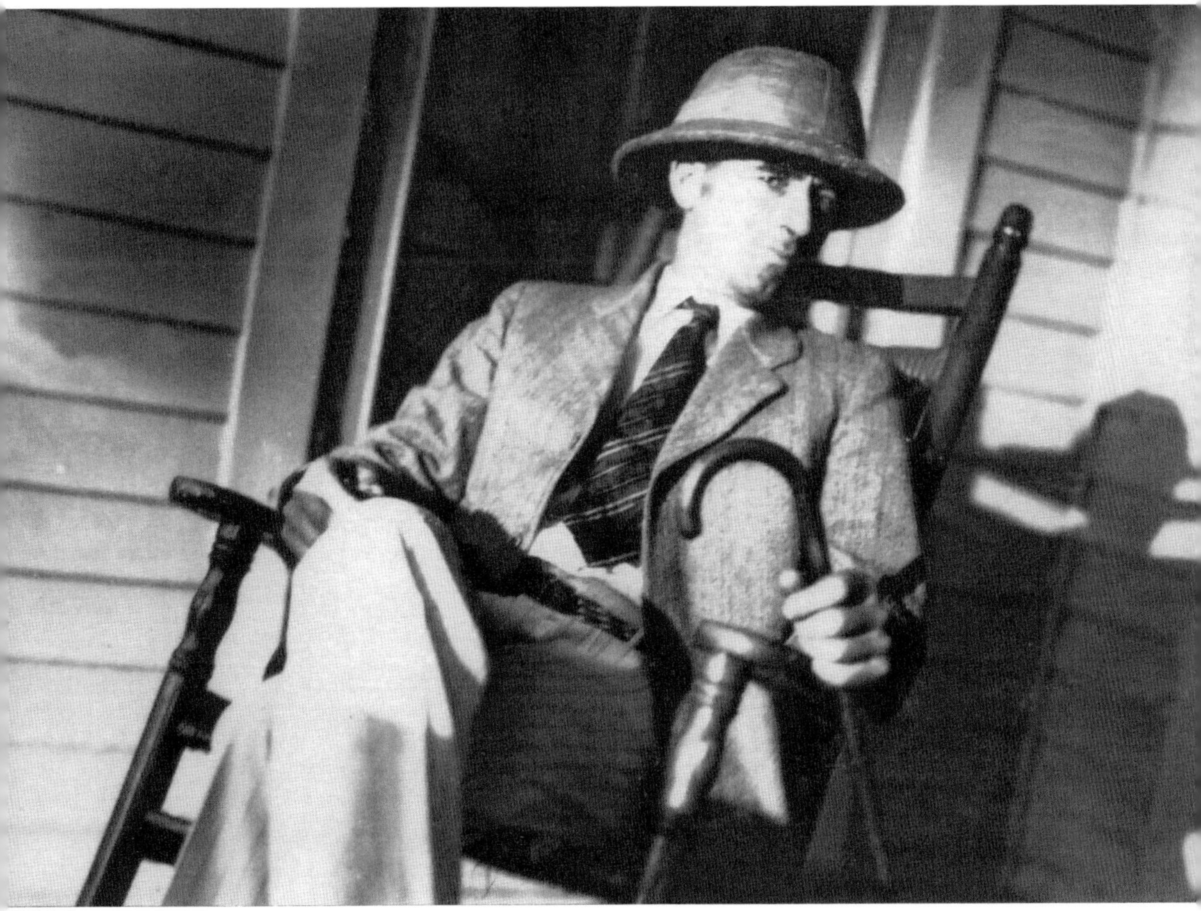

Dr. Edwin L. Rasmussen

Pioneer doctor of alternative medicine, Rasmussen continued in the profession of his father, a Danish naturopath who was an original member of the Battle Creek Sanitarium. The physician first visited Fort Myers in 1915 when in the US Auxiliary service, liked the town, and returned after World War I. He had a stormy career in the pioneer town, and was once shot at from ambush when he returned home one night from a late call. After 16 years, he left for Florida's east coast, only to return and open clinics that taught people how to stay well, as he put it. On his 90th birthday, he said he had stayed healthy by minding his own business. He died in 1972. He wrote an engaging memoir, *Medical Nostalgia*. (Courtesy of SWFMH.)

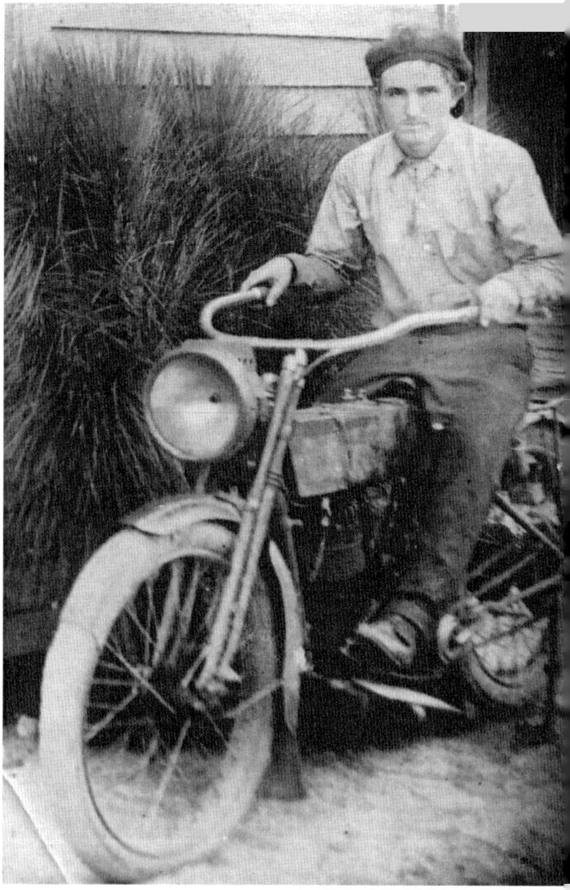

Frog Smith
Smith earned his nickname during the Depression when he caught and dressed a barrel of frog legs and shipped them to New York for some welcome income. Born in 1896, he came to southwest Florida in 1911, taking on a hodgepodge of jobs, including work on a yard-locomotive at age 14. It seems there's nothing he didn't try and do well, including riding his Harley motorcycle. A *Fort Myers News-Press* columnist for almost 40 years, he also published several books and other articles. Featured on CBS television's *On the Road* series with Charles Kuralt, he was a well-known folk artist and a storyteller in classic Florida Cracker tradition. He was given the 1975 Folk Heritage Award for Outstanding Contributions to Florida's Folklife. He died at 96. (Courtesy of SWFMH.)

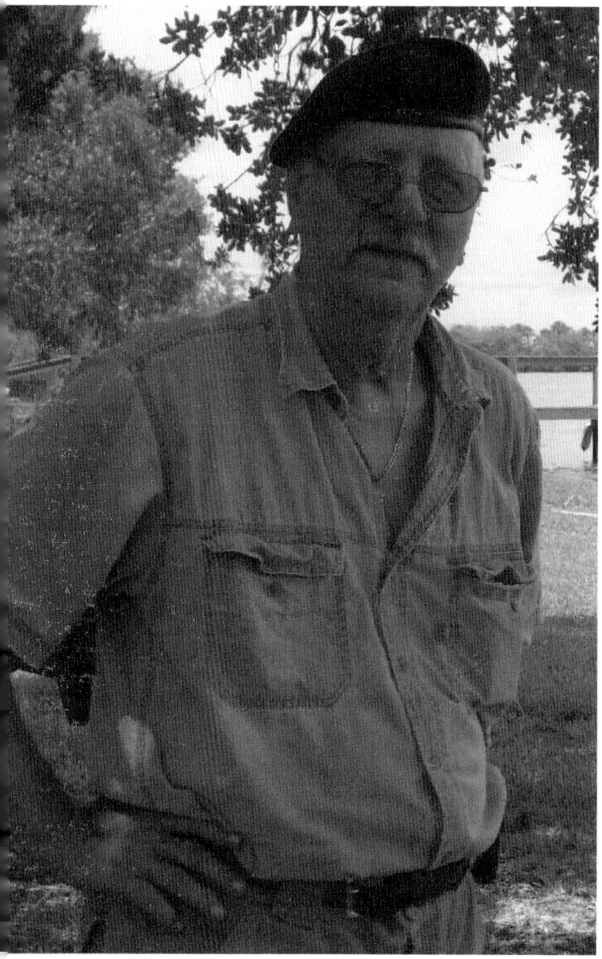

Don Wilkins
The sculptor's *Uncommon Friends* is the centerpiece of Centennial Park, and depicts Jimmy Newton with Thomas A. Edison, Henry Ford, and Harvey Firestone, who inspired Newton's book of the same title. Other notable projects include his sculpture of Coach Wes Nott; busts of Capt. Francis A. Hendry, Tootie McGregor Terry, and Connie Mack Sr.; and a memorial to the 2nd Regiment Infantry, US Colored Troops, stationed at Fort Myers during the Civil War. (Photograph by the author.)

CHAPTER THREE

Free Spirits

Artists, free-thinkers, writers, musicians, people who march to their own drummers—Fort Myers has had them all in abundance. Often unconventional, devoted to their own dreams and projects, and enviable for their self-assurance, they provide the sparkle, creativity, and ability to organize things that make a community out of the ordinary. Legends such as Effie Winkler McAdow and Jeanne Bochette have combined artistic ability, community spirit, and practicality to sustain their community for decades. Such people earn the distinguished title of "institution." Free spirits earn a well-deserved immortality. The performances of the Fort Myers Little Theatre still echo in the minds of locals, the music of Billy Nalle resounds through the years, and Dr. M.F. Johnson's Christmas Day snow spectacle, created out of love for his son, is still talked about.

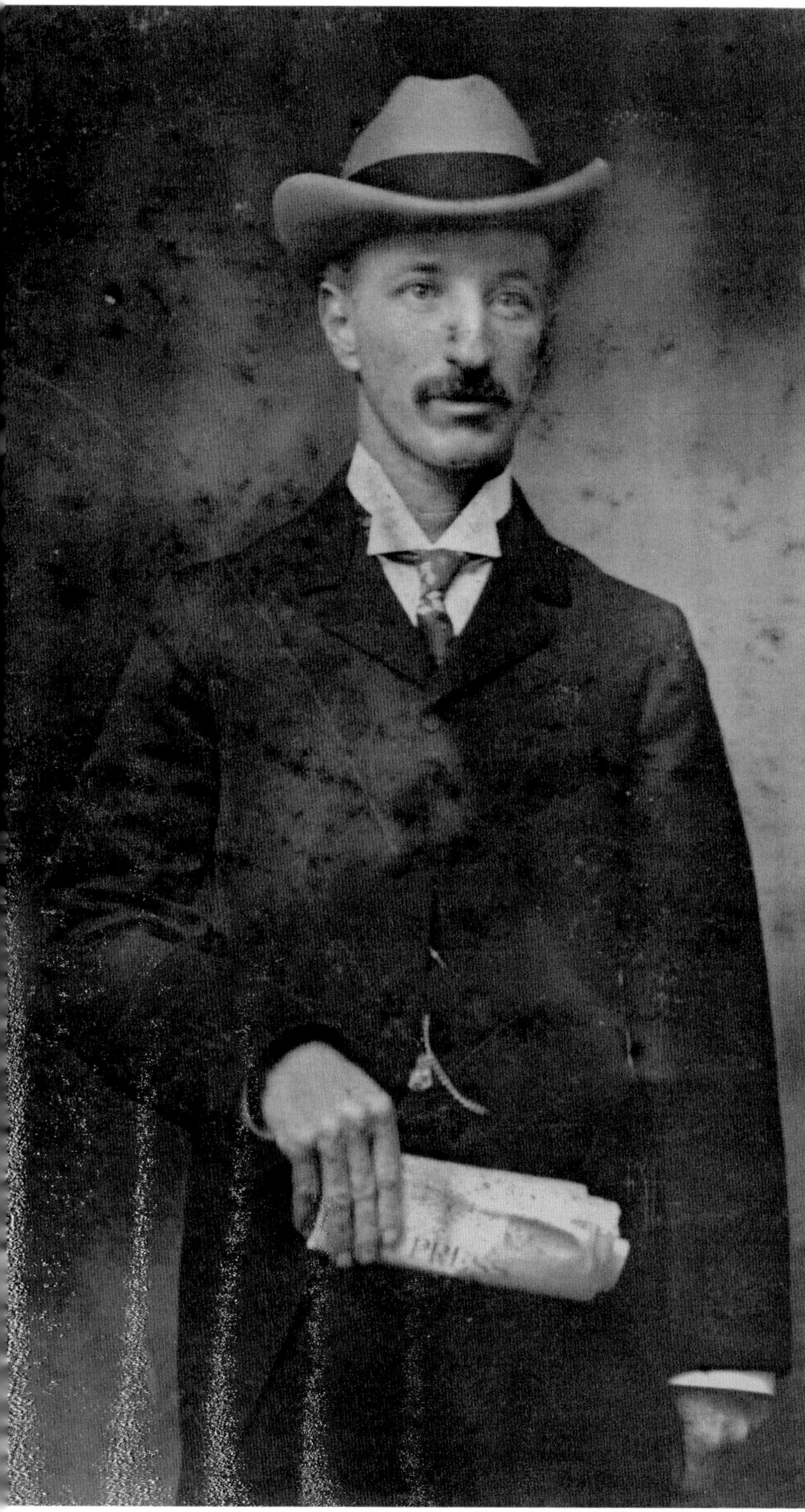

Philip Isaacs
A long-lasting squabble between two newspaper editors was put to rest in January 1897 with a merger. In 1894, Dr. W.W. Foose, the newly appointed political editor at the *Fort Myers Press*, had provoked readers' ire by questioning whether the prominent Hendry clan benefitted from political favoritism. A backlash spawned the creation of the rival *Tropical News* with Philip Isaacs as editor. The two editors engaged in vitriolic editorial fights to create what must have been an interesting newspaper scene for such a small town. However, the entertaining reading evidently did not result in financial profits, and during the next several months the *Tropical News* changed hands three times, with the two papers eventually consolidating in January 1897—with Isaacs surviving as editor. (Courtesy of SAF.)

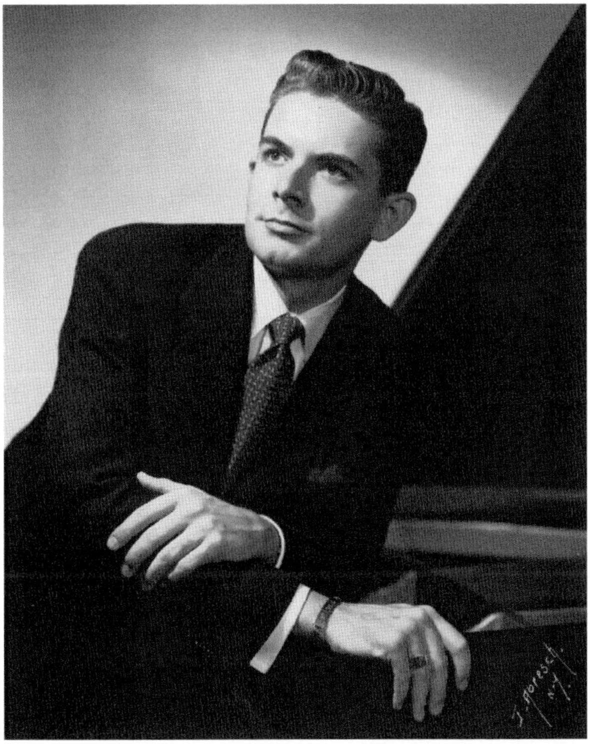

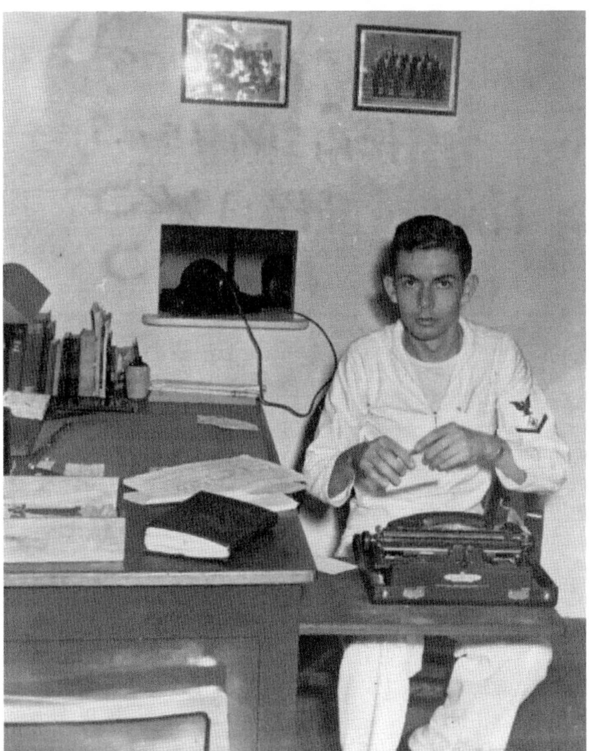

Billy Nalle

Nalle's talent made it evident that he would not carry on the successful mercantile business his father had founded in 1912. He was destined to be a musician and composer. Upon graduating from Fort Myers High School in 1939, Nalle was awarded the American Legion School Award and went on to study at the Juilliard School of Music in New York City on a full scholarship for piano and organ. He graduated in 1943, later doing postgraduate work from 1947 to 1948. He joined the US Navy in 1943 (below) and served as a touring musician to bases in the Pacific theater during World War II. Among his duties was the Pacific Area US Navy Entertainment Tour of 1945–1946. Along the way, he worked closely with Bobby Beers and Bob Fosse. After the war, Nalle's musical career flourished. He worked for 26 years as a pianist and organist on live television, eventually working for all the major networks in New York City and witnessing the new medium take shape. As early as 1948, the pianist played on the *Gloria Swanson Show*. He often doubled for screen stars whose roles required them to play the piano expertly on shows such as CBS-TV's *Studio One*, *Kraft Theater*, or *Lux Video Theater*. Nalle would play in the background, and the television camera would film the star's hands gracefully tickling the keys. Jack Lemmon was among the many actors he stood in for. He also appeared on Arlene Francis's *The Home Show*, accompanying her and Hugh Downs on piano. In 1975, he became the artist-in-residence at the Century II Center in Wichita, Kansas. At that center resided the world-famous 4/36 "Mighty Wurlitzer" organ that had been designed for New York's Paramount Theatre on Times Square, which opened in 1926. In 1993, he was inducted into the Theatre Organists Hall of Fame by the American Theatre Organ Society. In 1995, he retired to his native Fort Myers and died there in 2005. (Courtesy of SWFHS, Nalle Collection.)

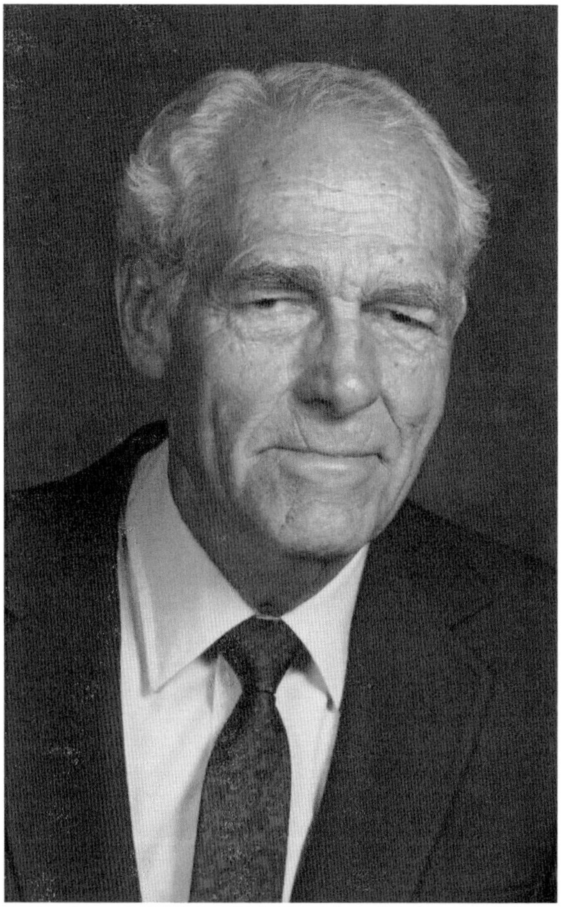

Richard Powell

Before discovering Fort Myers on a 1945 road trip, Powell was a reporter for the *Philadelphia Ledger* and a magazine writer. He became an overnight celebrity in 1957 with *The Philadelphian*, followed by *Pioneer, Go Home!* and *I Take This Land*, both set in southwest Florida. Woody Allen adapted *Don Quixote, U.S.A.* into the film *Bananas*, and Elvis Presley starred in *Follow That Dream*, an adaptation of *Pioneer.* Powell helped found the Fort Myers Little Theatre in the late 1940s. (Courtesy of Kevin McCarthy.)

Fort Myers Little Theatre

The Fort Myers Little Theatre resided in Patio de Leon, but when the historic theater was demolished, the group moved to the Edison Park Elementary School and evolved into the Edison Players. Actors appearing in *You Can't Take It With You* are, from left to right (front row seated) Mac McCreary, John Wyatt, Marge Wyatt, and Bill Sonnenberg; (back row, standing) Maureen Bashaw, Dan Henderson, Carroll Shands, Rick Anglickis, Guy Amason, Jinny McKay, Mike McInnis, and Dick Bashaw. (Courtesy of Marge Wyatt.)

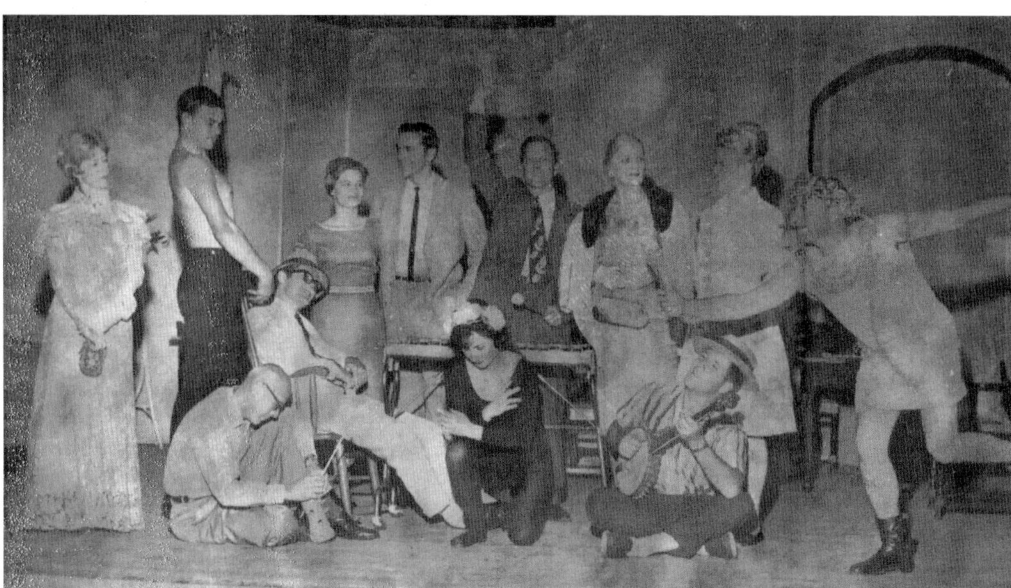

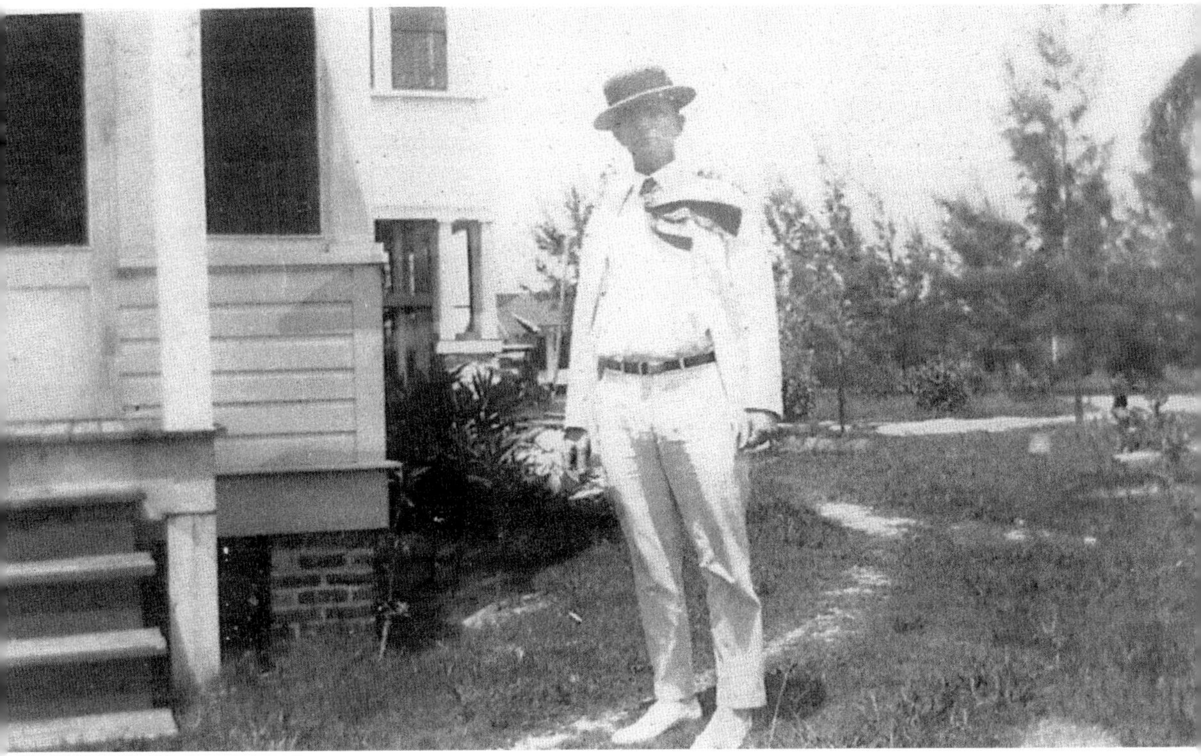

Dr. M.F. Johnson
Snow on Christmas morning was the surprise for anyone passing Dr. M.F. Johnson's residence in the late 1940s. The "snow" delivered from the ice company was a gift to his son, Franklin Jr., disabled from birth and requiring constant care. Locals remember that the doctor went all out for his son with holiday decorations and snow. He didn't advertise the gift, but people in the know looked forward to the spectacle each year. One of the first physicians to practice medicine in Fort Myers, he came to town in 1916. Also a businessman, he helped to found the Lee County Bank and built extensive rental properties. In 1963, he was the oldest practicing physician in Fort Myers and ran an office in the home famous for its snowy Christmas mornings. He died in 1968 at the age of 84. (Courtesy of SWFHS.)

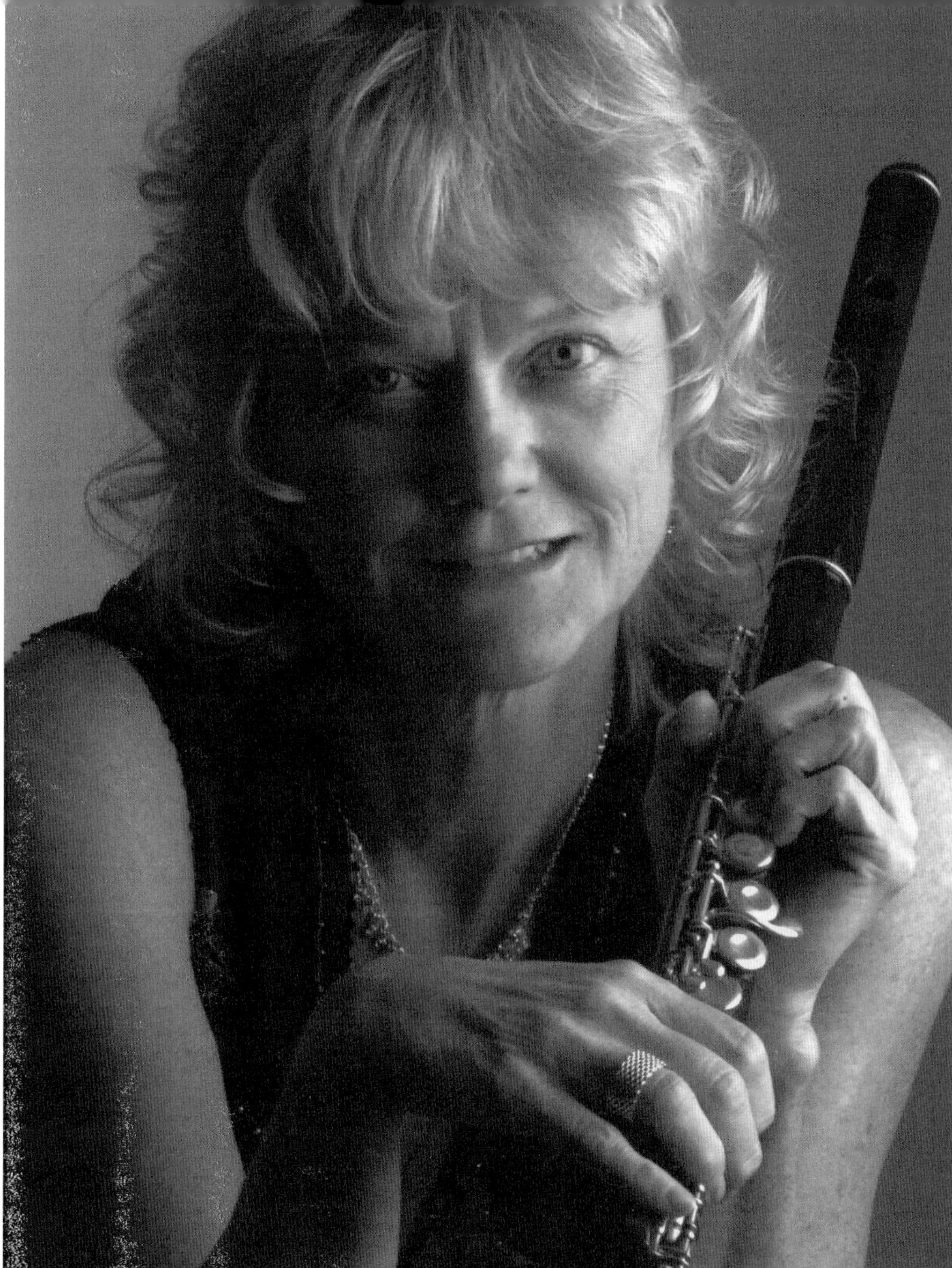

Kat Epple

The music of flautist and composer Kat Epple has been heard in film scores and television soundtracks, on recordings across the world, in digital orchestrations, and live concerts, in which she plays the flutes she has collected on her travels. Her music has earned her eight Emmy awards and a Grammy nomination. She has performed at the Guggenheim Museum, the Metropolitan Museum of Art, the United Nations, Palazzo dei Diamanti, Italy, and with the Merce Cunningham Dance Company as part of their *Legacy* tour. Also a peace activist, she was chosen as US ambassador for the Worldwide Peace Marker Project, a collaborative global art installation involving artists committed to peace, environmental stewardship, world health, global cooperation, and tolerance. (Courtesy of Kat Epple.)

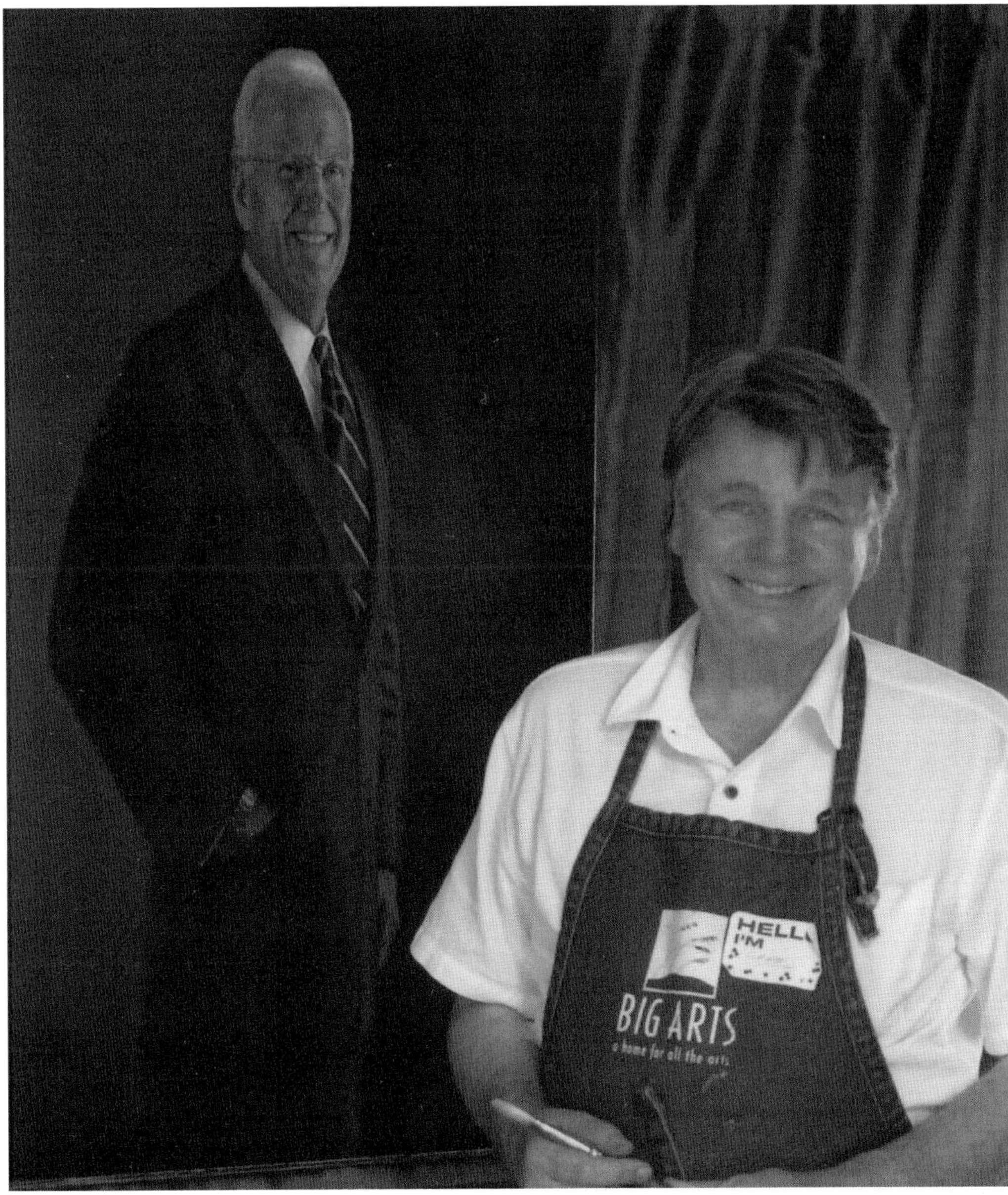

Greg Biolchini

An internationally recognized pastelist, painter, and portraitist, Biolchini has had over 30 solo shows, judged international exhibitions, and won dozens of awards. He teaches workshops in his studio on the north shore of the Caloosahatchee River and is in demand nationwide as a portrait painter. He is pictured with his portrait of Dr. Richard Pegnetter, founding dean of Florida Gulf Coast University. His work is in collections at Florida's State Capitol Building, the Edison & Ford Winter Estates, the Museum of Florida Art and Culture, and others. He felt especially honored by his community in 2006 when he was awarded the Angels of the Arts Visual Artist of the Year. A longtime arts advocate, he cofounded the Tower Gallery, Fort Myers' first art cooperative, with Jo Bainbridge Cobbett in the early 1980s. (Courtesy of Greg Biolchini.)

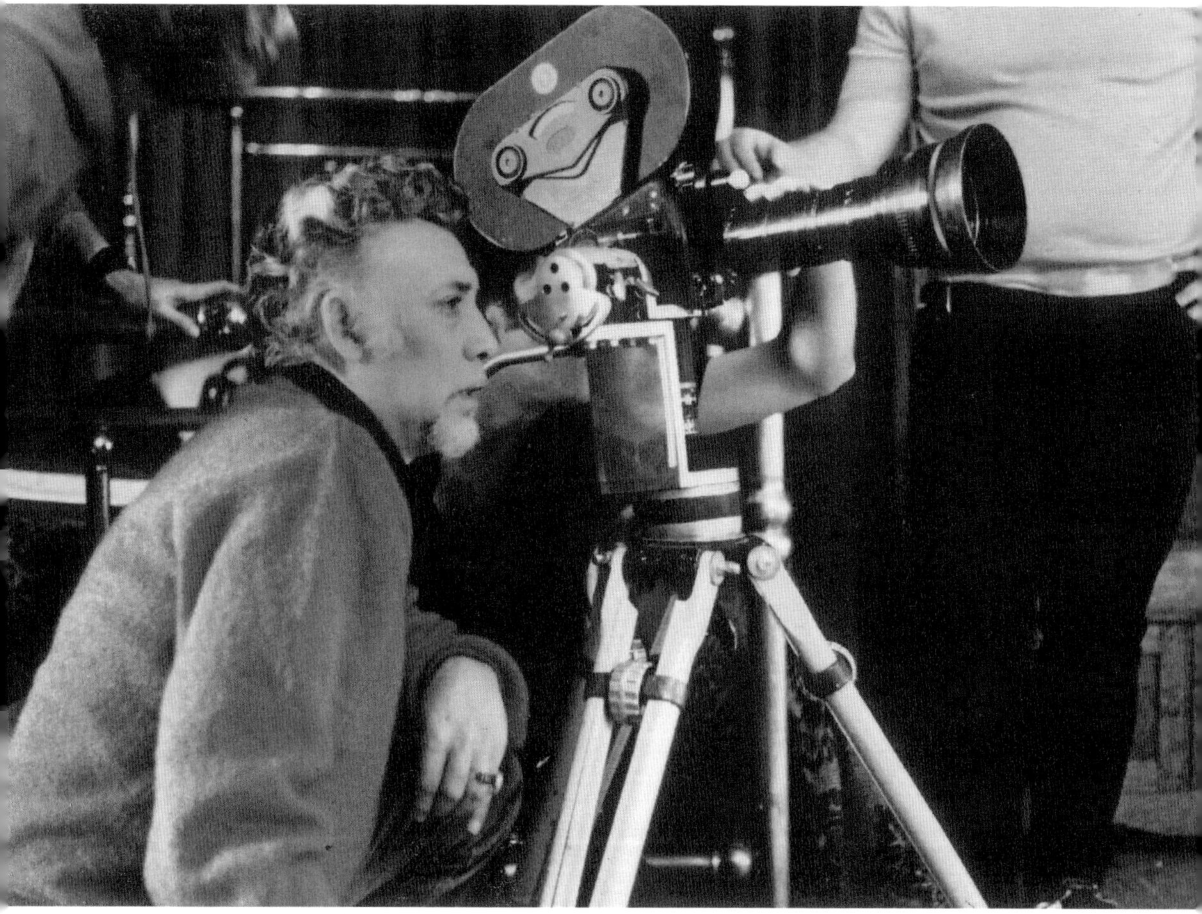

Gerard Damiano Sr.
In 1972, Damiano, the successful owner of New York City hair salons, created a media blitz as the director of *Deep Throat*. An iconic film in its genre, it was one of the most successful pornographic films with a nationwide general audience. The film's place in history was sealed in 2005, when W. Mark Felt, former number-two man at the FBI, disclosed that he was "Deep Throat," *Washington Post* journalist Bob Woodward's secret source of information during the Watergate investigation. Work as a professional photographer led to the start of Damiano's film career. Second in fame to *Deep Throat* was the 1973 *The Devil in Miss Jones*. He is pictured on the set of *The Story of Joanna* (1975). Damiano moved to Fort Myers in the 1990s after years as a seasonal visitor. He died there in 2008. (Courtesy of Damiano family.)

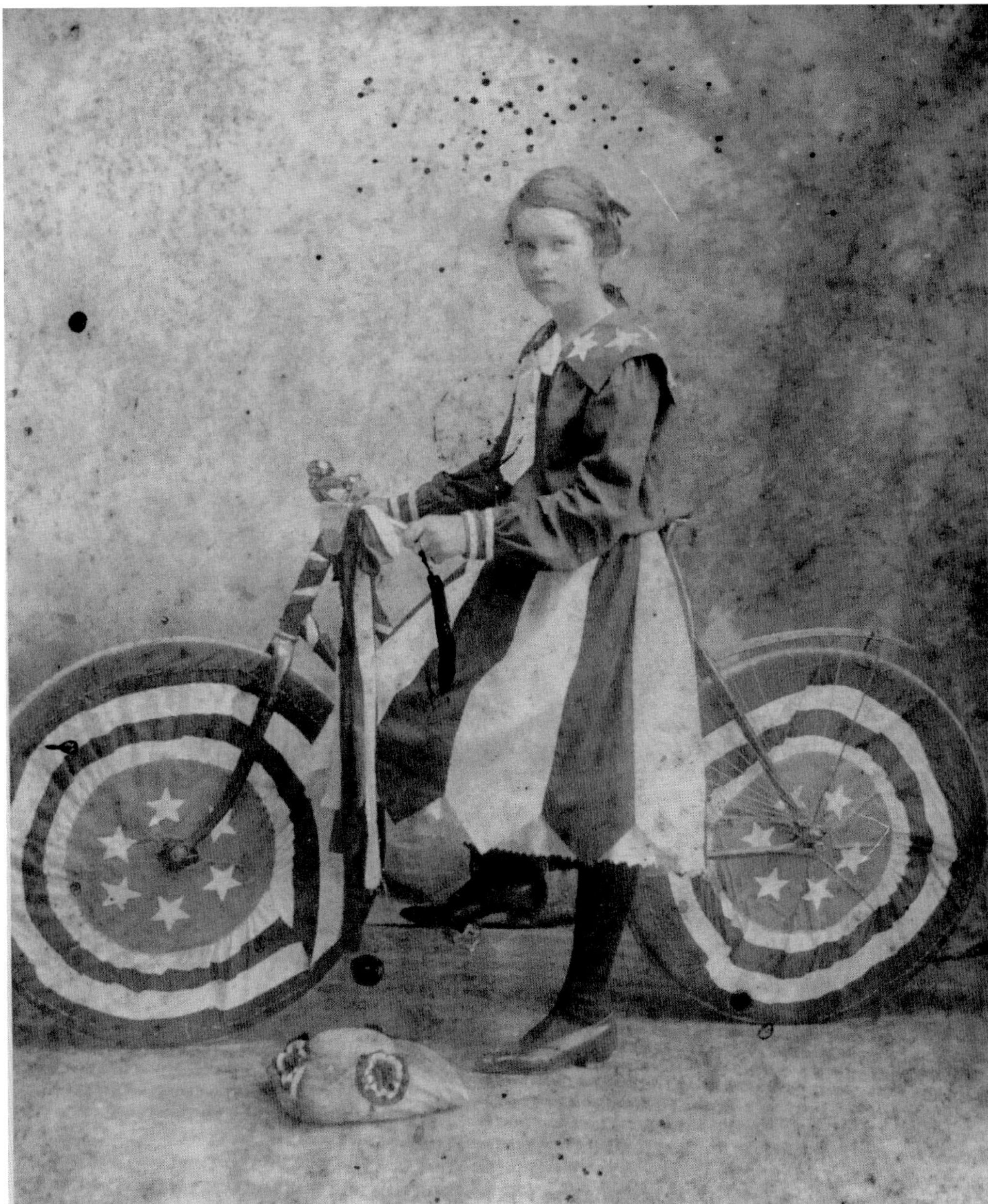

Geraldine (Carson) Vesper

This young bicyclist dressed patriotically for a parade had a 21-year career as society editor for the *Fort Myers News-Press*, following 10 years as Fort Myers correspondent for the *Miami Herald*. Born to the pioneering Frank Carson family, Vesper was known as a lady, in the old-fashioned and best sense of the word. She not only knew everyone, but she knew how to keep a confidence, when to reveal, and what to reveal. When she died in 1986, her colleagues remembered her as a professional who combined consideration for others, an ability to listen, and impeccable spelling and accuracy. In 1956, the Business and Professional Women's Club honored her as Woman of the Year. (Courtesy of SWFHS.)

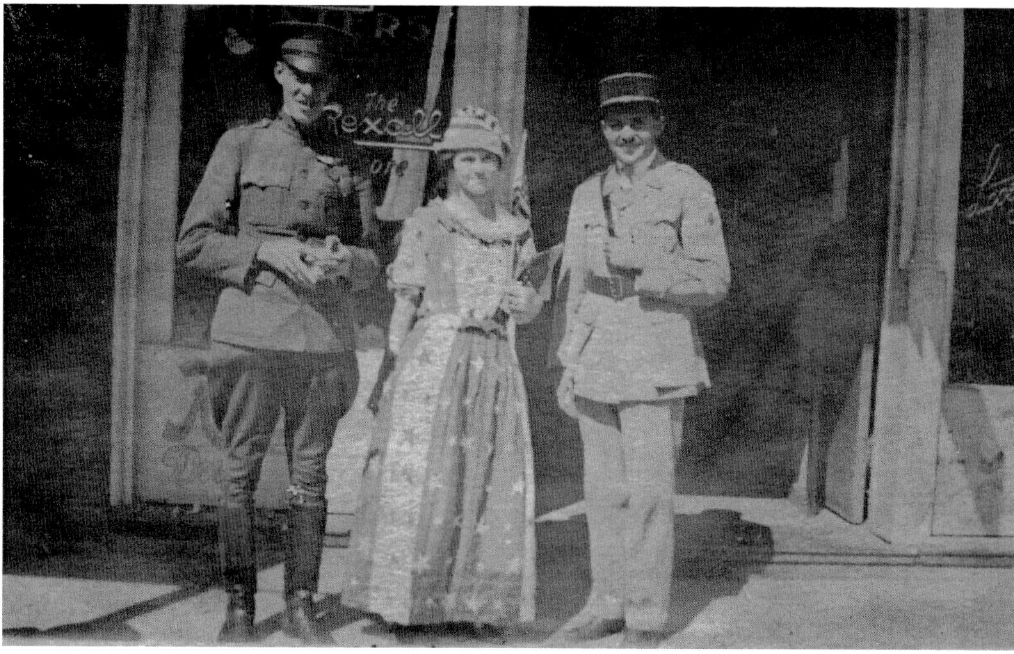
The
Rexall

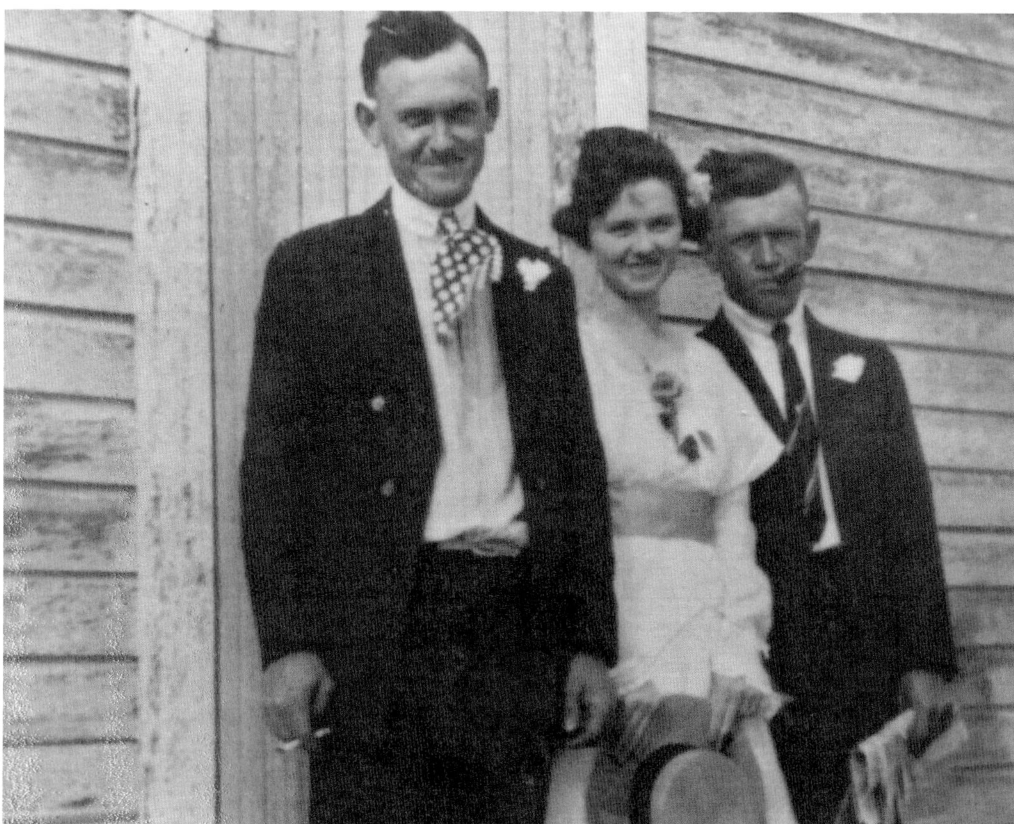

Ethel (Sherouse) Morrow (LEFT)

Dressed as Lady Liberty (left) and posing with soldiers stationed at nearby air fields, Ethel Sherouse exemplifies the festive spirit that swept through Fort Myers on Armistice Day, 1918. To celebrate the end of World War I, she joined the crowds riding through town in an open car, honking the horn and waving a flag. During World War I, she managed McCrory's Five and Ten. Soon afterwards, the high-spirited redhead would meet Harry Morrow at a skating rink. They tied the knot in January 1921 at the Edison Estate, where her grandfather was a caretaker (below). She entertained her children and grandchildren with tales of swimming and fishing with the famous inventor in his "cement pond." With her are Harry Morrow (left) and her brother Clarence Sherouse. (Both courtesy of SWFHS.)

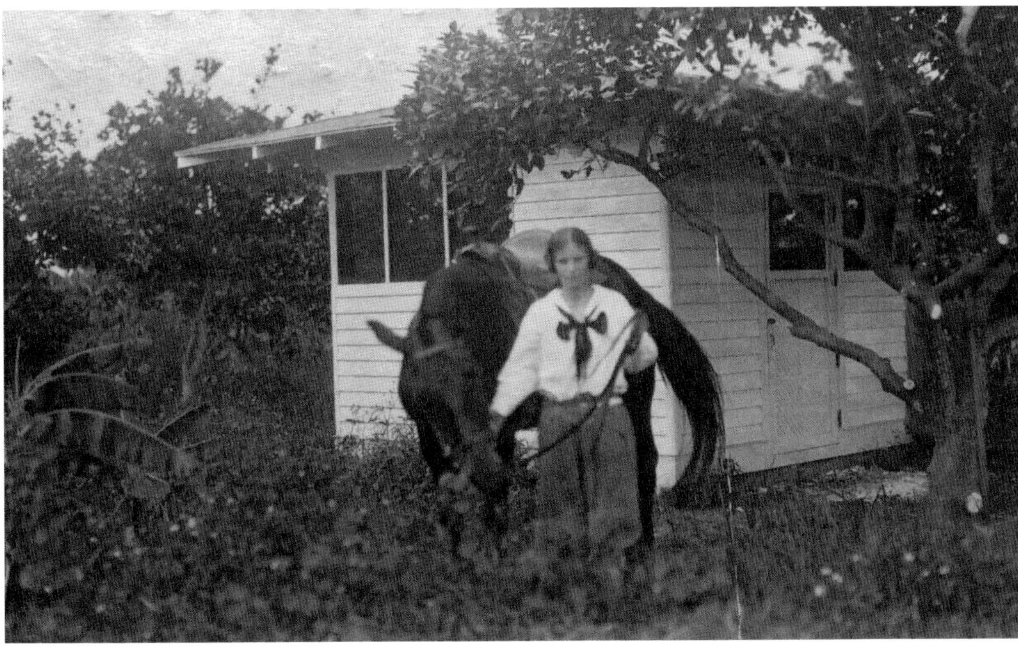

Lois (Alexander) Congdon

This avid equestrian posing with horse Don Pedro came to Fort Myers with her family in 1926 via her native Nebraska, and then California and Hawaii. In 1937, Lois Alexander graduated from Florida State University and accepted a position as the first principal and teacher—with janitor privileges—at the one-room Beach Elementary School in Fort Myers Beach. At the height of the tourist season, she taught all 38 pupils in first through third grades. In later years, she also taught at J. Colin English, Tice, Villas Elementary, Edison Park Elementary, and Orangewood Elementary Schools, from which she retired in 1975. Throughout it all, she was active with many organizations, including the Alliance for the Arts, the Calusa Nature Center and Planetarium, the Southwest Florida Community Foundation, and the Fort Myers Woman's Community Club. Even after retiring from teaching, she pursued extensive education-related volunteer work, serving as president of the Teacher's Association of Lee County, holding county- and state-level offices for the Retired Educators, and serving on the Lee County School Board's Centennial Committee. During the 1980s, she served on the board of the Southwest Florida Historical Society. In 1986, she received the Community Services Award from the American Association of Retired Persons, which honors volunteers who have made outstanding contributions to their communities. In 1958, Congdon and husband James opened Fort Myers Tropical Garden to the public. The major tourist attraction of the 1950s and 1960s was created by Congdon's father, Frederick Hall Alexander. She recalled that when the Edisons visited the gardens, her father would always have a bouquet of roses for Mina Edison. (Courtesy of SWFHS.)

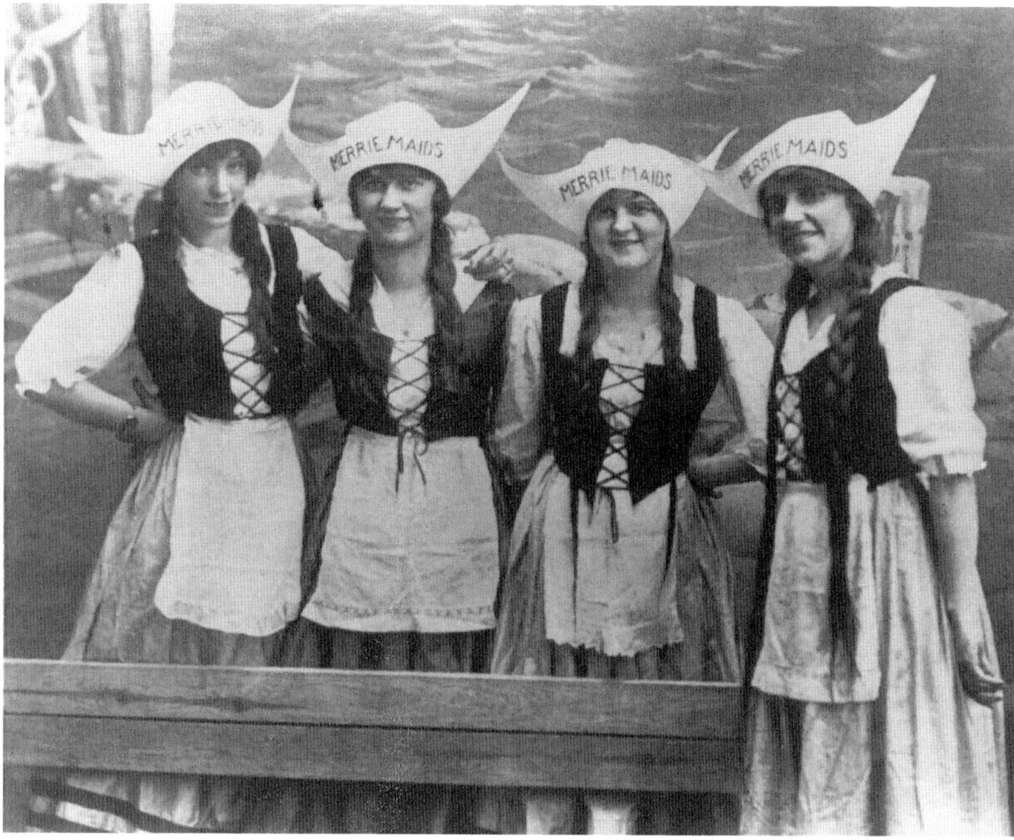

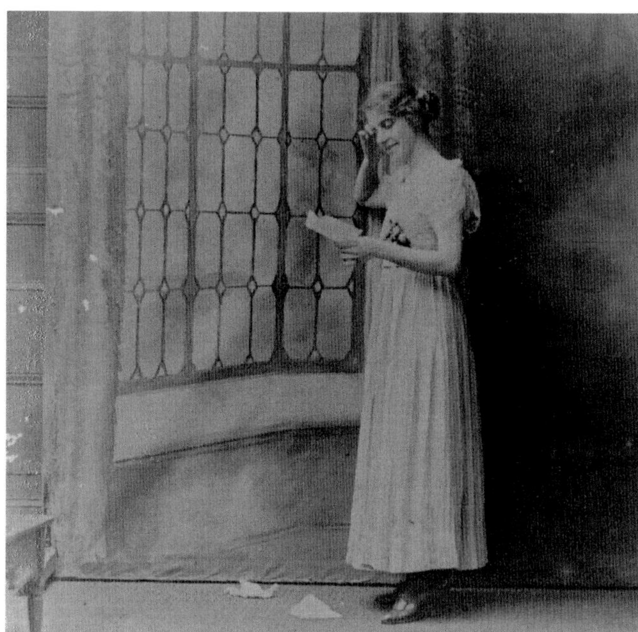

Mary Hart (Stebbins) Philips
Philips was born in 1888 to true pioneers. Her father, Charles Hyde Stebbins, was one of the signers of the document incorporating the town of Fort Myers in 1885. After her father died, Mary moved with her mother Ida Blount (Stebbins) English, to nearby Alva, where she attended school as a young girl. In 1907, she became the first woman from Lee County to graduate from college. Musically talented, she and three friends formed the group the Merrie Maids (above) and toured the United States performing plays and musicales. In 1922, she married Prof. Fred Philips, an accomplished musician who came to Fort Myers to join the high school faculty. She died in 1964. (Courtesy of SWFHS.)

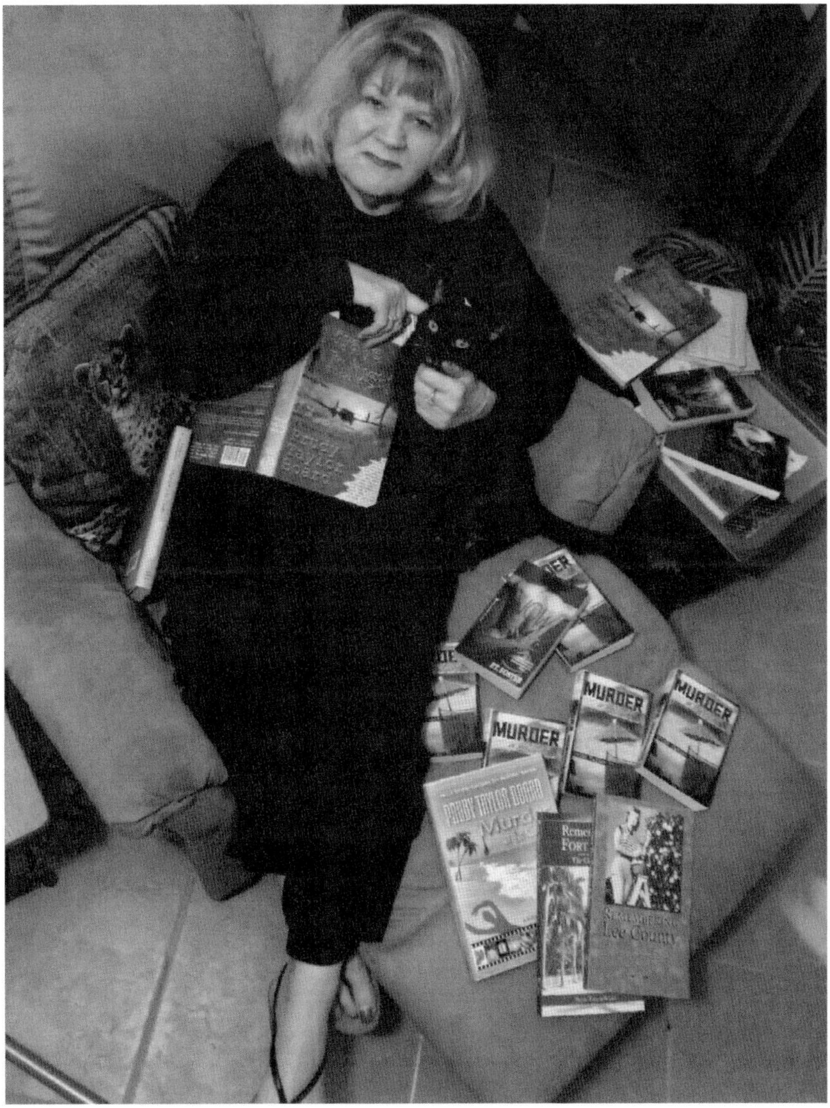

Prudy Taylor Board
As early as second grade, Board knew she wanted to be a writer. Despite discouragement from high school teachers who said she would never make a living writing, she pressed on, receiving encouragement from unexpected sources. Frank Lodwick, the Fort Myers High School Band director, personally visited her father to say she was too smart for the bank job she took after graduation, that she ought to be in college, and that a group of Elks Club members had agreed to start a fund. Never mind that a family trust fund was on hand for the budding writer's education—how could her supporters know that a dispute with her executrix grandmother over her choice of college held up her plans? She persevered, and today has published 25 books, including histories of her native Fort Myers and Lee County, novels set in southwest Florida, and others. Along the way, she wrote for the *Fort Myers News-Press*, was an assignment editor and on-camera reporter for local television stations, edited several magazines, and presented writers' workshops in several states. Her proudest moment was being appointed co-chair of Fort Myers' year-long centennial celebration in 1985. (Courtesy of Prudy Taylor Board.)

Robert Macomber

Author of the award-winning Honor Series of naval novels featuring Peter Wake, Macomber is also a maritime commentator for Florida PBS documentaries and a defense consultant. He has appeared as guest author and speaker aboard the *Queen Mary 2* and other luxury liners. Among his awards are the Patrick Smith Literary Award for Best Historical Novel of Florida, and the American Library Association's 2008 W.Y. Boyd Literary Award for Excellence in Military Fiction. (Courtesy of Robert Macomber.)

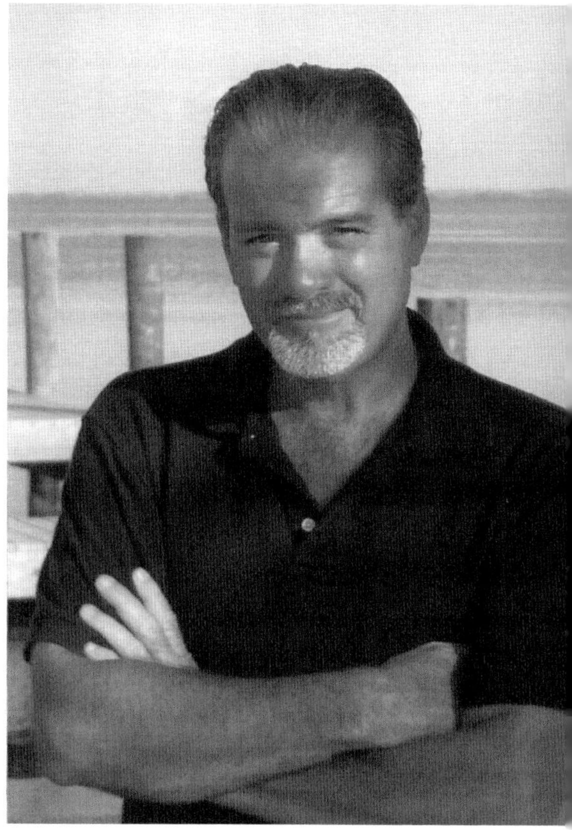

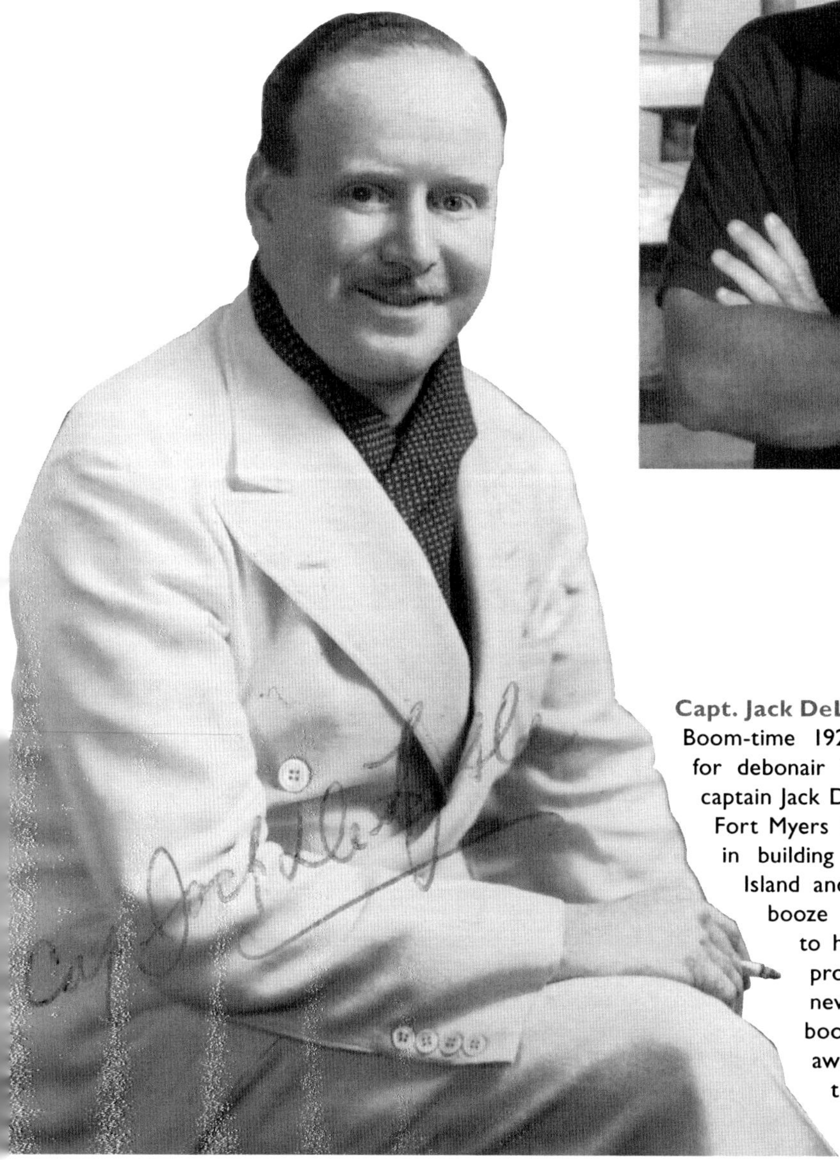

Capt. Jack DeLysle

Boom-time 1920s was the perfect stage for debonair World War I British army captain Jack DeLysle. He built a casino on Fort Myers Beach and was instrumental in building a bridge between Estero Island and the mainland. Charges of booze smuggling added intrigue to his persona, but never were proven. In 1925, he started the newspaper the *Palm Leaf.* The boom ended, the casino washed away in the 1926 hurricane, and the *Palm Leaf* didn't survive the Great Depression. (Courtesy of SWFHS.)

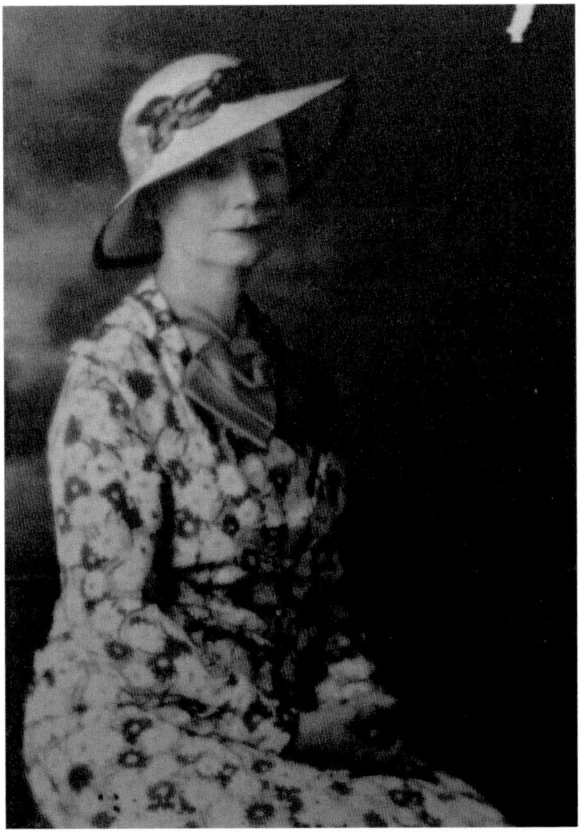

Effie (Winkler) McAdow

Classically trained "Miss Effie" (left, circa 1928) was a musical inspiration to her community for nearly three-quarters of a century. The 20-year-old arrived from Memphis in 1900 to join her brother and father, Dr. W.B. Winkler. She started teaching piano, organ, and voice, and frequently accompanied visiting artists. Offered a European tour with the Dolly Sisters, she refused to leave Fort Myers. In 1929, she became Lee County's first music supervisor, a position she held for 25 years. Active in civic life, she was a founding member and a president for the Woman's Community Club. When Thomas Edison heard her enchanting voice, he asked her to record "Danny Boy" on his famous invention. She was still teaching only days before she died at the age of 94. Circa 1940, she bicycles with her husband Perry Lamme McAdow on Boca Grande. (Left courtesy of SWFMH; below courtesy of Margaret Garner and Barbara Brown.)

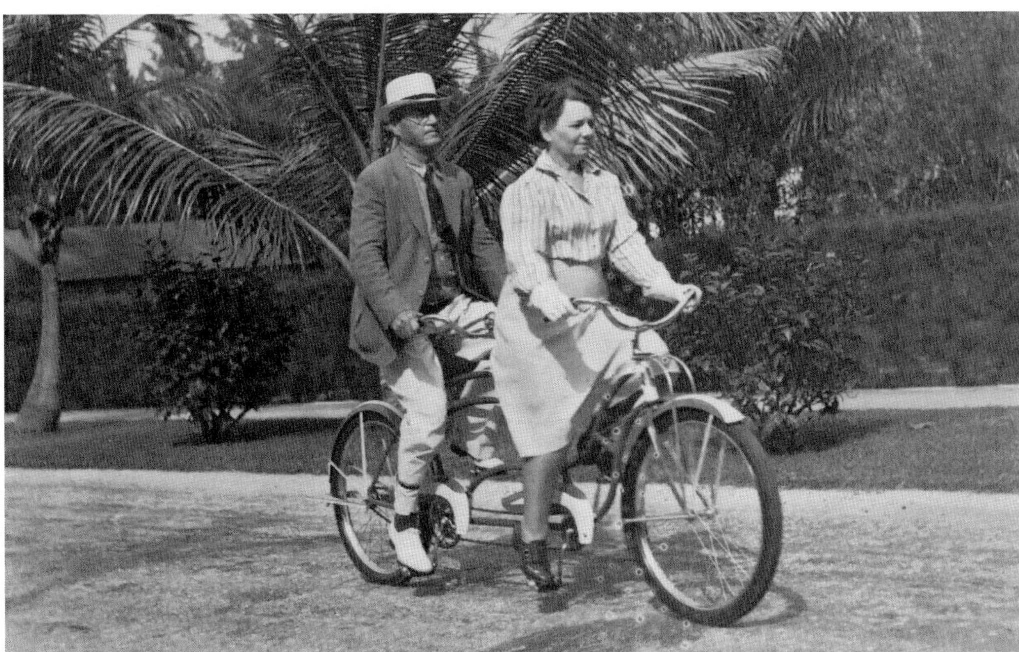

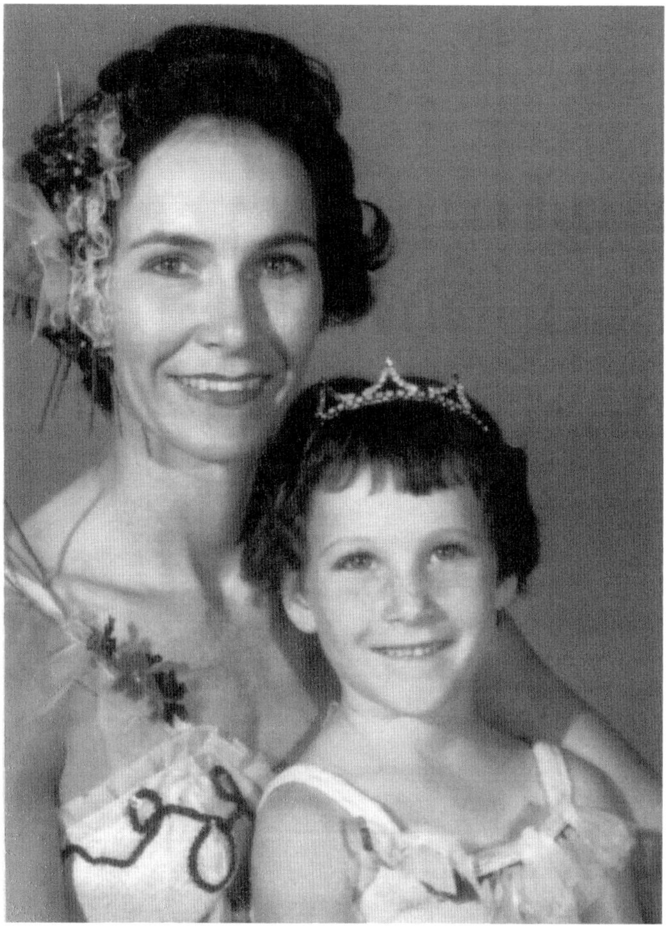

Jeanne Bochette
After having studied in New York City and England's Royal Ballet, Bochette danced at the Roxy Theatre and with the Rockettes at Radio City Music Hall. She chose to finish her last year at Rollins College rather than stay in the Big Apple. She subsequently came home, married, and founded Studio Bochette in 1951. The studio is located in her father's former machine shop. Her honors include Rollins College's Lifetime Achievement Award; the Angels of the Arts Awards for Lifetime Achievement and Arts Teacher of the Year; and the Greater Fort Myers Chamber of Commerce "Grand Dame" award in 2010. She is pictured with daughter Alyce. (Courtesy of Alyce Bochette.)

Alyce Bochette (RIGHT)
Family lore has it that Bochette started her dance training at about the age of two, because her mother finally relented to her cry, "Mommie-Jeanne, take me with you." Virtually growing up in her mother's dance studio, she was performing from an early age. She vividly recalls rehearsing and performing as a shepherd in the operetta *Amahl and the Night Visitors* at the age of four or five, along with her mother. She studied on scholarship with the Joffrey Ballet at New York University's Tisch School of the Arts, earning a BFA. For more than 20 years, she toured with major modern dance companies directed by Rachel Lampert, May O'Donnell, and Doug Varone. After joining the renowned Mark Morris Dance Group in 1988 upon its relocation to Brussels, Belgium, she collaborated with Mikhail Baryshnikov, Yo-Yo Ma, Peter Sellers, Lou Reed, Liza Minnelli, and Ben Vereen. Her performances have been captured on film by PBS's *Dance in America*, A&E, Ovation Television, CBS Cable, Bravo, and the BBC. Since returning to Fort Myers in 1995, she has codirected Dance Bochette, the studio founded by her mother Jeanne. In 2010, she choreographed *Salvage*, a collaborative evening-long concert incorporating movement, music, video, poetry, and fabric and light. Inspired by and performed in the historic Sidney & Berne Davis Art Center, the sold-out performance was received with a standing ovation. Among her hometown art mentors, she lists painter Gale Bennett, piano teacher Arlo Diebler, and vocal teacher Tom Walters—and most certainly, her mother. Bochette says the longevity and contributions of the family business make her feel woven into the cultural fabric of the community. (Photograph by Robin Cornett, courtesy of Alyce Bochette.)

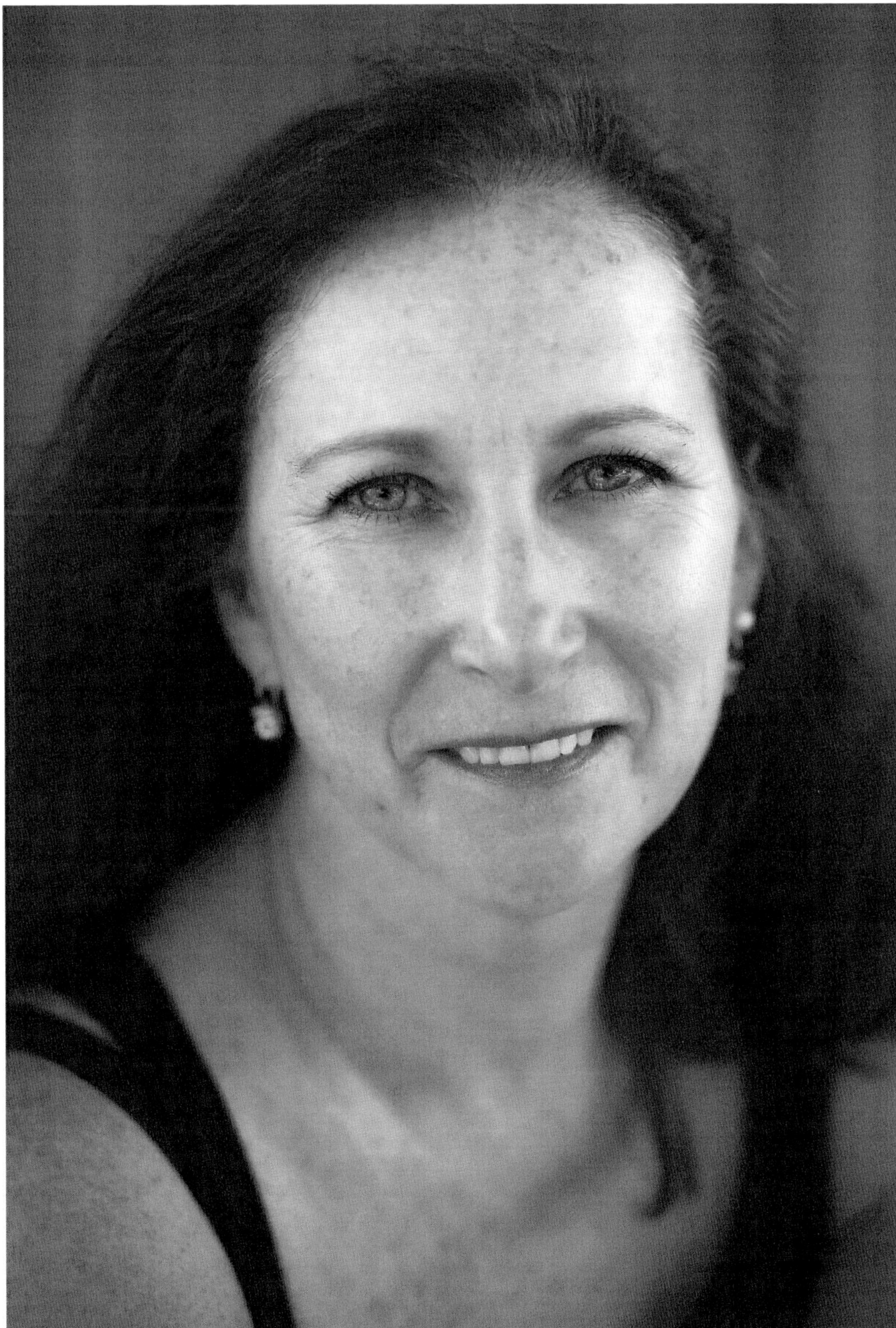

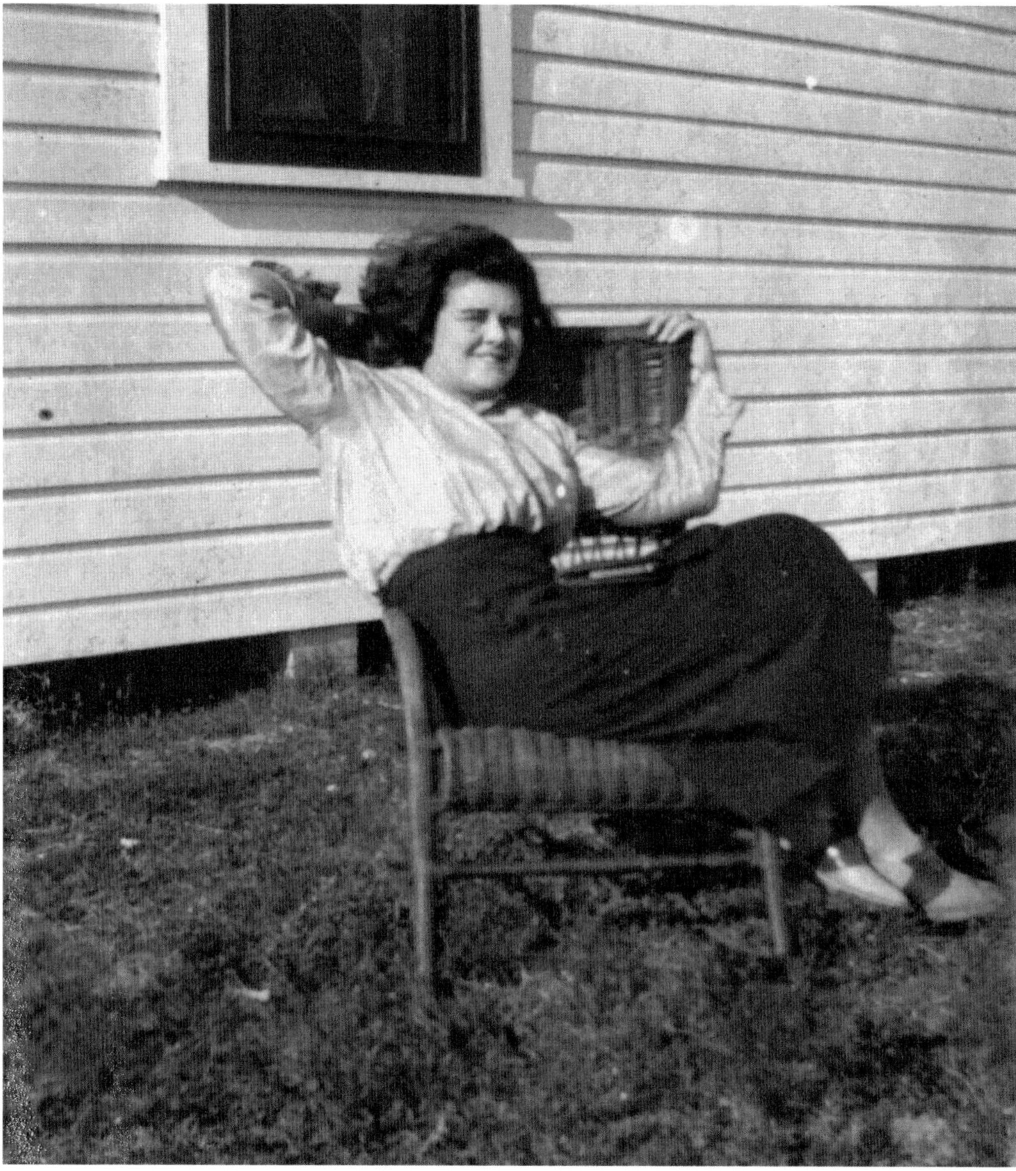

Margaret Mickle

In 1913, plucky 10-year-old Margaret Mickle got her first big scoop after setting off in a skiff to photograph a former president of the United States. Anchored off her family's Captiva Island beachfront home were scientist Russell J. Coles and Teddy Roosevelt. The skiff overturned, but she swam with the camera overhead. As the crew helped her aboard, she asked, "Where's Teddy?" and was told he was unavailable. Overhearing her, Roosevelt said, "Anyone who calls me Teddy can see me." For her audacity, she was rewarded with dinner, a .22 rifle, an authentic autographed photograph, and a unique pair of fish-skin slippers. She worked briefly for Lee Memorial Hospital before pursuing a writing career with the *Tropical News* and the *Fort Myers News-Press*. As *Press* Society editor for 20 years, she started a popular gossip-filled column called "Local Lowdown." To the delight of readers, at age 83, she came out of retirement in 1986. (Courtesy of SWFHS.)

CHAPTER FOUR

Community Builders and Advocates

Clubs, community leaders, volunteers, role models, and mentors—they are crucial in weaving a community together. In retrospect, the community can only wonder, what would life be like without them? The works of Boy Scout master H.O. Kight, volunteer Ruth Lovrin, and community activist Evelyn Sams Canady have changed lives for the better. Without tireless women like Olive Stout, would there have been the long and rich history of women's clubs and even a library system? When would Fort Myers' first modern school have materialized without the generosity of Col. Andrew D. Gwynne? And what would the town have been without the delight of park concerts and parade music, all provided by the first local arts organization, the Fort Myers Concert Band?

Rotary Club of Fort Myers

The Rotary Club of Fort Myers was chartered on April 1, 1922, as the fourth club in the state, with Ora E. Chapman as president. Frank Stoneman, editor of the *Miami Herald,* was the guest speaker at the formal presentation of the charter three weeks later. Guest for the club's 30th anniversary in 1952 was Marjory Stoneman Douglas, author of *The Everglades: River of Grass*. Identified members and friends frolicking in League Field in the late 1920s are, from left to right (standing) Harry Satchel and Edward L. Evans; and, from right to left (standing), are Judge Nathan Stout (holding cymbals), Ben King, and Capt. Arthur N. Wintle (in captain's hat). The others shown are unidentified. (Courtesy of SWFHS.)

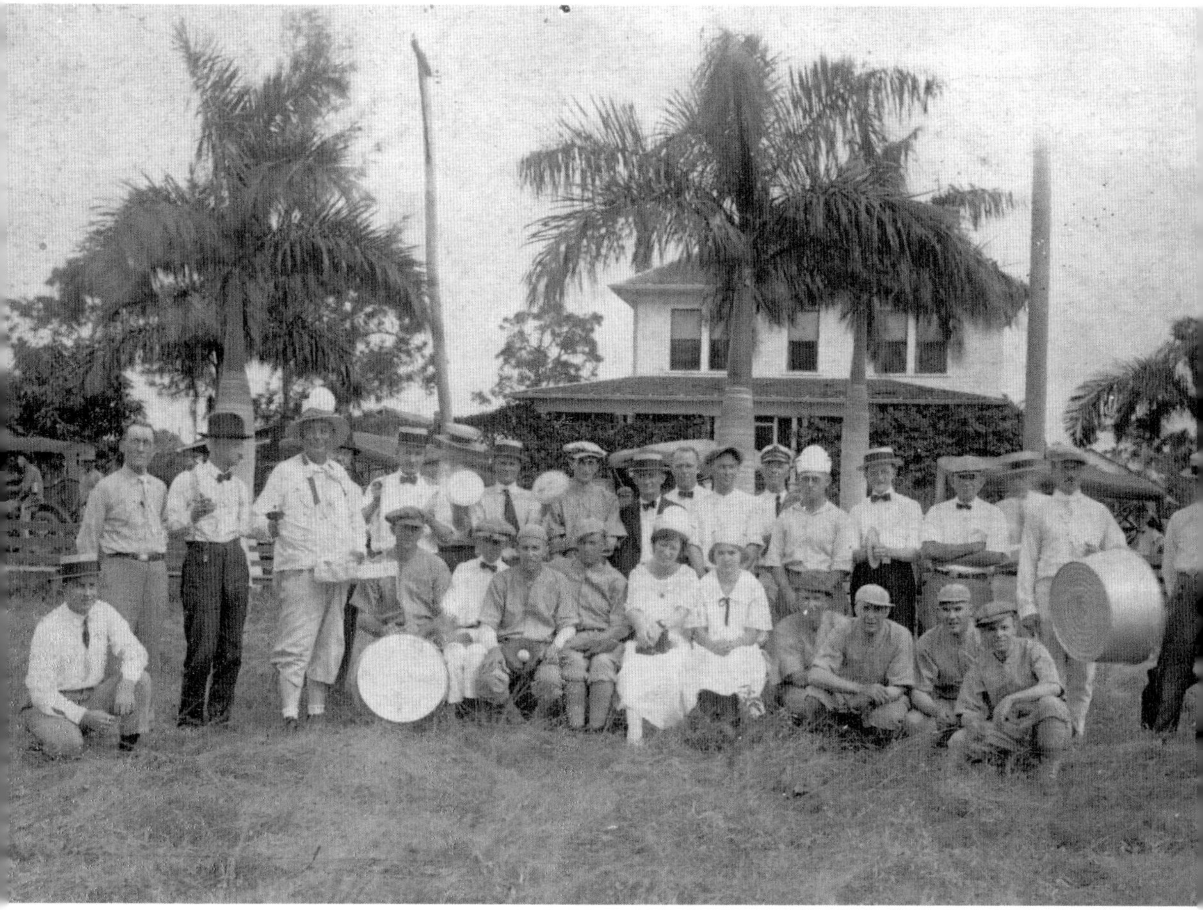

H.O. Kight (RIGHT)

Boy Scout leader H.O. Kight is remembered as a fount of knowledge on scouting and an exemplary mentor. From 1927 until 1936, he was a council executive for the Royal Palm Council. He resigned that paid position and became a volunteer. He earned his eagle badges in his youth and was a member of Order of the Arrow, the Boy Scout of America's National Honor Society for campers. Kight was the scout master of East Fort Myers' Troop 18 from 1946 to 1953. Doug Bartleson remembers the scout master as a natural trainer who inspired scouts to lead and attain eagle status. Kight personally funded a complete woodshop so his troop could earn all their wood badges. He died in 1966. (Courtesy of SWFHS.)

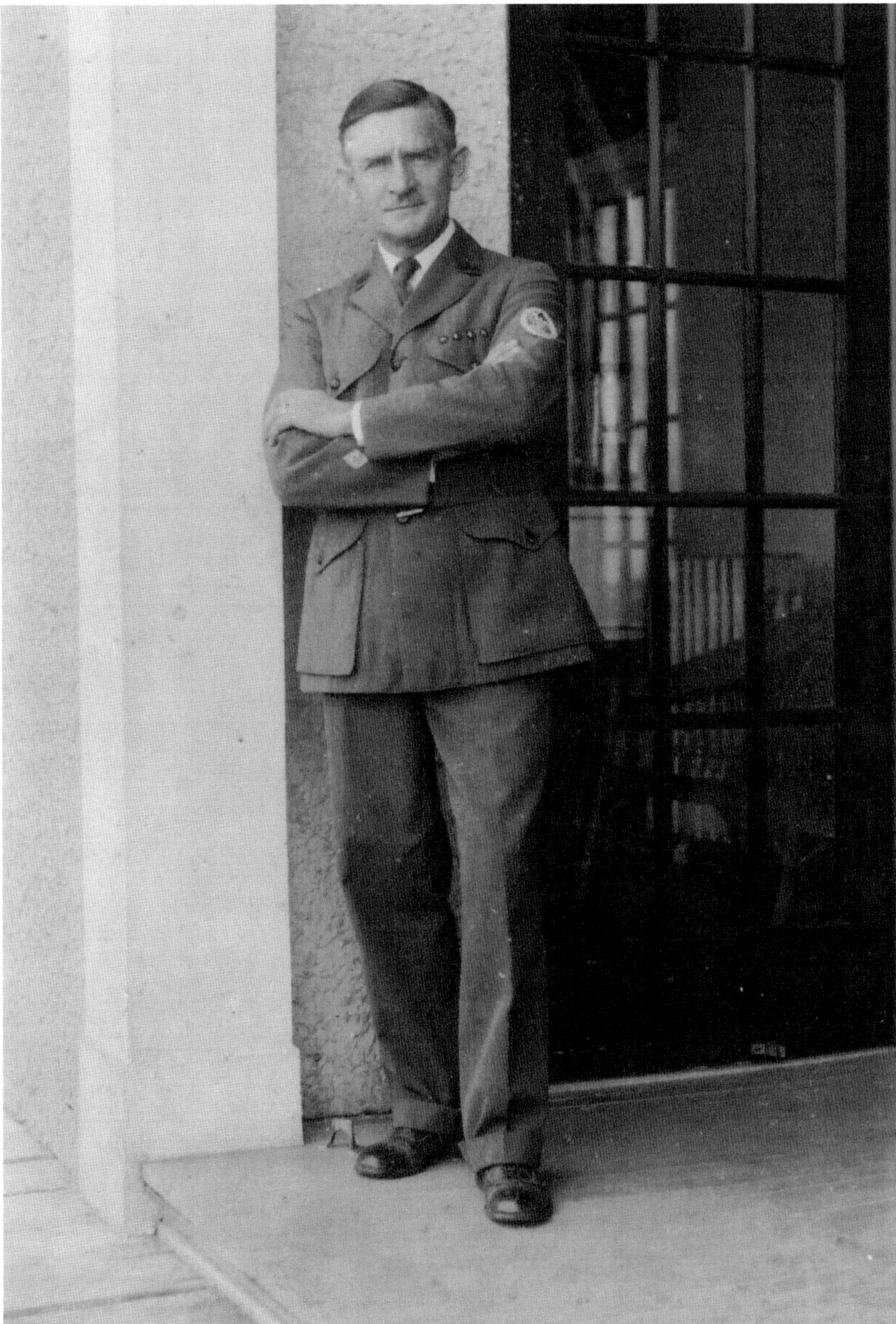

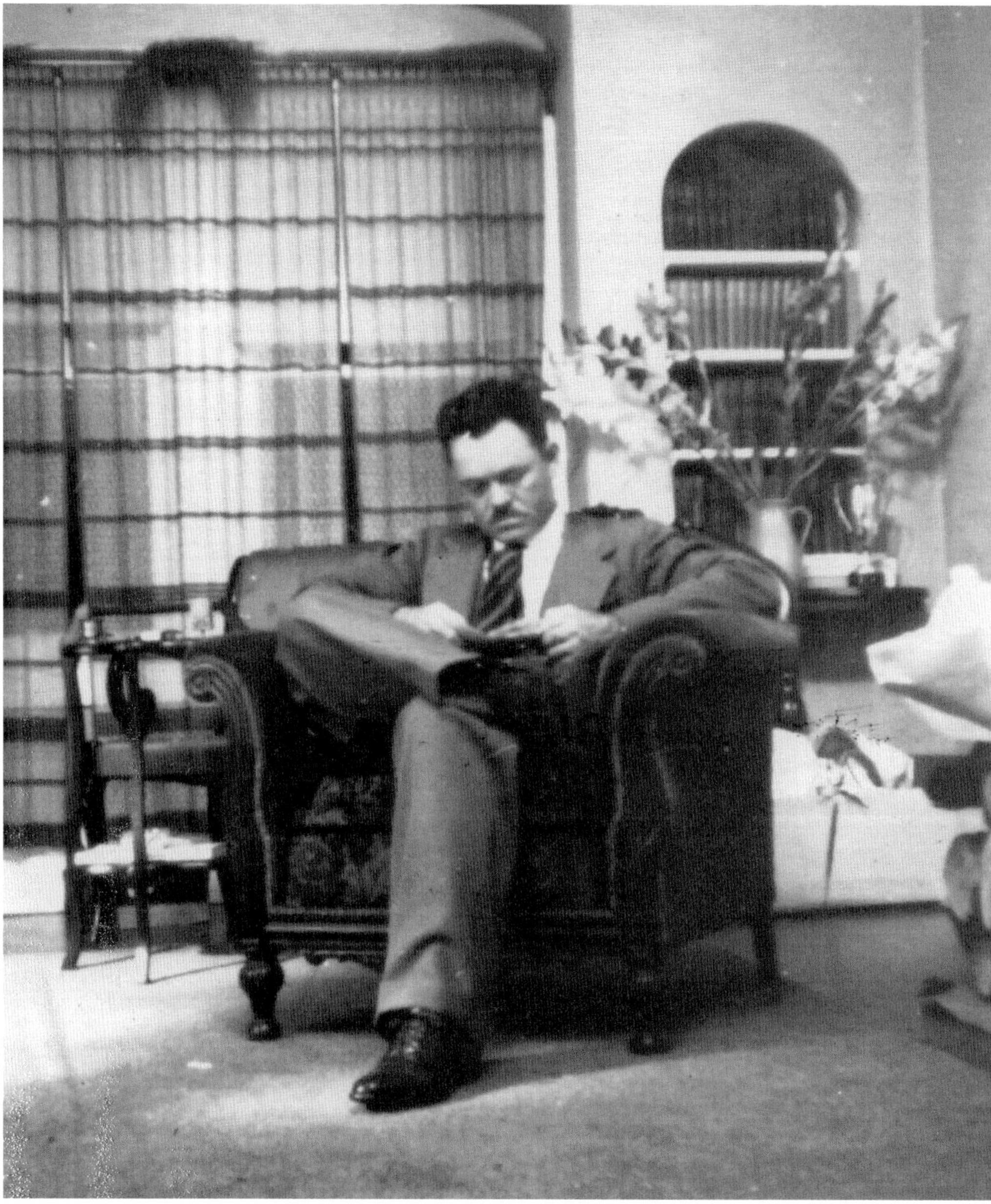

Dr. Fred Bartleson

Born in 1904, Bartleson moved from Jacksonville, Florida, to Fort Myers as a teenager. During his 33-year practice, he delivered more than 1,500 babies. So trusted was he that some patients traveled more than 100 miles to consult him. He helped to establish the migrant clinic at Harlem Heights in the Iona agricultural area. In the photograph, Dr. Fred, as he was affectionately called, takes a break from his busy rounds at the hospital. He served as the first president of the Fort Myers Lions Club, as a school board trustee, and was appointed to the first Water Management (Flood Control) Board for the State of Florida. He was a Master Mason, Scottish Rite Mason, York Rite Mason (Knight Templar) and a Noble of the Shrine. He died in 1967. (Courtesy of SWFHS.)

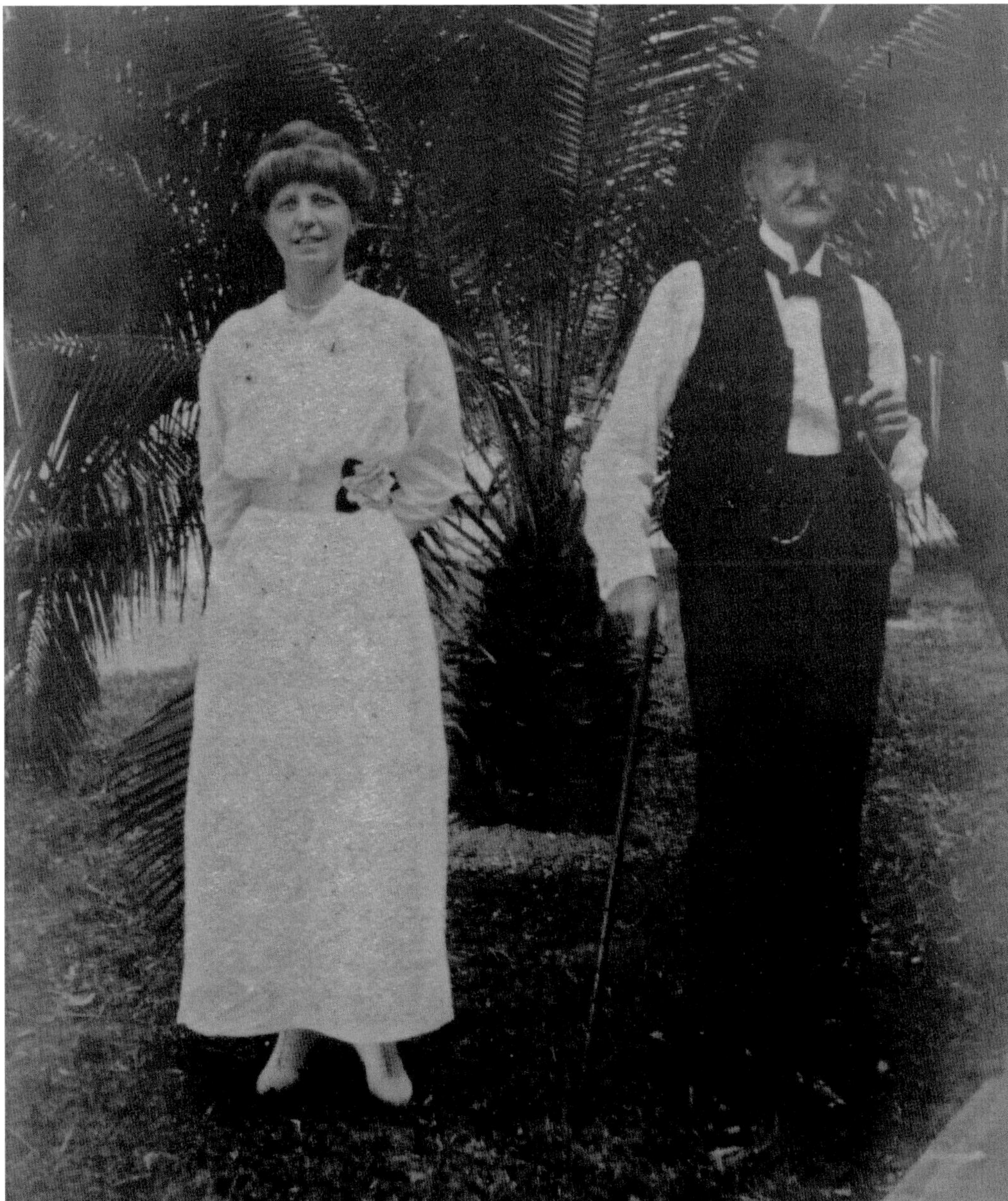

Col. Andrew D. Gwynne

In 1909, a wealthy winter visitor observed the serious overcrowding of the inadequate Fort Myers schools. Gwynne, a Memphis cotton broker and wholesale grocer, remarked to his wife that if the town ever got motivated to build a better school, he would be happy to help fund it. Lucky for Fort Myers, she remembered that vow after the colonel died the following summer. The matching funds that the Gwynne family pledged made possible the town's first modern school. In fact, when it opened in 1911, it was praised as one of the best facilities in the state. The school board unanimously agreed to name the school the Andrew D. Gwynne Institute. The building is still used for educational purposes. Gwynne is pictured with his daughter-in-law, Katie Lloyd Gwynne. (Courtesy of SWFHS.)

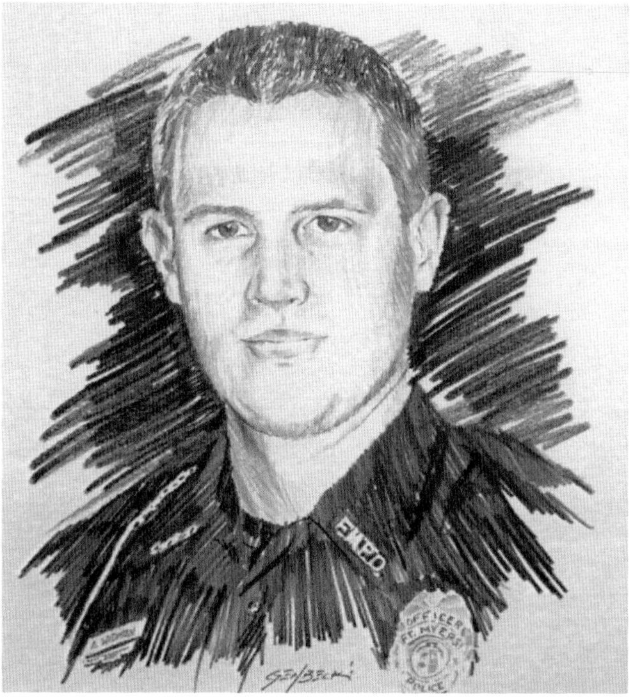

Officer Andrew Widman
Fort Myers police officer Andrew Widman was only 30 years old and had served only a year and three months when he was killed in the line of duty in 2008. He was shot while responding to a domestic dispute at a downtown business. The tragedy led to a new law, the Officer Andrew Widman Act, passed by the Florida Legislature in 2011 and intended to help judges keep repeat violent offenders off the streets. (Courtesy of Fort Myers Police Department.)

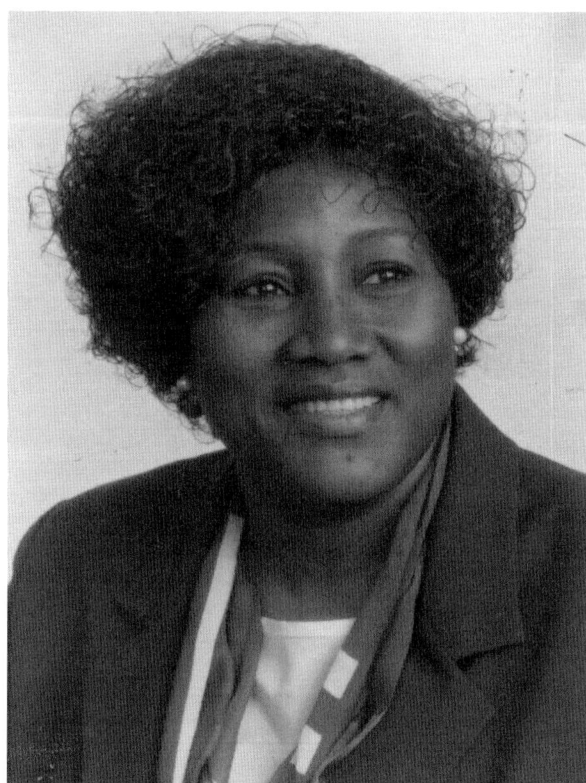

Melvin Morgan
In 1983, Gov. Bob Graham appointed Morgan to serve on the county commission, the first black to do so. In 1961, she began a career teaching physical education and social work. She has served on the board of trustees for the Edison & Ford Winter Estates and the Southwest Florida Community Foundation. As a board member of the Lee County Black History Society, she was part of the effort to found the Williams Academy Black History Museum. (Courtesy of LCBHS.)

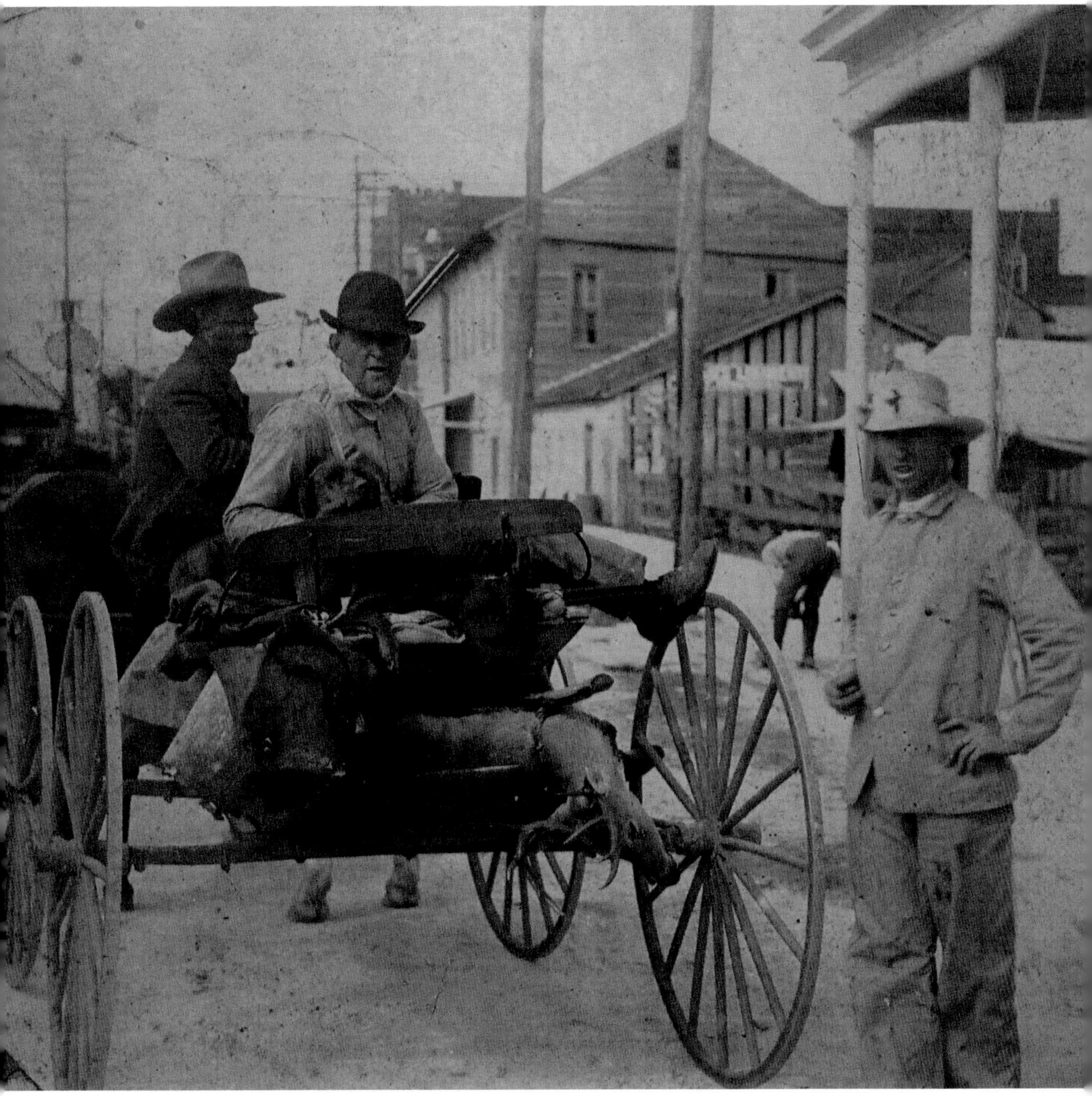

Harry A. Laycock

After several devastating fires just after the turn of the 20th century, Fort Myers decided it needed to organize a volunteer fire department. Laycock, pictured with the hunting dog, became chief in 1905 and convinced the town council to buy a Watrous gasoline fire engine and 1,000 feet of hose for $2,200. Horses or volunteers heaved the cart-mounted engine through the streets. Water was supplied by artesian wells, the river, or cisterns. Laycock's background in technology suited him to the job. After college, he had installed telephone systems around the state. He came to Fort Myers in 1903 to sell electrical machinery, accompanied by his mother, Mary Laycock. He continued as unpaid chief until 1916 and steadily worked to upgrade fire-fighting equipment and take the department into the modern age. The other men are unidentified. (Courtesy of SWFHS.)

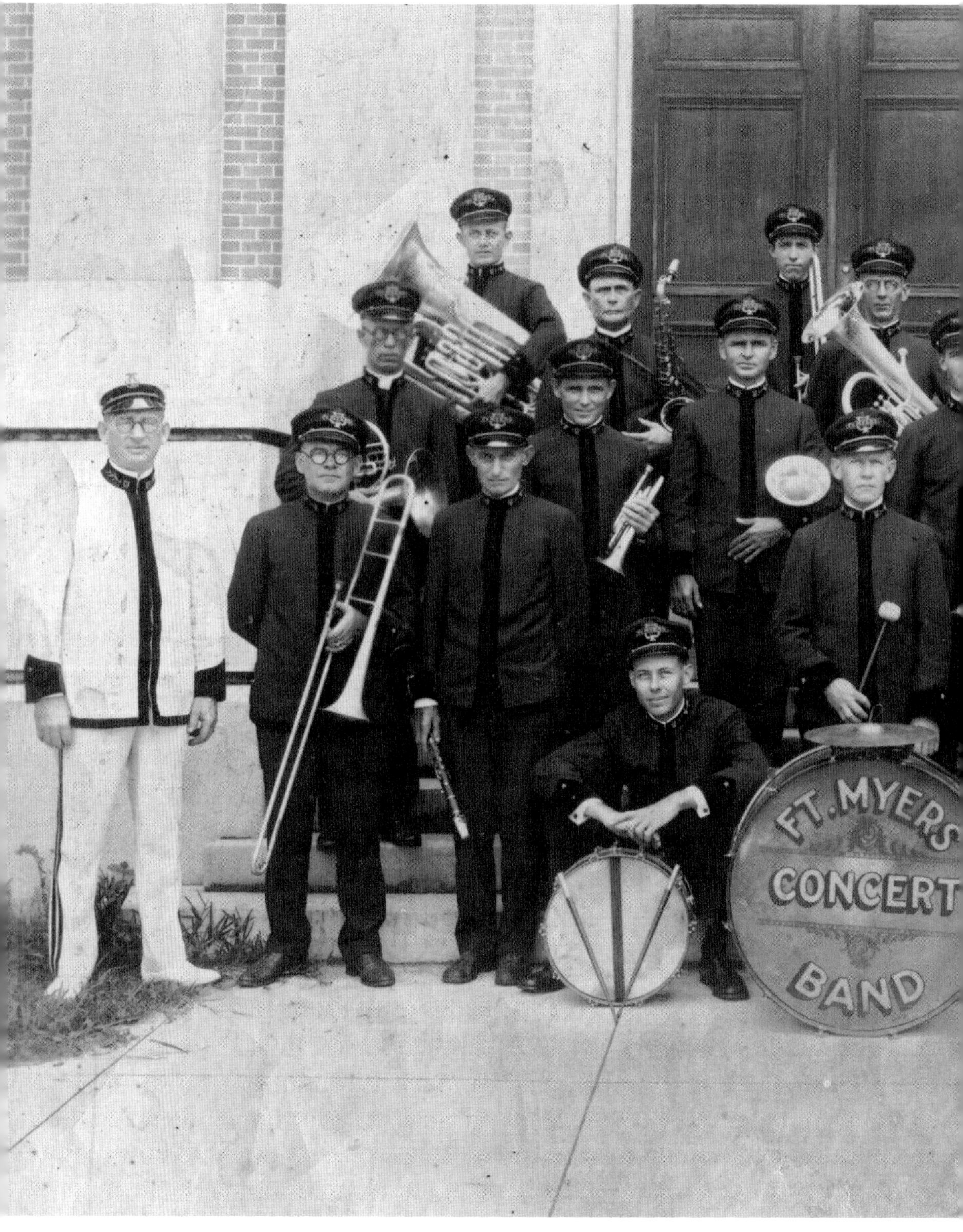
FT. MYERS
CONCERT
BAND

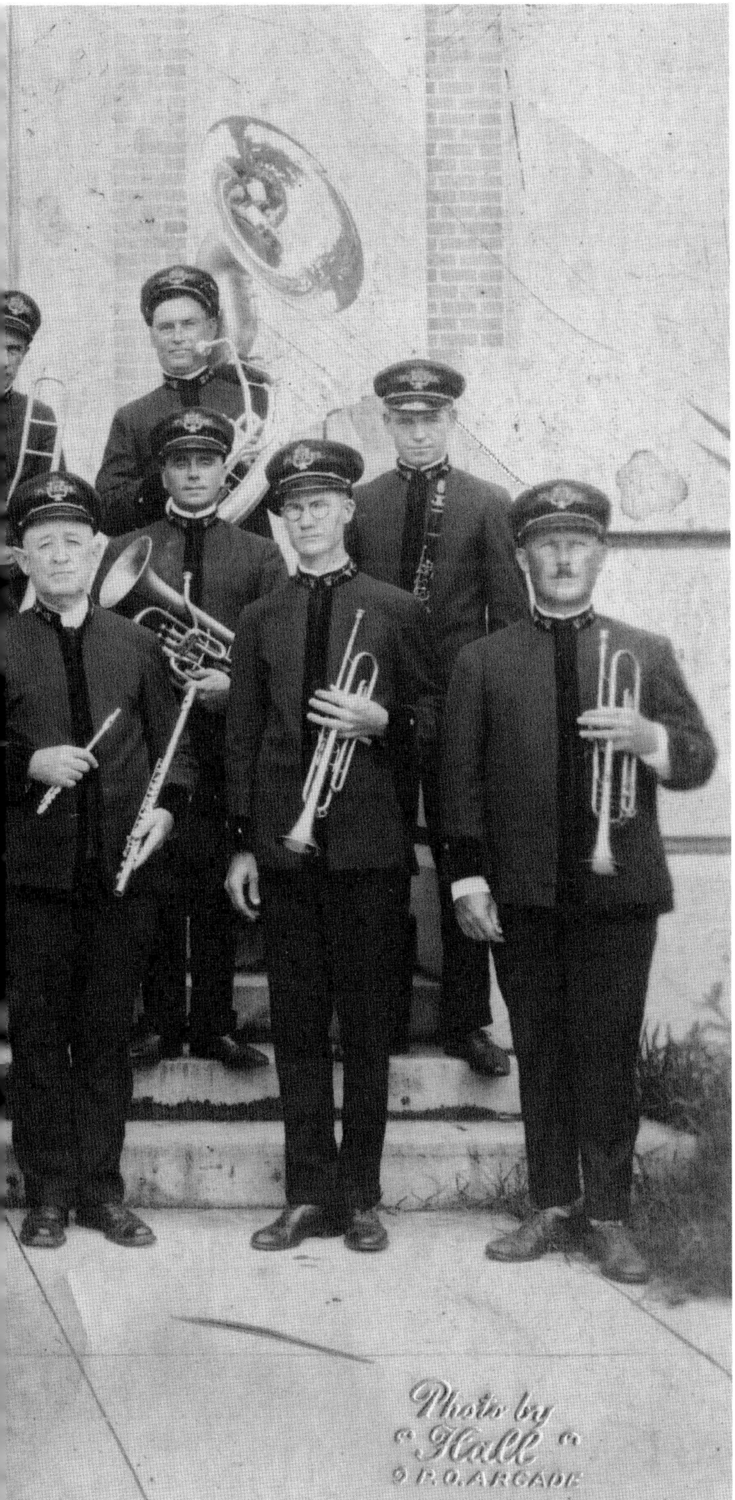

Fort Myers Concert Band Musicians organized the town's first band in 1885. One of their first gigs was serenading honeymooners Thomas and Mina Edison. For decades, they performed at celebrations, parades, and park concerts. In this c. 1925 photograph are, from left to right (first row) Bert King, George Peterson, George Zweifel, Morris McWilliams (kneeling), Harry Morrow, O.S. Vaughn, Bob Moger, and Charlie Lienard; (second row) D.A. Page, Oscar Sheets, Leslie Sheets, Nick Lienard, Albert Jackson, and Orion White; (third row) Ralph McWilliams, H.C. Willis, Bob Thompson, George Dupuy, Harvey Lutes, and George Haas. (Courtesy of SWFMH.)

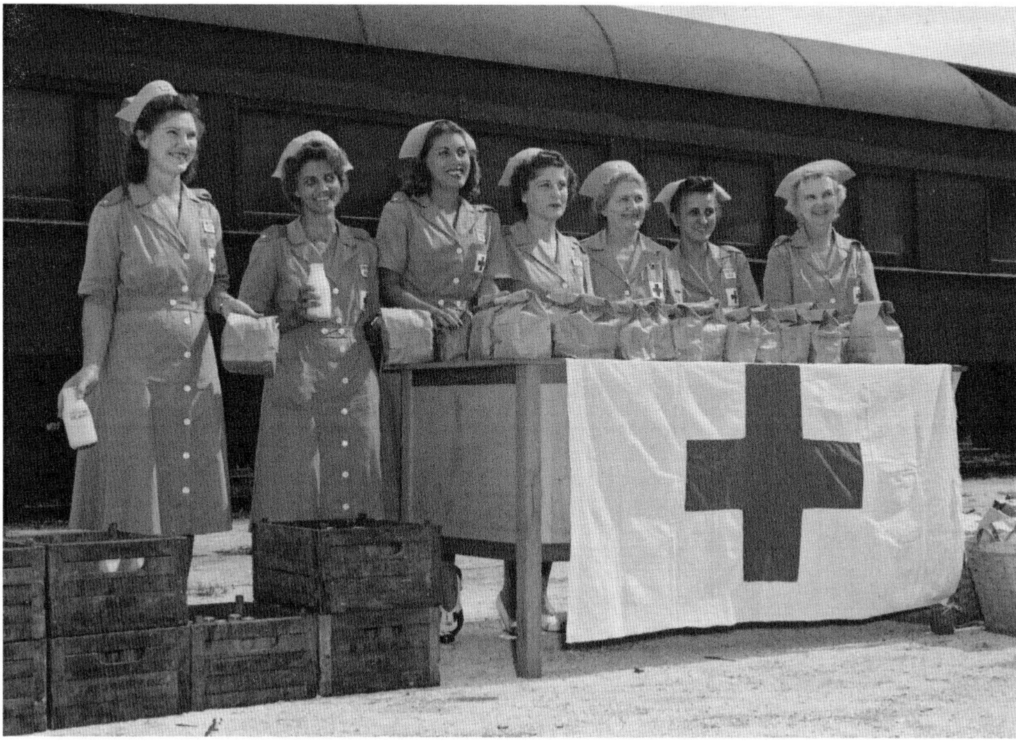

Fannie Thaggard
Among the cheerful volunteers of the Lee County Chapter of the American Red Cross is Fannie Thaggard (left). During World War II, she distributed refreshments to soldiers at the train station, volunteered at the Buckingham Air Base Hospital, and at the USO. She won many blue ribbons for her baking at the Southwest Florida Fair and a Pillsbury award for her coconut cake. Other volunteers are, left to right, unidentified, Barbara Hendry, Evelyn Kingston, Dot Hendry, unidentified, and Penny Parkinson. (Courtesy of SWFHS.)

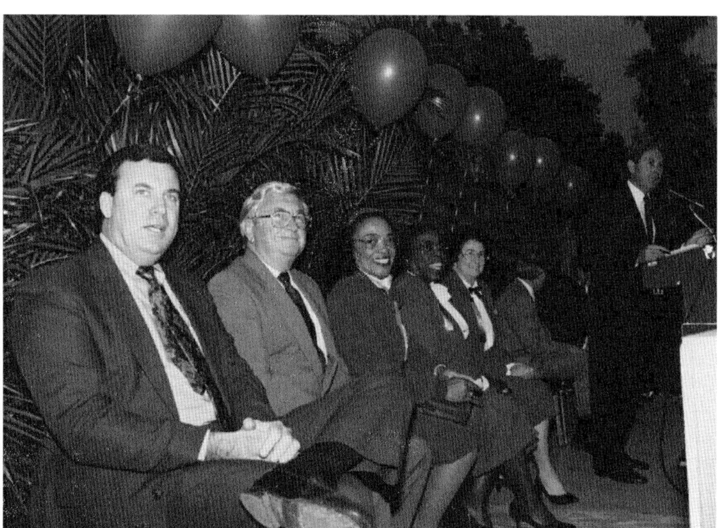

Dr. Anne Murphy Knight
Knight was a teacher at Edgewood Elementary School when elected to the Fort Myers City Council in 1984. She was re-elected in 1988, in an era when the council began to reflect the community's diversity. Knight (seated center) sits with fellow officials, from left to right, Bruce Grady, Richard Bashaw, Veronica Shoemaker, Joan Pigott Porter, and Mayor Billy Smith (standing). (Courtesy of LCBHS.)

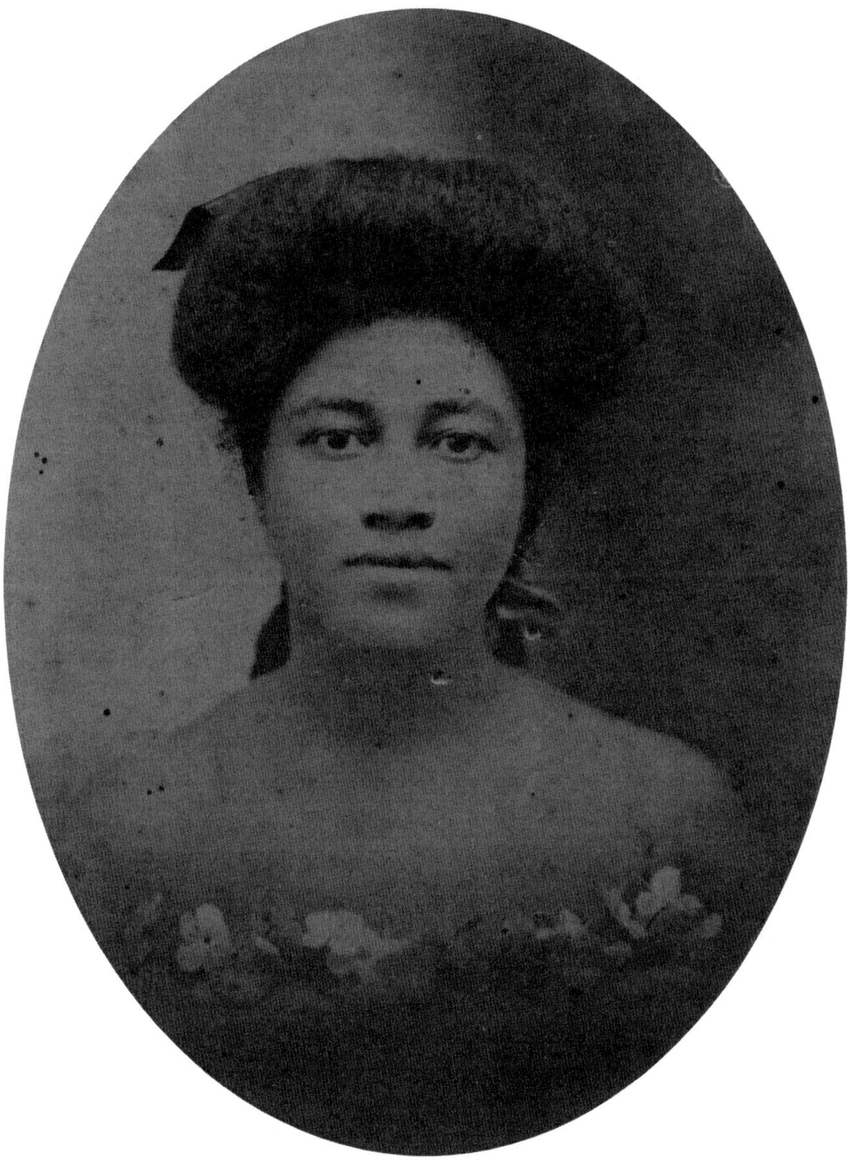

Dr. Ella M. Piper
Civic activist and philanthropist Dr. Ella Piper established the first beauty parlor and chiropody office in Fort Myers. Among her clients were Mrs. Thomas Edison and Mrs. Henry Ford. When her mother died in 1926, she continued the annual Christmas tree party she had started at her home, an event that continues today. Her personal philanthropy included providing scholarships, food, and clothing to neighbors and housing Negro League baseball players denied hotel accommodations. She helped finance Williams Academy, a school for blacks, and Jones-Walker Hospital, the first for nonwhites in Fort Myers. She helped to establish a black chapter of the American Red Cross. When she died in 1954, she willed her home and property to the city, stipulating that it be a community center to serve seniors and young children. The new Dr. Ella Piper Center, built on the Mango Street site in 1976, carries on her work, best summed up by local historian Vivian Hill: "Dr. Piper was like a godmother to so many people." In 2010, Mango Street was renamed Dr. Ella Piper Way to honor her. (Courtesy of SWFMH.)

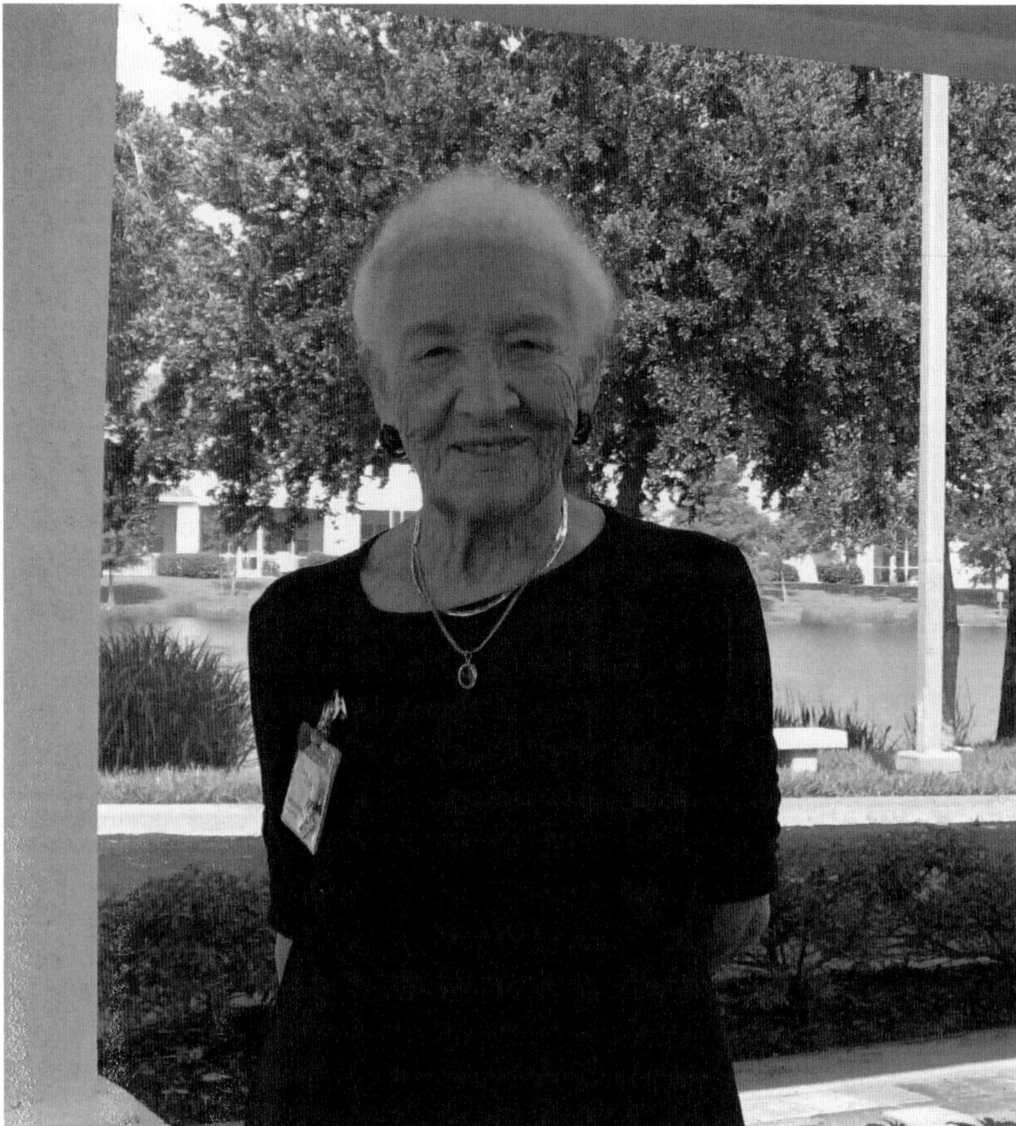

Ruth Lovrin

Born in Pennsylvania in the Pocono Mountains, Lovrin left home at 17 and went into nurse's training in New Jersey. She says volunteering teaches her that being active and maintaining a sense of humor makes you feel better and live longer. One of the first things she did when she moved to the Fort Myers area in 1973 was to volunteer at Lee Memorial Hospital. Three decades ago, she started volunteering at Hope Hospice too, determined to provide patients and families with the end-of-life support her husband needed a year before the hospice movement reached Fort Myers. One of Lovrin's main points—and the hospice movement's too—is that the caregiver needs support (if even for an afternoon) in order to maintain the physical and emotional stamina to care for the terminally ill family member. She put it simply, "Everybody's going to die, so if you can make it easier, that's very rewarding." She is a recipient of the President's Volunteer Service Award for 10,000 hours of volunteer work. (Photograph by the author.)

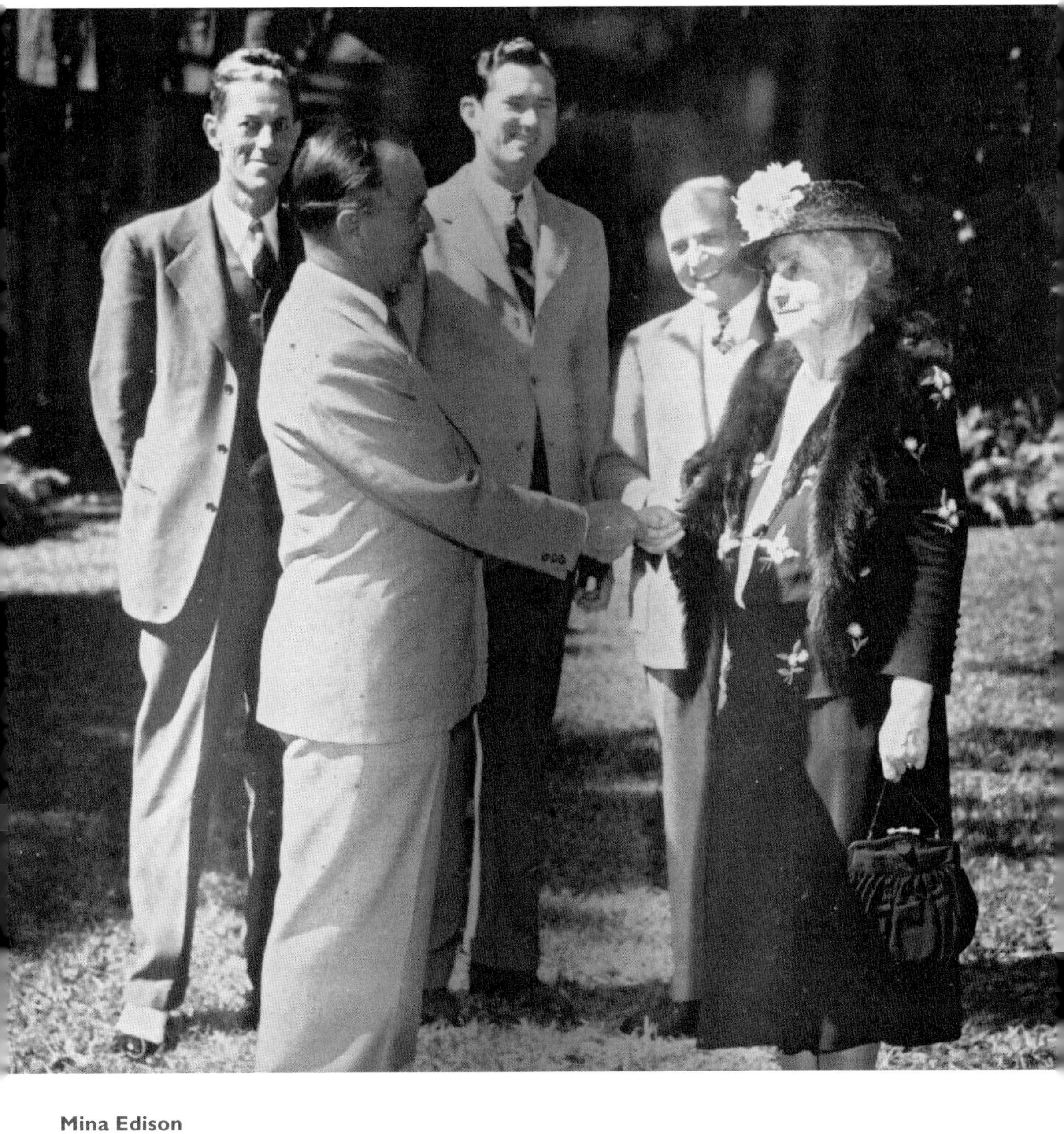

Mina Edison

In this 1947 photograph, Mina Edison, widow of Thomas A. Edison, presents the deed to their winter home, Seminole Lodge, as well as the laboratory and grounds, to the City of Fort Myers as a memorial to her husband. Here, Mayor David G. Shapard accepts the gift. Also present are, from left to right, Frank Carson, Edison Pageant of Light president; Graydon Jones, Junior Chamber of Commerce president; and Sidney Davis, Edison family friend and presider at the deed-presentation ceremony. The famous couple, who came to Fort Myers in 1886 while on their honeymoon, spent most of their winters at their estate thereafter. When she died later that year, Mina Edison's long activity in the community and the social life of her winter home came to an end. (Courtesy of SWFHS.)

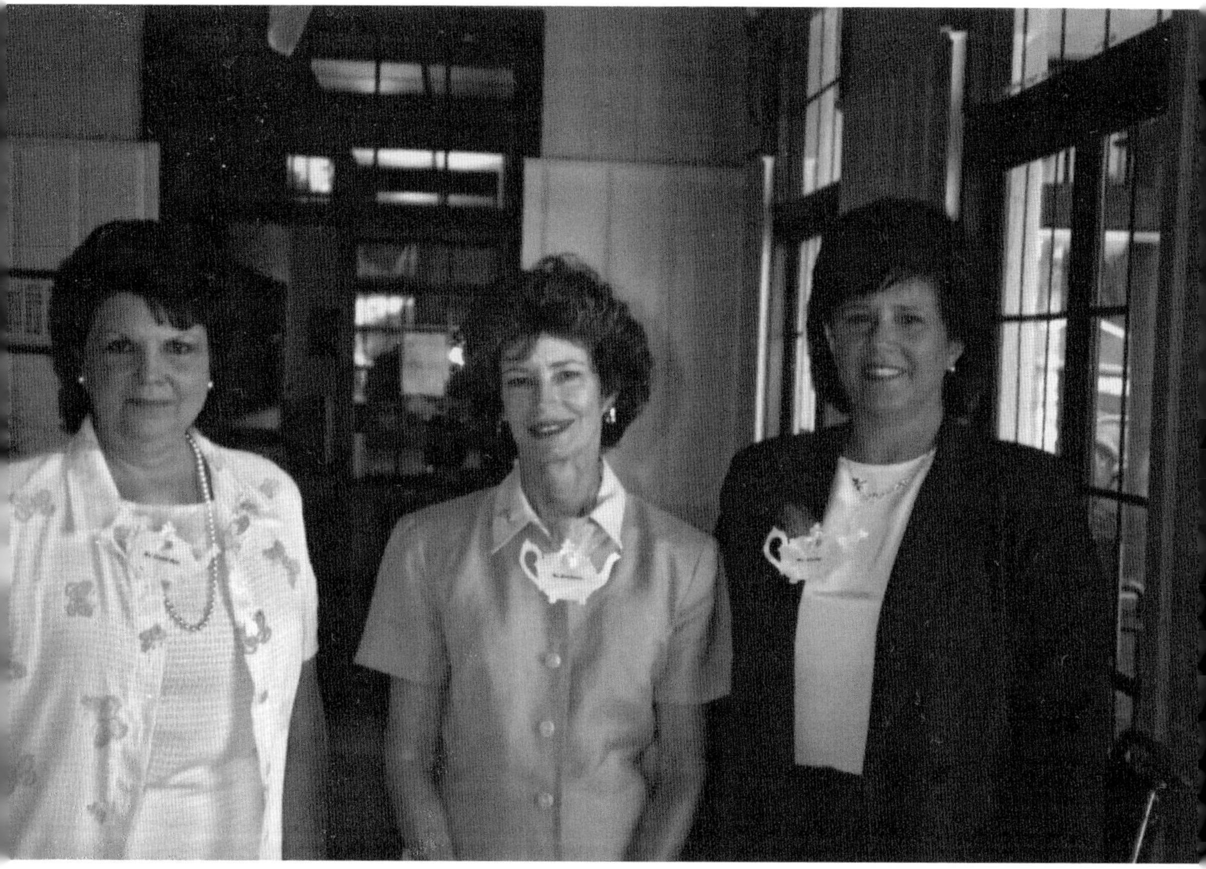

Fort Myers Woman's Community Club

Few organizations can rival this club for its enduring legacy of community spirit and love of Fort Myers. Although incorporated in 1927 as the Woman's Community Club of Fort Myers, the organization has two forerunners, the Woman's Auxiliary, which met in 1885 at the home of Julia Hanson, and the Woman's Club, organized in 1900 at the home of Olive E. Stout. In 1938, the community club joined the Junior Chamber of Commerce to help Ronald Halgrim create the first Edison Pageant of Light, which commemorated the birthday of the inventor. The club has hosted the pageant's Coronation Ball ever since. Starting in 1956, the Annual Holiday House has been the organization's gift to the community. Since 2008, the event has been held in the historic Murphy-Burroughs and Langford-Kingston Homes. In the 1998 photograph taken at the annual Pink Tea are, from left to right, Mary Lee Mann, Teta Roberts, and Jane Ball, all past presidents. (Courtesy of Fort Myers Woman's Community Club.)

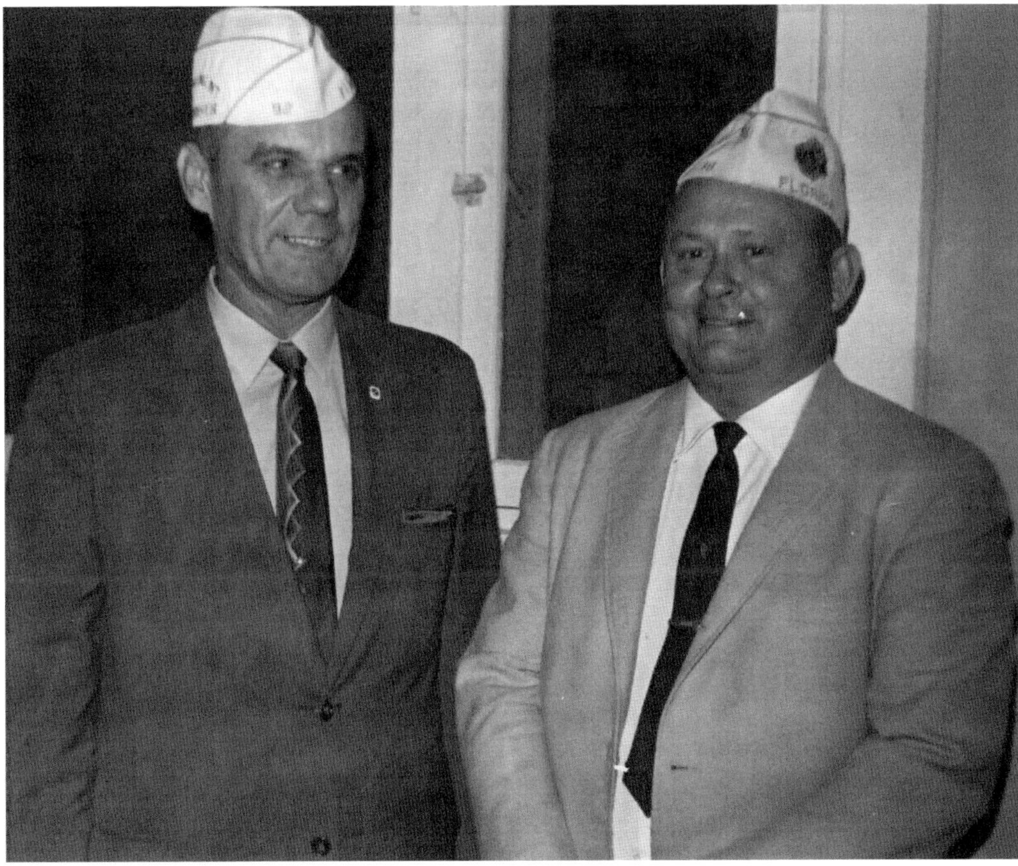

Park Pigott

Pigott dedicated himself to reestablishing American Legion baseball in Fort Myers. By the time he died in 1972 at age 58, the former minor-league catcher had coached American Legion baseball for 25 years. He was the first employee of the Lee County Parks and Recreation Department and eventually became the director. He started the Terry Park baseball field and fairgrounds and supervised the redesigning and rebuilding of Terry Park to accommodate major-league teams who were in residence for spring training. A plaque at the park honors his contributions. He was also active in the Fort Myers Boys Club, Elks Lodge, and the PTA. At his death, he held the office of vice-commander, the second-highest American Legion state post. He is (right) pictured with an unidentified legionnaire. (Courtesy of AL.)

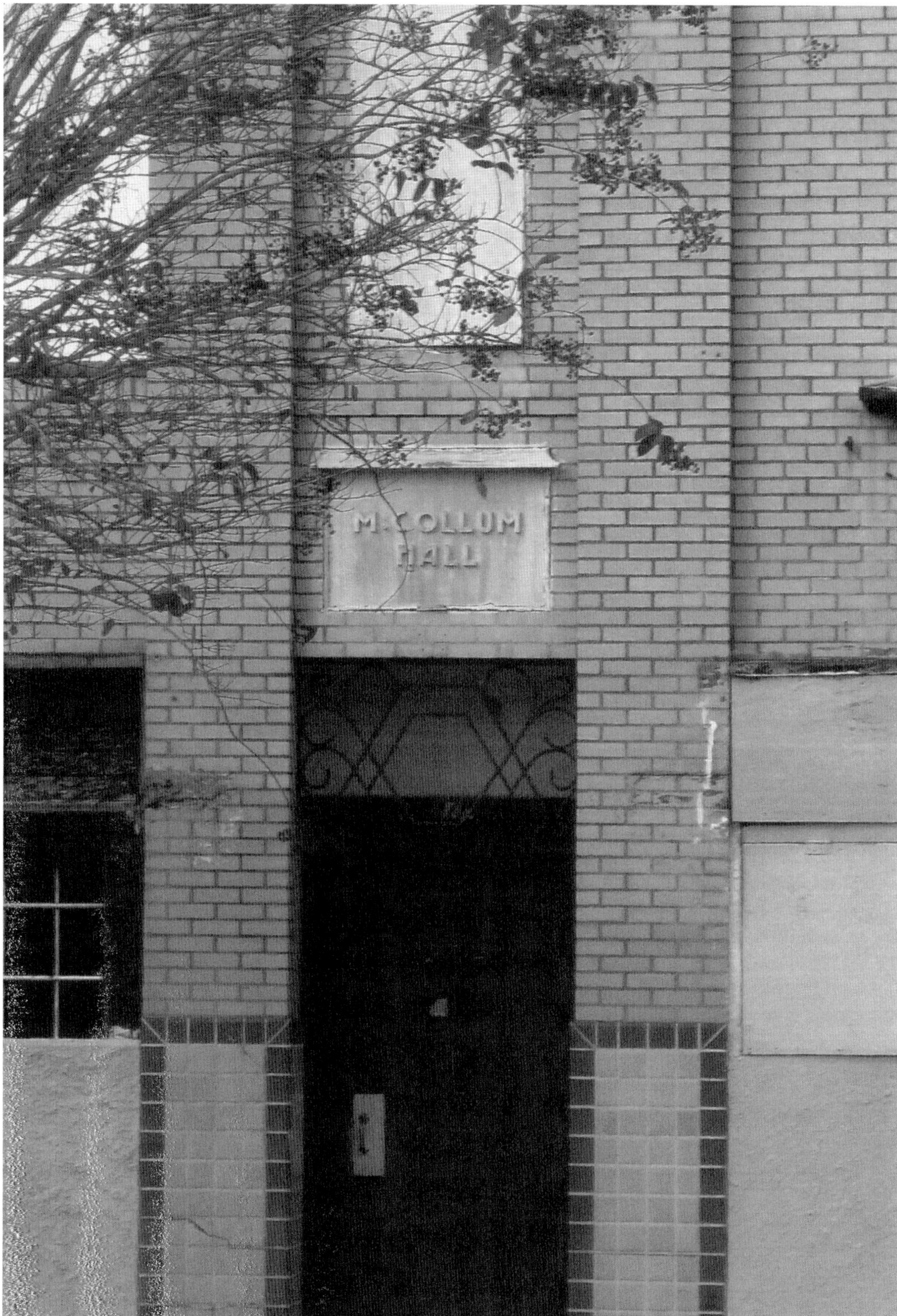
McCOLLUM
HALL

Clifford McCollum Sr. (LEFT)
McCollum built his Art Deco hall in 1938. At the center of Dunbar, it was a vibrant component in the social and economic life of the black community. The racially segregated upstairs dance hall attracted the greatest of music legends for several decades, including Duke Ellington, Louis Armstrong, B.B. King, Otis Redding, and Count Basie. The lower level housed a variety of thriving businesses and a USO for black soldiers from Buckingham Army Air Force Base in World War II. The historic hall is being restored and redesigned as McCollum Place, which will house retail, restaurants, and a reception hall. (Photograph by the author.)

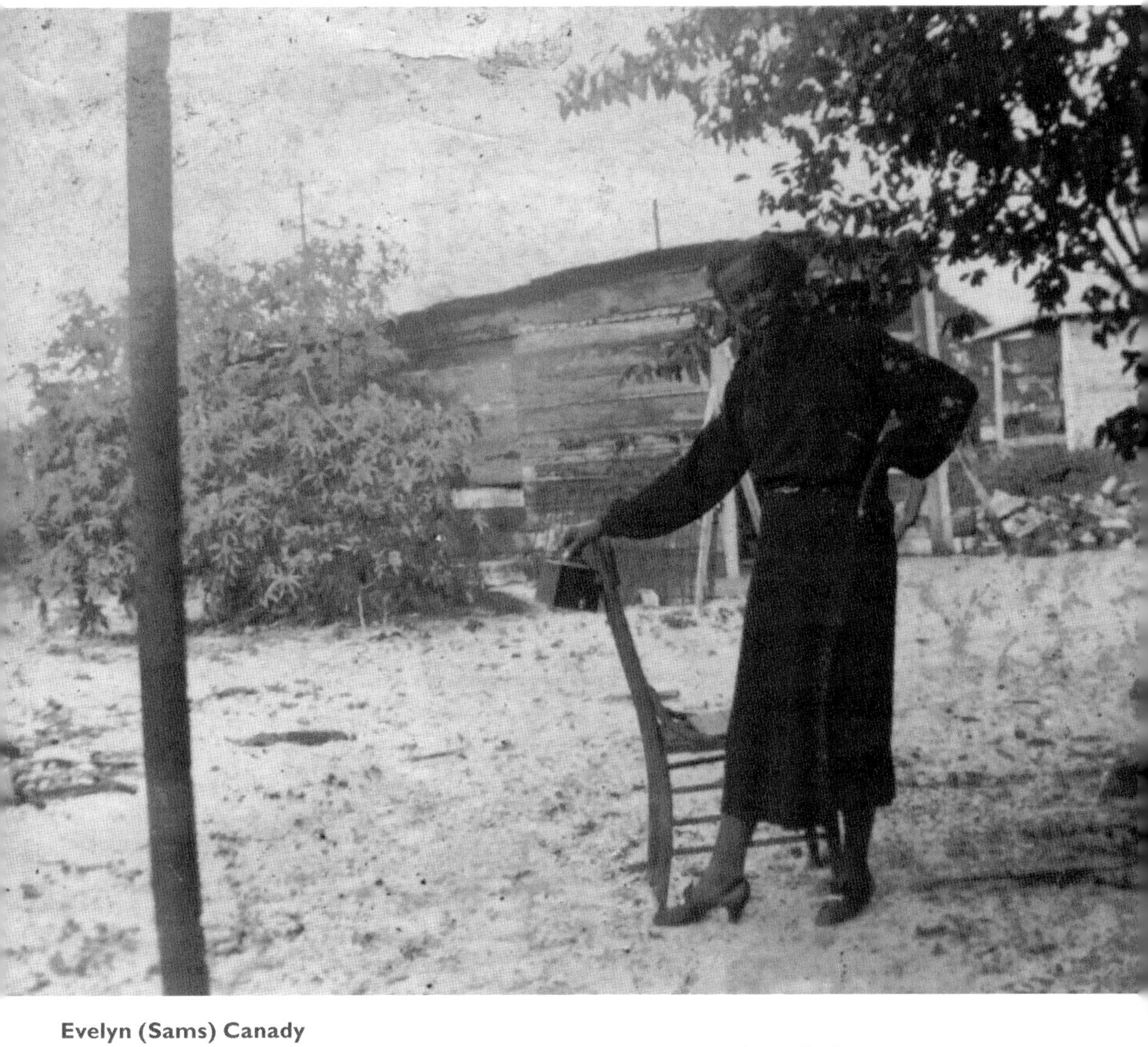

Evelyn (Sams) Canady
Born in 1908 in Archie, Florida, Canady came to Fort Myers in 1916, where she became an important educator and civic and religious worker in the black community. She founded Dunbar's Easter Parade in 1946, a tradition that today attracts tens of thousands of people. She also helped to found the Dr. Ella Piper Center and Dunbar High School, which opened in 1929 and gave local black students the opportunity to earn a high school education without moving away from home. She taught in Lee County schools for 47 years, 25 of them at Dunbar Elementary. (Courtesy of LCBHS.)

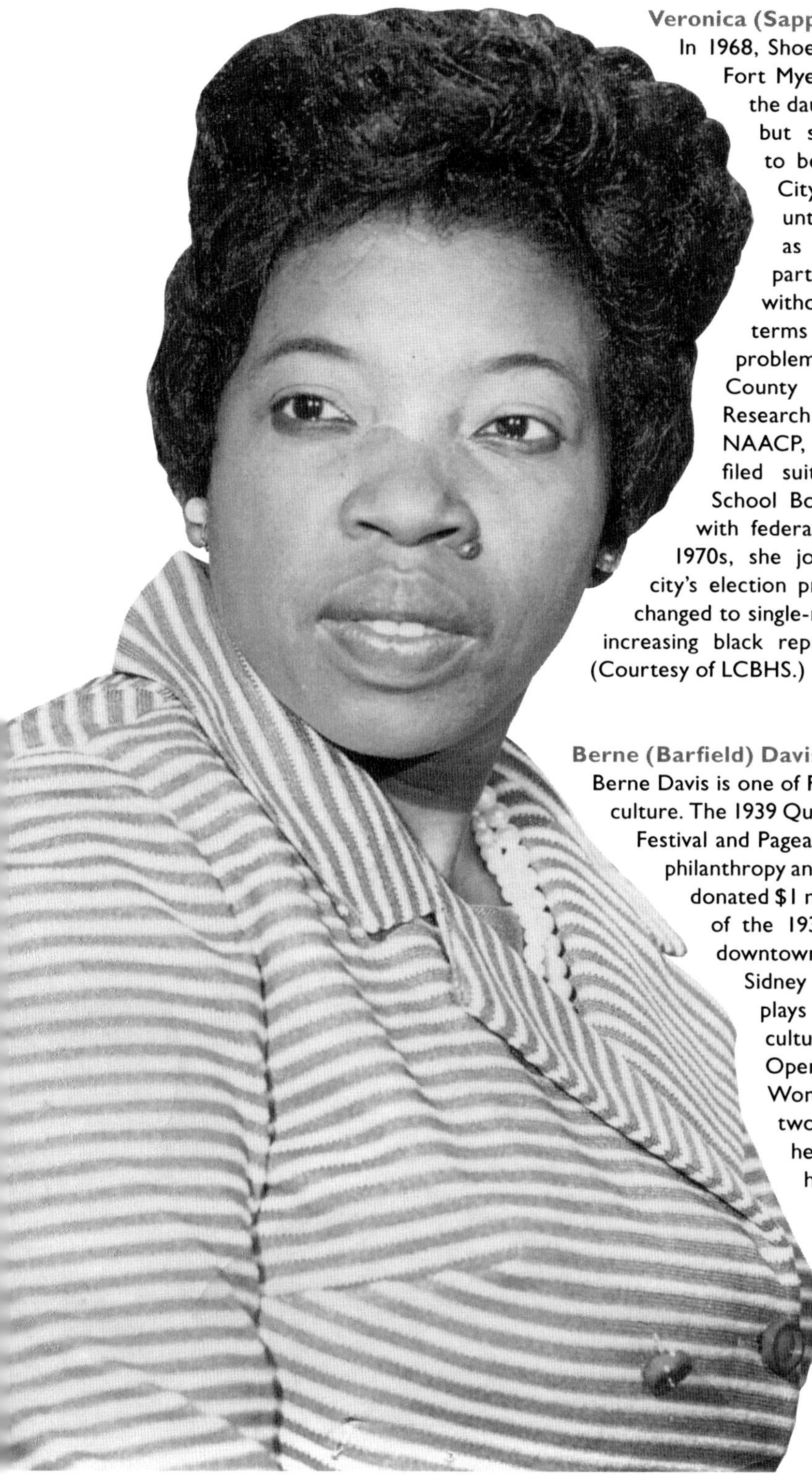

Veronica (Sapp) Shoemaker

In 1968, Shoemaker was the first black in Fort Myers to run for office. It took the daughter of a preacher 14 years, but she became the first black to be seated on the Fort Myers City Council in 1982 and served until 2007. Her chief interests as a politician were societal, particularly serving all citizens without bias. Other efforts of her terms were resolving school busing problems and establishing the Lee County Black History Museum and Research Center. As president of the NAACP, she and other black citizens filed suit against the Lee County School Board over its noncompliance with federal desegregation laws. In the 1970s, she joined a suit challenging the city's election process. As a result, the city changed to single-member voting districts, thus increasing black representation on the council. (Courtesy of LCBHS.)

Berne (Barfield) Davis (RIGHT)

Berne Davis is one of Fort Myers' angels of arts and culture. The 1939 Queen of Edisonia for the Edison Festival and Pageant of Light is revered for her philanthropy and personal grace. In 2006, she donated $1 million toward the restoration of the 1933 WPA-built post office in downtown Fort Myers. Christened the Sidney & Berne Davis Art Center, it plays a central role in downtown culture and revitalization. The Opera Guild and Fort Myers Woman's Community Club are two of her civic interests. With her in the photograph is her husband, Sidney, noted for his service to the community and his men's clothing store established in 1934. He was instrumental in arranging the deeding of the Edison Winter Estate to the city by Mina Edison, a personal friend. (Courtesy of SWFHS, Nalle Collection.)

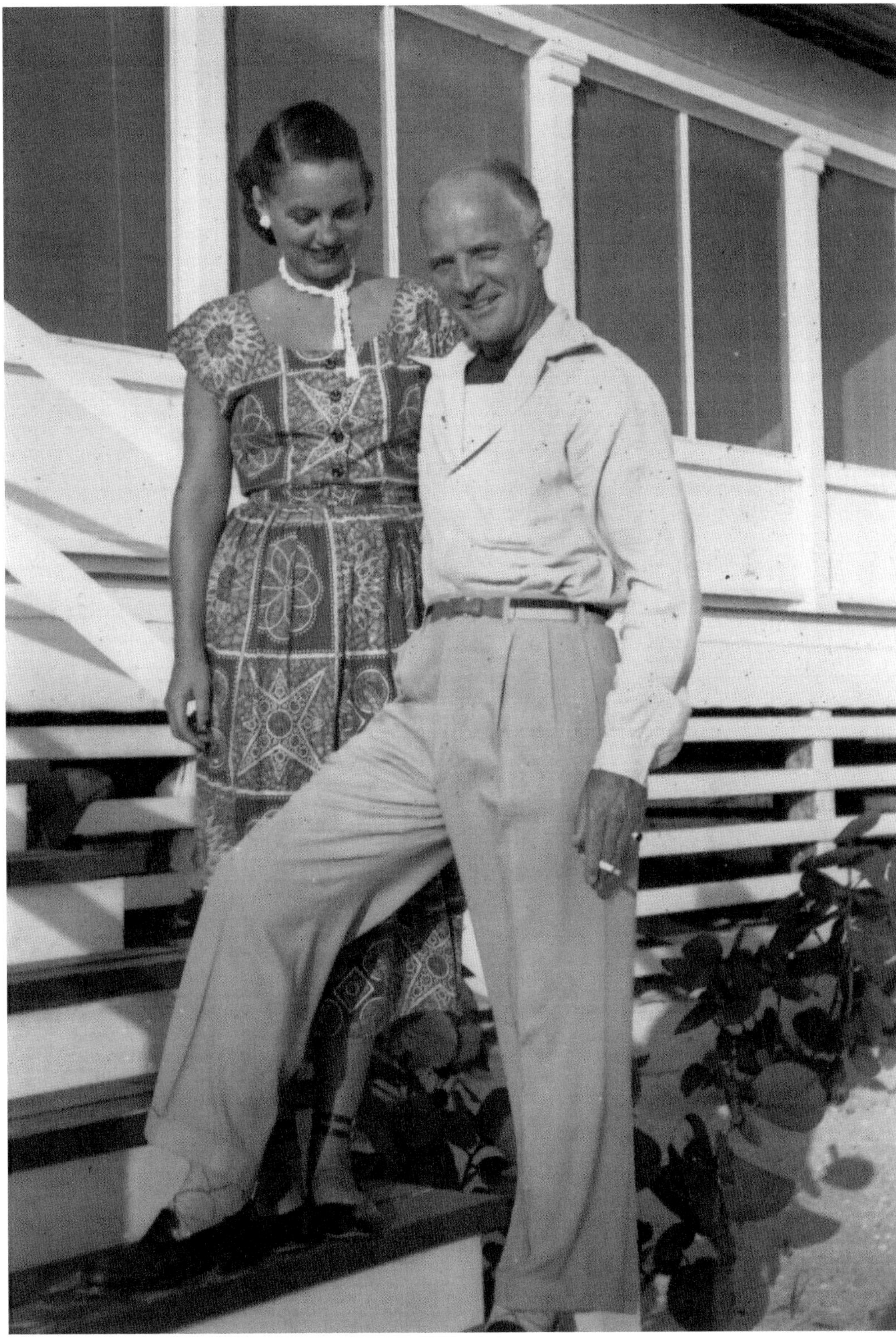

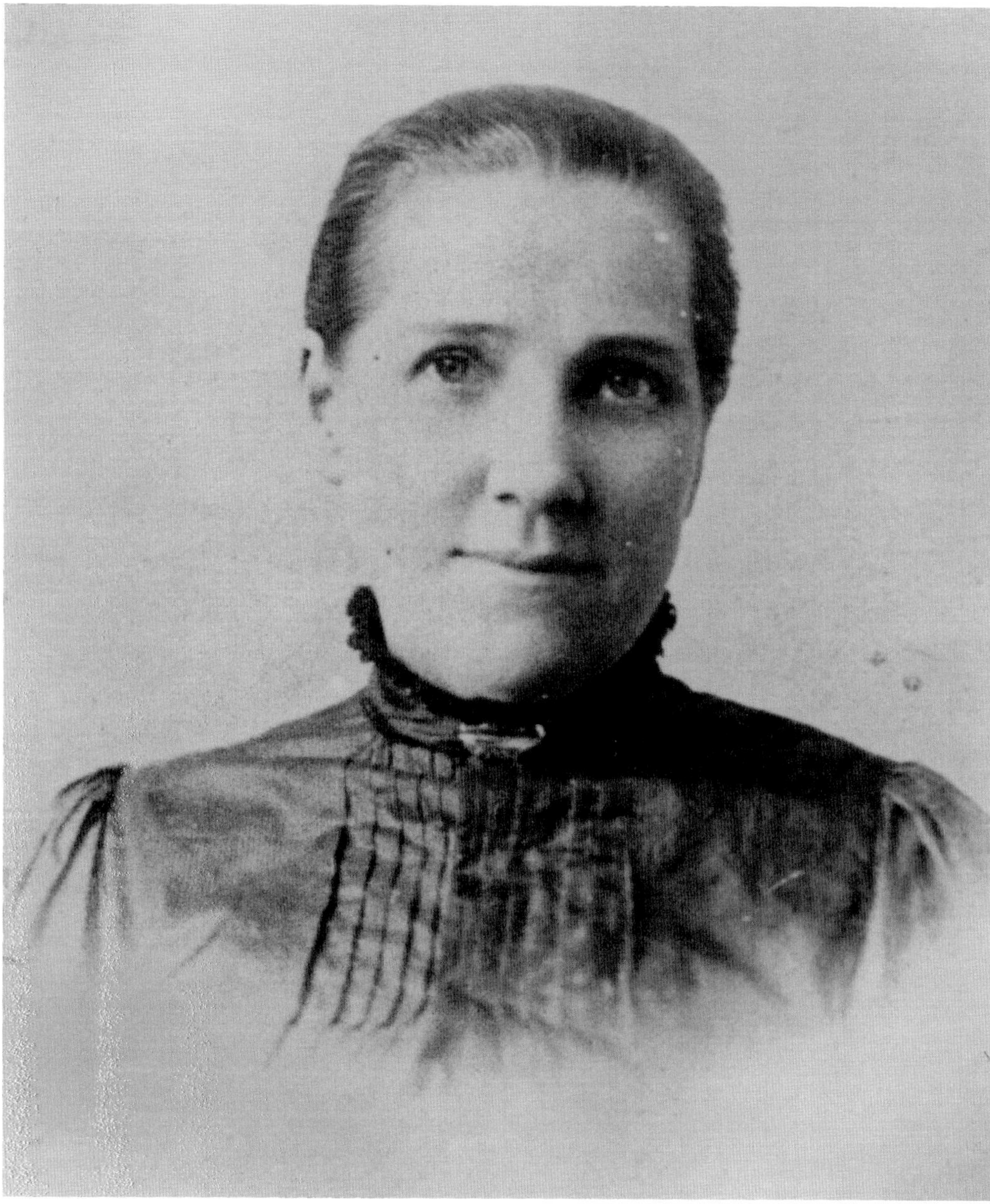

Olive Stout

Stout came to the area on the same steamer that brought Thomas A. and Mina Edison on their honeymoon in 1886. The former schoolteacher and independent-minded woman from Wisconsin was scouting for a newspaper to buy and operate with her husband Frank, a newspaperman. She bought the one-year-old *Fort Myers Press* from the widow of Stafford Cleveland, and the family owned and operated it for 27 years. Stout dedicated herself to being a civilizing influence on the cow town. Concerned about rowdy behavior in the streets and saloons, she joined the crusading Women's Christian Temperance Union to clean up the town. She was instrumental in the women's clubs and founding the public library, and she twice served as postmistress. She died in 1930 at age 83. (Courtesy of SWFHS.)

CHAPTER FIVE

Visionaries

Every town owes much to those who can imagine beyond the limits of the here and now, whether they are inventors, social activists, Renaissance women, or born environmentalists. Visionaries have the uncanny ability of knowing what's important, even when faced with the indifference, hostility, or perplexity of fellow citizens. The confirmation of others is not the goal. Realizing a vision is. For John Blalock, the vision was educational equality, and for Charles Edgar Foster, it was teaching others to love southwest Florida's land, water, and sky as he did. John Morgan Dean brought advanced and civilizing city-planning concepts to Fort Myers almost a century ago, and Bertha May Boomer painted the landscape she loved and had the astounding idea of cofounding a museum in little Fort Myers.

Bertha May Boomer

Born into a prominent Chicago family in 1880, Boomer came to southwest Florida in 1894 to the Koreshan Unity, an Estero utopian society. An accomplished musician and painter, Boomer graduated from the Art Institute of Chicago and studied in Europe. After moving to Fort Myers, she and curator and collector Mrs. C.E. Briggs opened the Lee County Museum, the city's first, in the mid-1930s. Boomer loved sketching outdoor scenes, swimming, and picnicking. In the photograph, she sits (far right) with a group of unidentified picnickers. She died at Fort Myers Beach in 1941, run over by a truck at a swimming party. (Courtesy of SWFMH.)

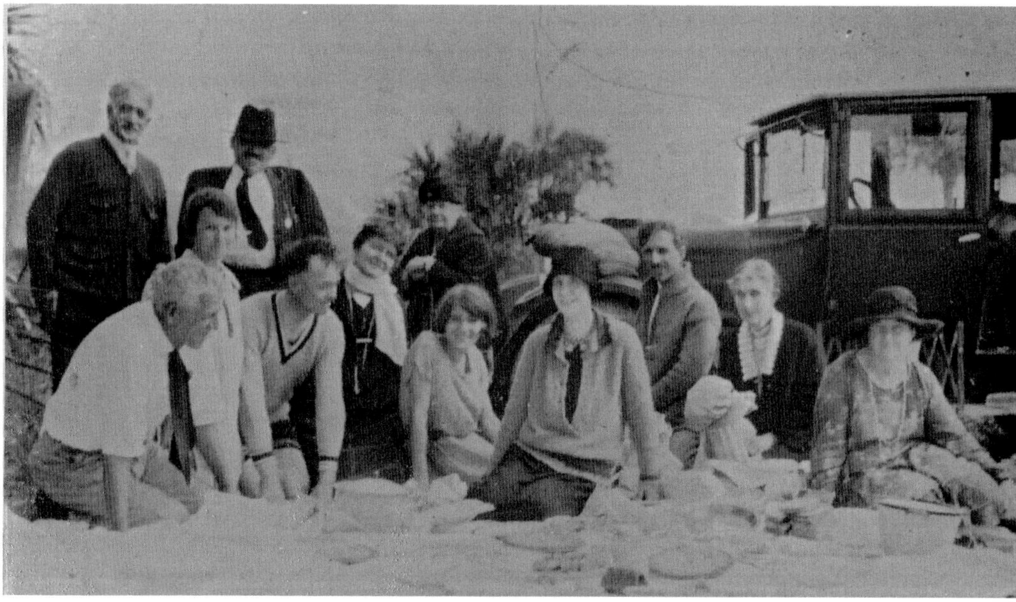

John Blalock (RIGHT)

On August 4, 1964, a Fort Myers father risked his reputation and his very life for a principle. The suit *Rosalind Blalock, et al.* v. *the Board of Public Instruction of Lee County, Florida, et al.* was filed in US District Court in Tampa. Lead plaintiff John H. Blalock, in tandem with the National Association for the Advancement of Colored People, and on behalf of his daughter Rosalind and 33 other black students, sought the racial integration of the public schools as required by the US Supreme Court's 1954 decision in *Brown* v. *the Board of Education*. His love for his daughter provided the catalyst for the suit. Planning a career in science, Rosalind knew she was not getting the education she needed to succeed in college. She wanted to transfer from the all-black Dunbar High School to the better-equipped all-white Fort Myers High School. She was denied enrollment. Blalock's wife Mildred says that fear or difficulty didn't matter to him, for his wartime service had prepared him to fight. "He was fighting for himself and for his daughter." Born in Lamar, Georgia, in 1924, he met Mildred, a Fort Myers native, at an Armistice Day event at Buckingham Army Air Base. He served in the Air Force Transportation Corps conveying personnel to the front lines. The two married in 1944 when he was on furlough. He later volunteered for Korea, leaving with the rank of staff sergeant and declining promotion to lieutenant to come home to his family. Ultimately, the federal court ordered Lee County to integrate what had been a biracial or dual system. It was 1971 before the school system was deemed compliant with federal integration laws, but the cases went in and out of court for more than three decades, as the county's desegregation plans were debated and ruled upon. The results of the fight for educational equality were too late for Rosalind in high school, but not for her siblings and thousands of other students who benefitted later. She went on to earn a degree at Alabama's Tuskegee Institute and later pursued graduate work. (Courtesy of Mildred Blalock.)

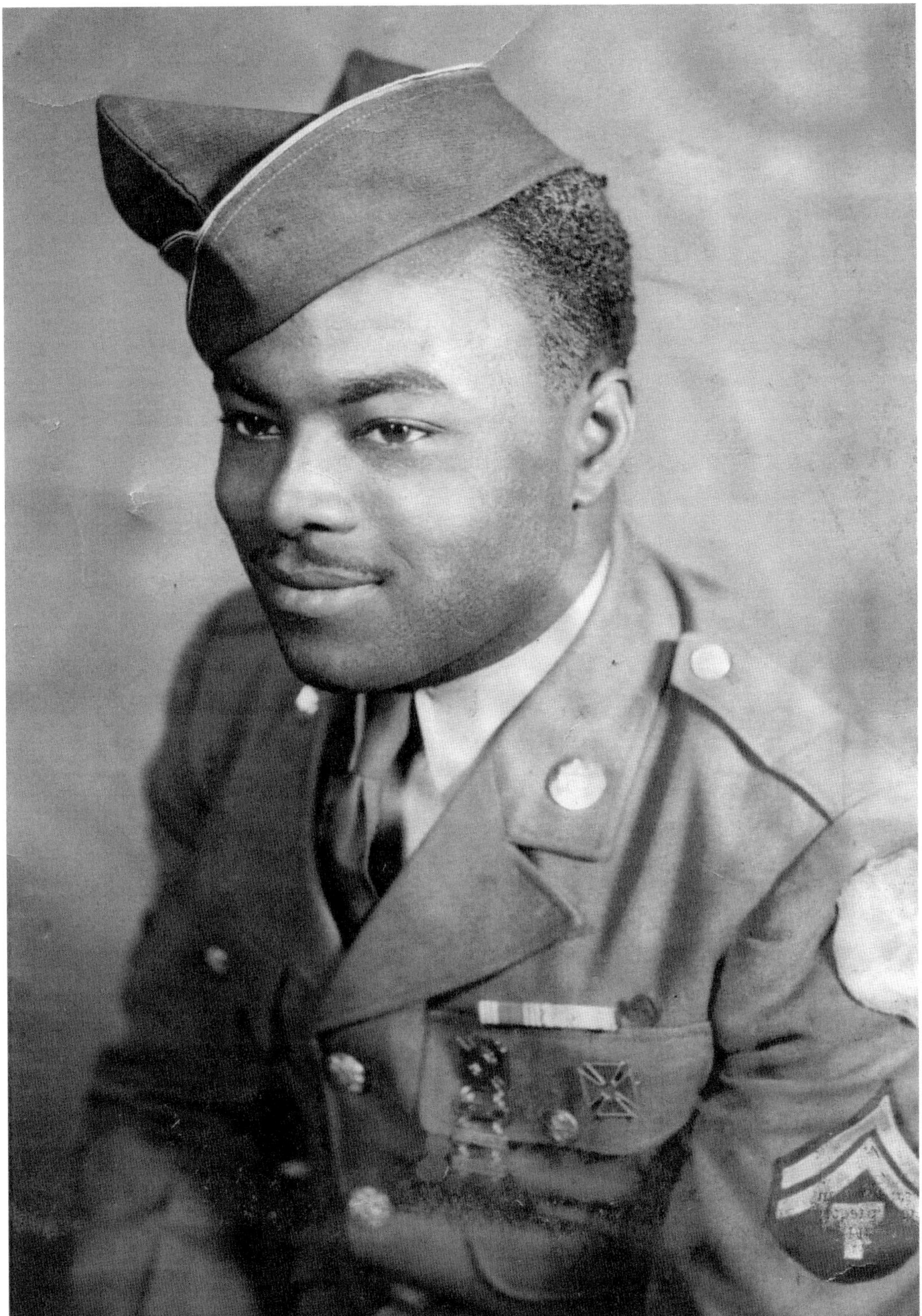

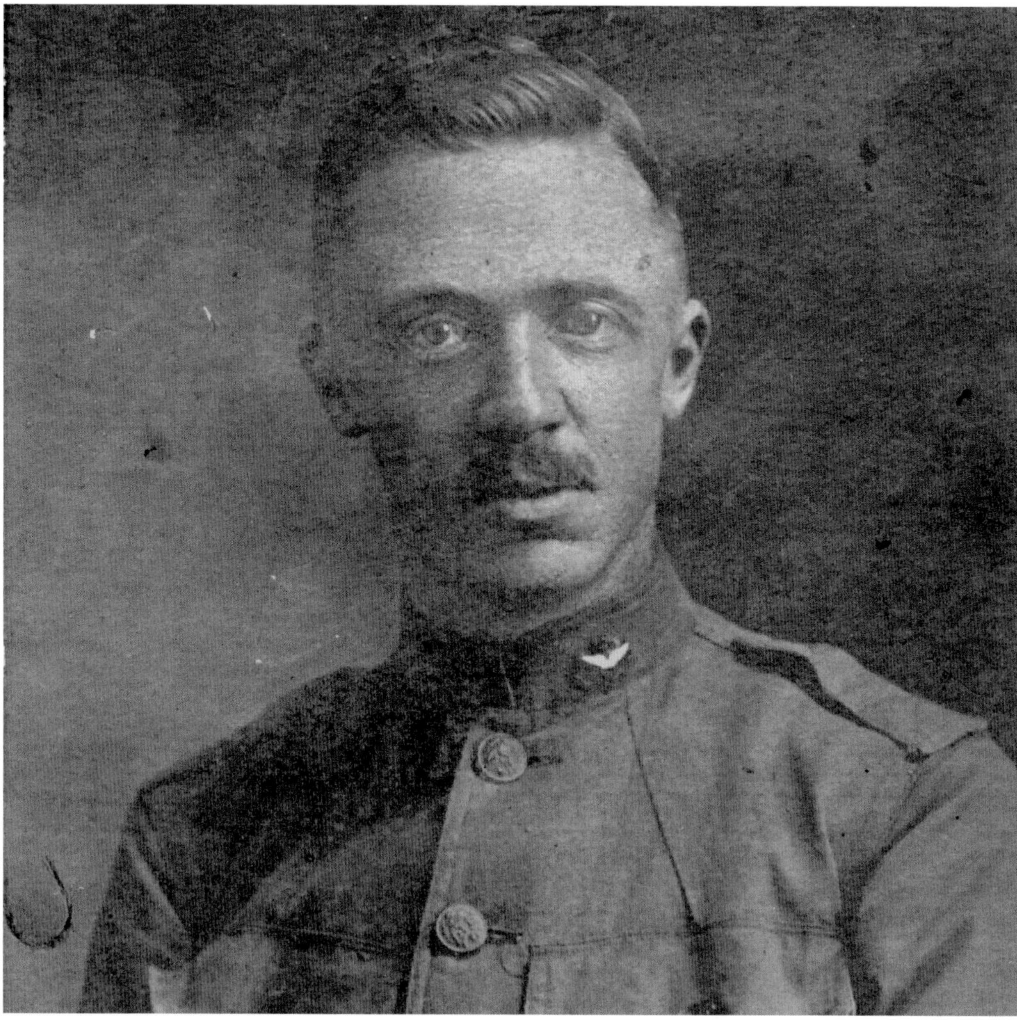

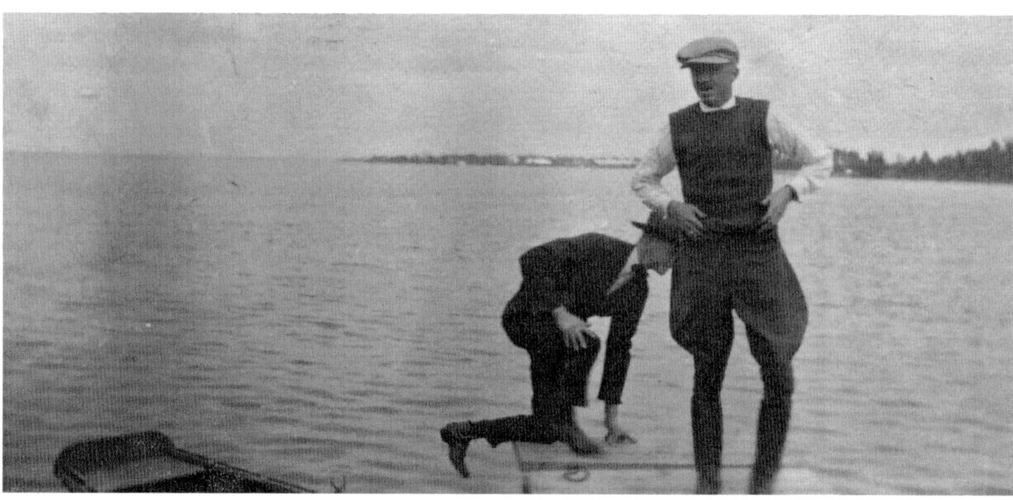

Capt. Channing Page (LEFT)

Fort Myers' own World War I flying ace was born in Philadelphia, Pennsylvania in 1893. After graduating from the University of Virginia, Page moved to Lee County with his parents in July of 1915. He became the first Floridian to receive a commission as an officer in the Army Aviation Corps, but not before being rejected twice. The determined young man succeeded only after traveling to Washington, DC, and convincing Florida's state senators to intercede on his behalf. Among the awards Page received were the Distinguished Service Cross and the Croix de Guerre. On March 2, 1920, local headlines announced the "MOST APPALLING TRAGEDY EVER KNOWN IN LEE COUNTY." Page, along with G. Hunter Bryant, Lee County tax assessor, and Thomas H. Colcord, his mechanic, was killed in the Curtiss Sea-Gull hydroplane in the photograph (below). That very morning, while talking to a member of the press, the pilot had foretold the turbulent weather he might encounter, but expressed confidence that things would be fine. Fortuitously, before he left, Page joked to the editor of the *Fort Myers Press*, "And listen, Mort, cut that 'hero stuff' when you write a piece about the trip. If anything happens be sure to write a good story about it. So long." Lee County's first airport was renamed Page Field in his honor in 1942. (Above, courtesy of AL; below, courtesy of SWFMH.)

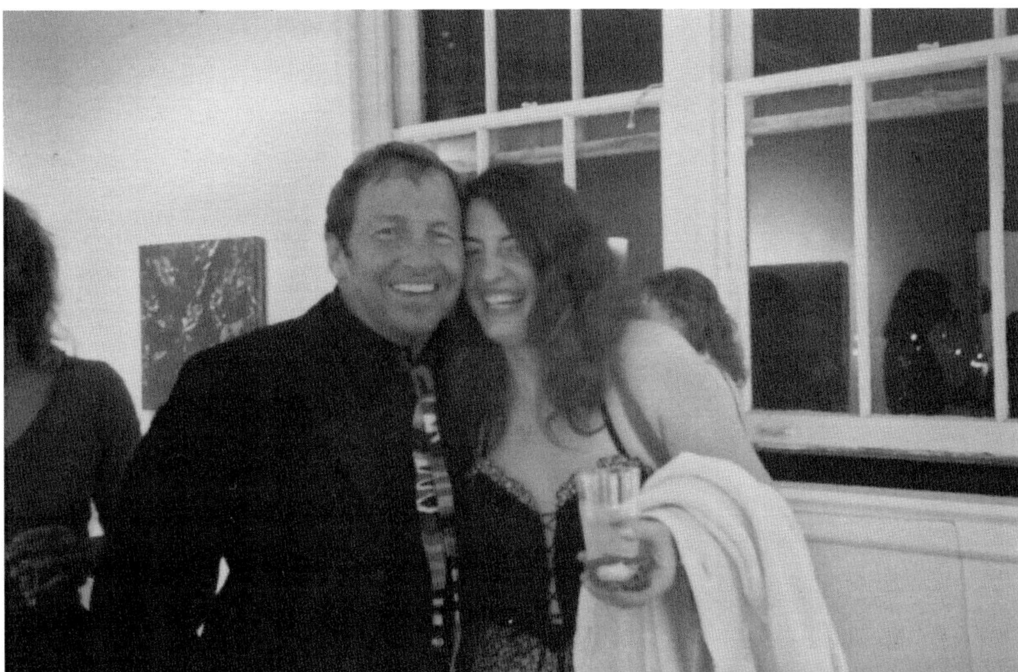

Robert Rauschenberg

Beginning in the 1950s, world-renowned artist Robert Rauschenberg enriched the art and community life of Fort Myers, when he bought land on sparsely populated Captiva Island. In the 1970s, he began a long association with Edison State College's gallery, which was renamed the Bob Rauschenberg Gallery in 2004. He was a major supporter of many local organizations, particularly the ACT Auction, Abuse Counseling and Treatment's annual gala fundraiser, for which he always donated work. The BIG Arts scholarships for young artists bear his name, and he was also known for his commitment to environmental causes and groups such as the Corkscrew Regional Ecosystem Watershed (CREW) Land and Water Trust. He designed International Earth Day posters in 1970 and 1990. The artist was also known for his personal generosity, mentoring, and support of other artists. With him in the photograph is Brenda Collison. (Courtesy of Greg Biolchini.)

Stanley Hanson

The "white medicine man" to the Seminoles, Hanson spoke their language fluently and earned tribal trust as their confidant and counselor. His writings are the most authoritative record of that culture, and many of his papers and archives reside at the National Anthropological Archives at the Smithsonian Institution. Also active in civic affairs, he served as city tax collector and three terms as councilman and was one of the original Tamiami Trail Blazers. As Florida's district inspector for the US Migratory Bird Law, he surveyed bird populations and protected the rookeries of native birds such as roseate spoonbills and egrets. In a 1915 newspaper interview, he wondered if a woman wearing an aigrette on her hat realized that it represented not only the death of the parent bird, but the death of three to five chicks who starved to death on the nest. He died in 1945. (Courtesy of SWFMH.)

Julia (Allen) Hanson (RIGHT)

Historian and writer Julia Allen Hanson was called the "mother of all women's clubs." For half a century, she was so influential in community affairs that it is difficult to imagine what Fort Myers would have been without her progressive influence. She was a founder of the first woman's club in 1885, a forerunner to the present Fort Myers Woman's Community Club. Born in London, England, in 1843 to a prominent family, the titian-haired beauty was painted by Byrne Jones and Sir John Millais, and her social circle included famous authors, celebrities, and royalty. Dedicated to the welfare of the Seminoles and bird conservation, she worked to pass laws on both issues. Wife of Dr. William Hanson and mother to Stanley, she died in 1934. (Courtesy of HFA.)

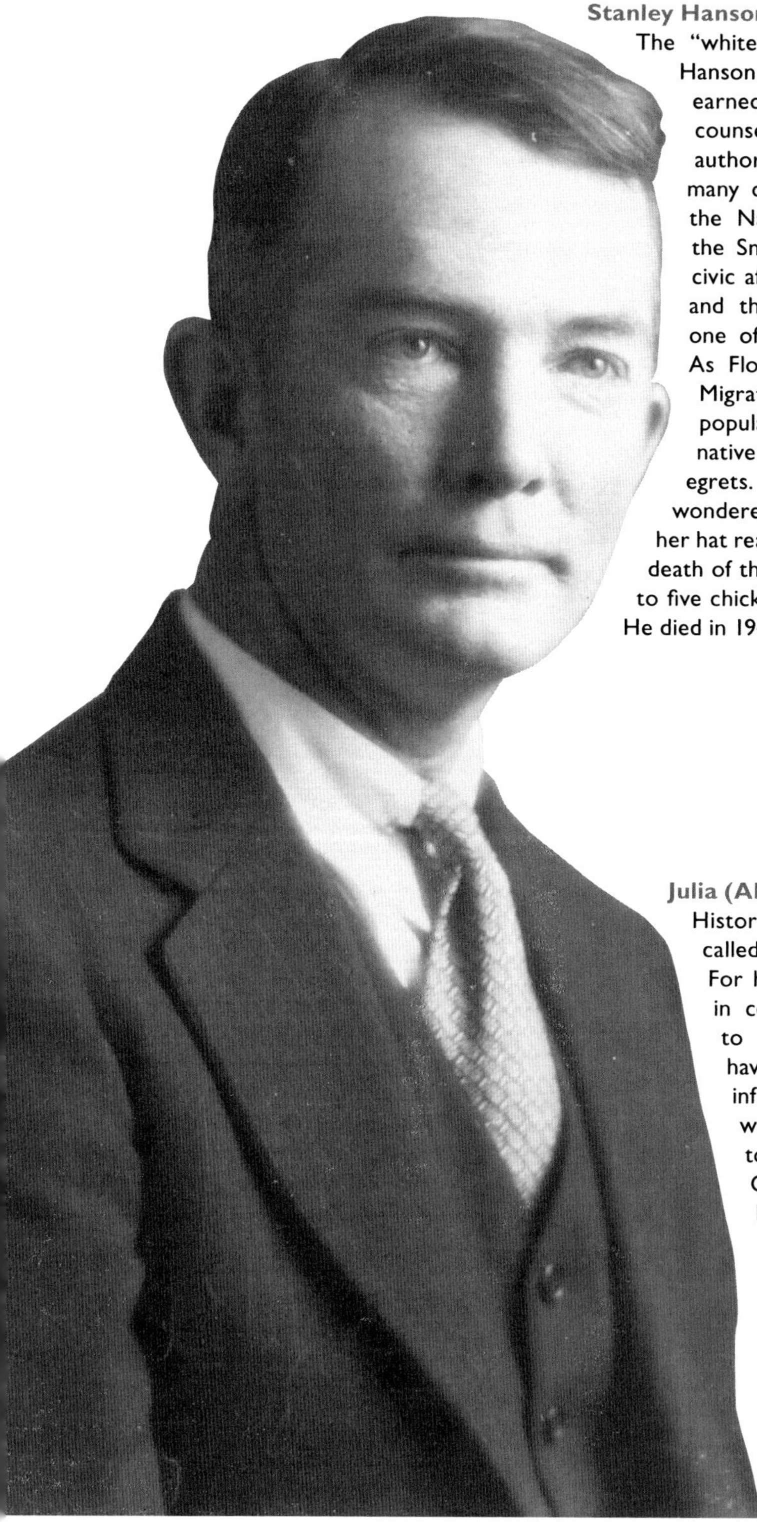

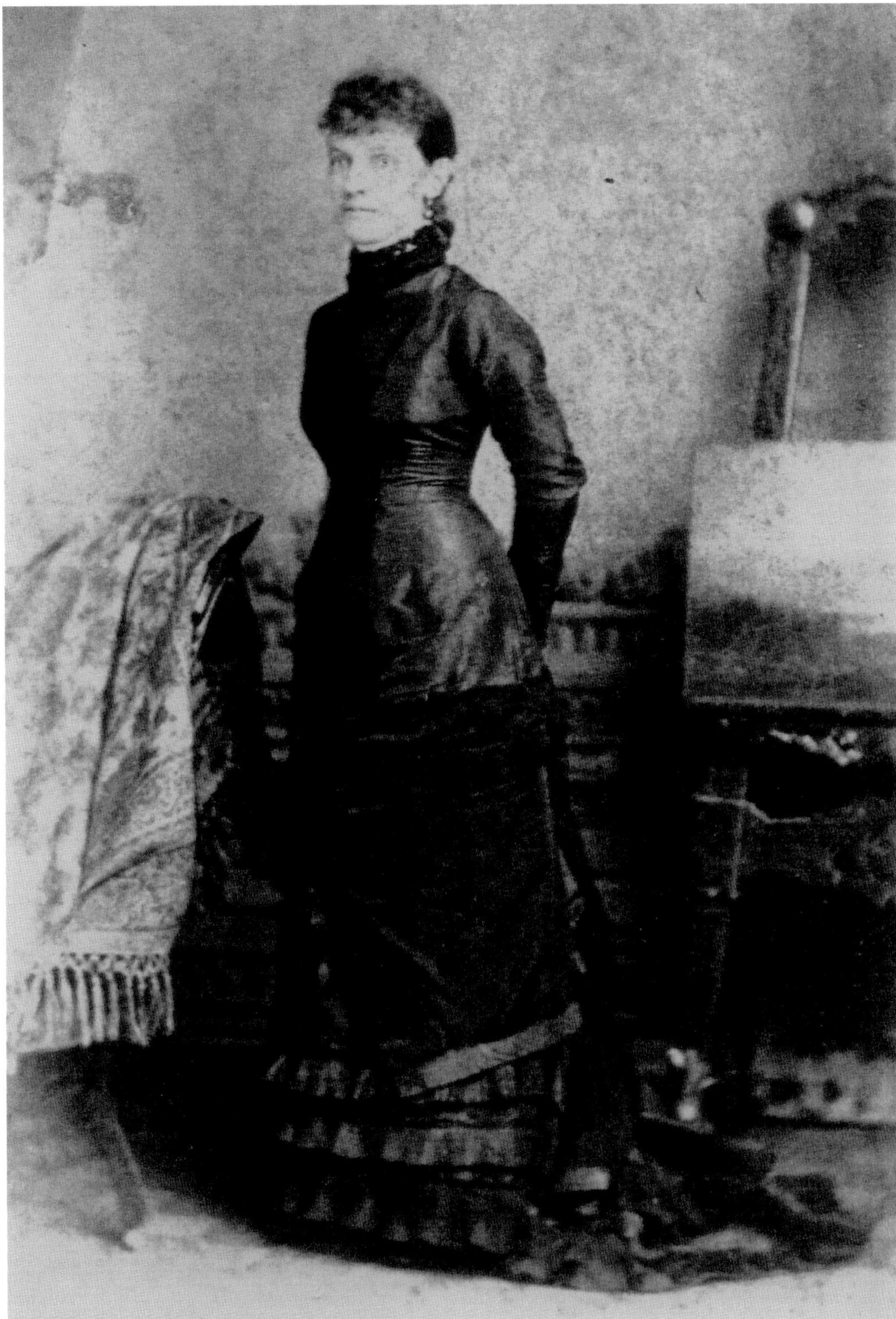

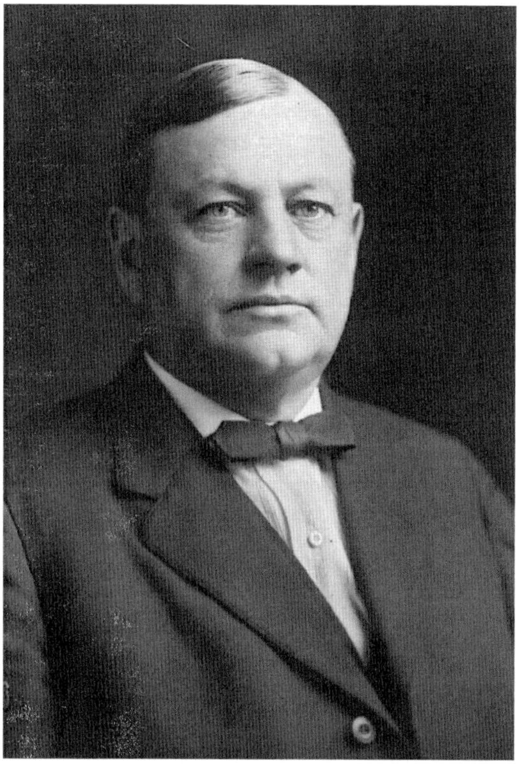

John Morgan Dean

A developer and businessman, Dean first arrived here in 1898 from Rhode Island for a hunting trip. He was among the group of wealthy seasonal visitors who, in the early 20th century, invested in and significantly shaped the future of Fort Myers. In 1900, he bought significant tracts of riverfront property and developed Dean Park, now one of the city's historic neighborhoods. He died in 1938. (Courtesy of Rhoda Hopson Ingram.)

Bruce Gora

Everyone recognizes the work of architect Bruce Gora, notably the Alliance for the Arts and Temple Beth-El. In 2004, Gora/McGahey Associates in Architecture received Southwest Florida's American Institute of Architects (AIA) Design Award. In 2006, the chapter awarded him the W.R. Frizzell Medal of Honor. He died in 2008 at the age of 58 and posthumously received the Angels of the Arts Artist Lifetime Achievement award. Gora's rhythm and blues band, the Juice, is part of his legacy. (Courtesy of Carolyn Gora.)

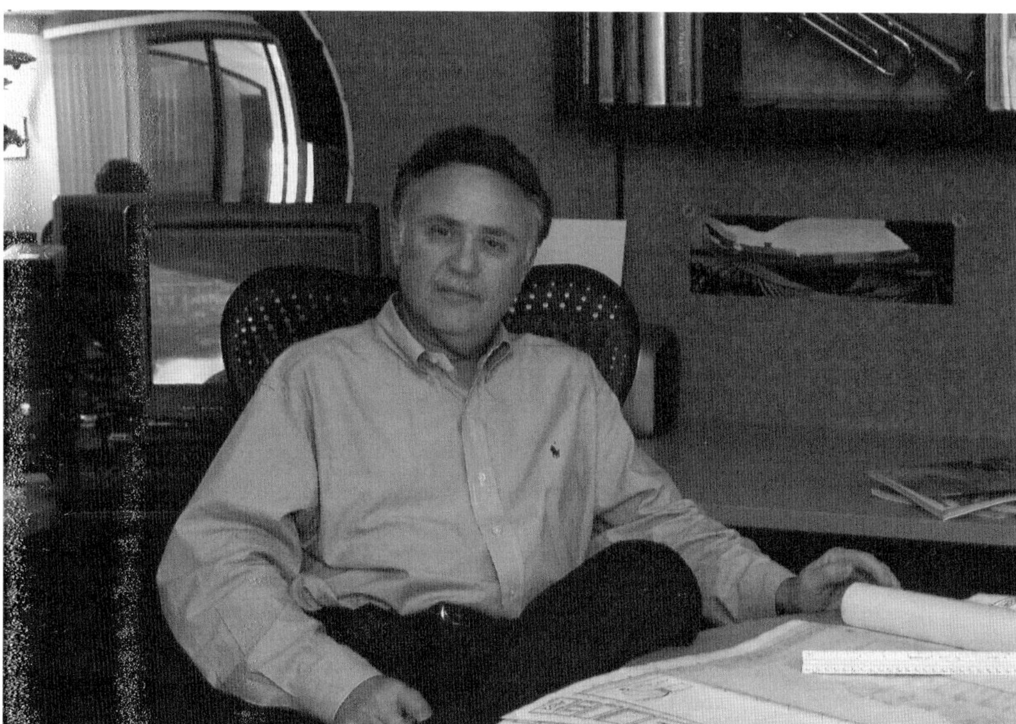

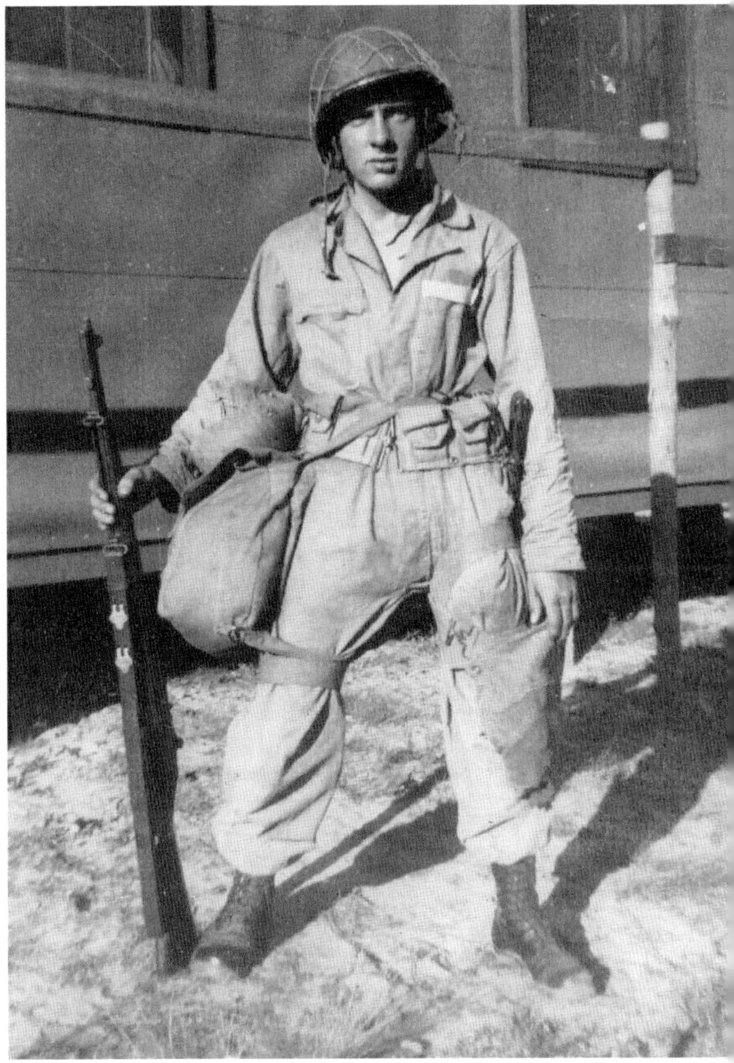

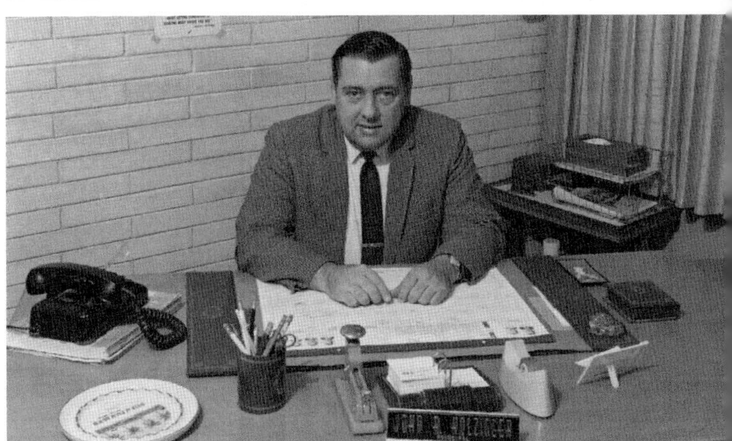

John Holzinger
At the close of 1968, the staff of the *Fort Myers News-Press*, by overwhelming consensus, named the statewide teacher walkout as the year's top story. In the opening days of the walkout, 58 percent of teachers and 20 percent of principals in Lee County walked out after failed state-level negotiations. What united the teachers, most of whom were non-union, was their determination to improve support for education. Textbooks, better libraries, basic supplies, teachers for students with special needs, overcrowding—all were among the needs. Villas Elementary School principal John Holzinger was one of the cause's most stalwart supporters. A native of Lancaster, Pennsylvania, he had volunteered while quite young during World War II, fighting as a paratrooper in New Guinea, so fighting was not new to him. He came to Florida in 1956 for a teaching job in Venice, and several years later joined the Lee County system. It was while he was principal at Villas Elementary School in Fort Myers that the teacher's strike occurred and his principles were put at stake. He persevered in the fight to gain ground for the students. One former colleague recalls his enthusiasm as he led fellow strikers in song while playing his guitar. Gradually, teachers began to return to work, sensing that the walkout as a political tool was not in tune with public opinion. The strike was called off statewide about three weeks later and Holzinger was demoted to teaching shop at another school. Years later, he characterized the teachers who walked out as "wide-eyed idealists." He still championed the cause, but questioned the methods, given the lack of widespread public support. He retired from the Lee County School District in the late 1980s after 40 years as an educator. He died in 1990. (Courtesy of Holzinger family.)

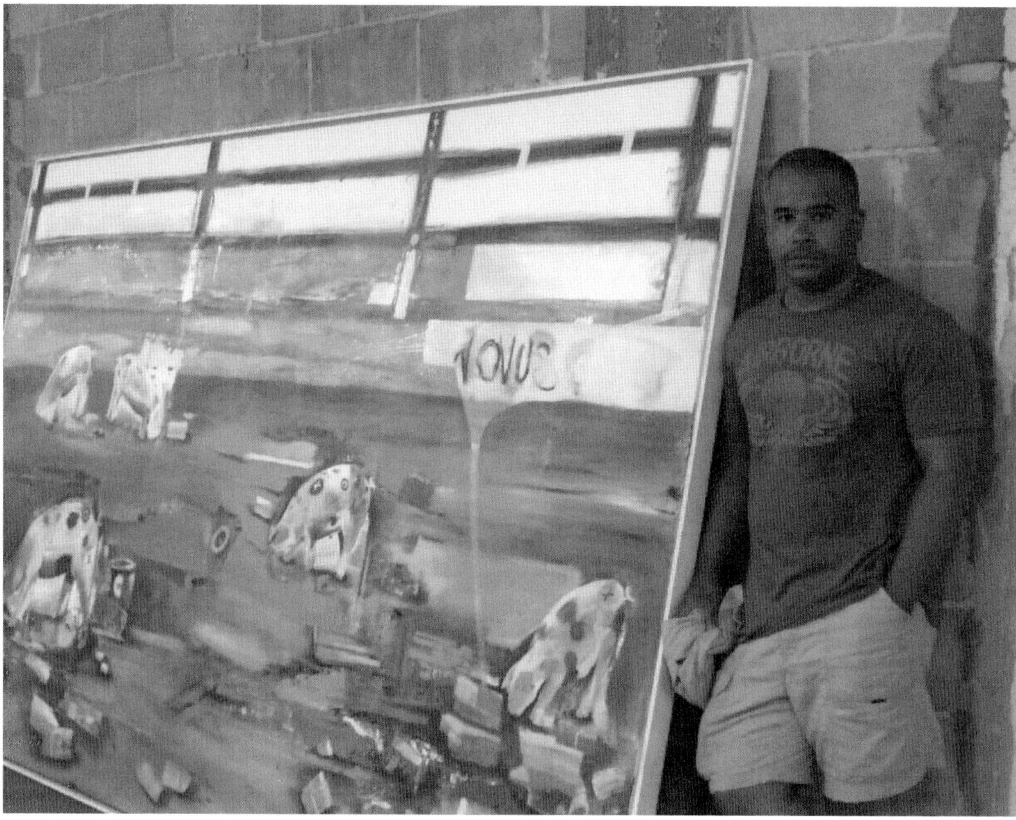

Marcus Jansen
The child who painted on newspaper or scrap paper—any surface available—is now a major artist of Urban Expressionism who exhibits worldwide and whose work resides in prestigious collections. Many of Jansen's large-scale works weave photographs, typeface, newspaper clippings, money, labels, texts, spray paint, circles, and arrows with fluidity, a pastiche of modern life. They reflect the turmoil, chaos, and tawdry beauty that characterize the urban landscape. Born in New York City in 1968, Jansen began to realize himself as an artist while growing up amid hurling subway cars awash with color and cartoon-like characters. He cites the influences of cubism, Dadaism, abstract expressionism, and the artists Robert Rauschenberg and Jean-Michel Basquiat. Educated at the Berufsfaschule fuer Gestaltung/Design in Germany, he traveled widely in Western Europe as a youth. In the 1980s, Jansen was introduced to the legendary graffiti writer WESTONE, and in the late 1990s, he returned to New York after military service in the Gulf War. He was selected Ford Motor Company's Centennial artist in 2003. In 2005, the Southwest Florida Museum of History commissioned him to create an exhibit capturing Fort Myers from an urban-expressionist and historical perspective. That same year, he received the Angel of the Arts "New Artist of the Year" award. His work is now in the collections of the New Britain Museum of American Art, Moscow Museum of Modern Art, and the Smithsonian Institution, among others. His major artistic collaborations include work for Warner Brothers, Ford Motor Company, and the FIFA World Cup. In 2011, Jansen was selected by Absolut Vodka for its "Absolut Blank" campaign, in which artists such as Andy Warhol and Keith Haring have been previously honored. He was also commissioned to paint four original works to represent the four lines of Illuminum, the London-based perfume chosen by Katherine Middleton for her wedding to Prince William. In a 7,000-square-foot studio converted from a 1920s garage, he paints in historic downtown Fort Myers and is also the founder of the "UNIT A" Studio Museum, opened in 2012 in Fort Myers. (Photograph by the author.)

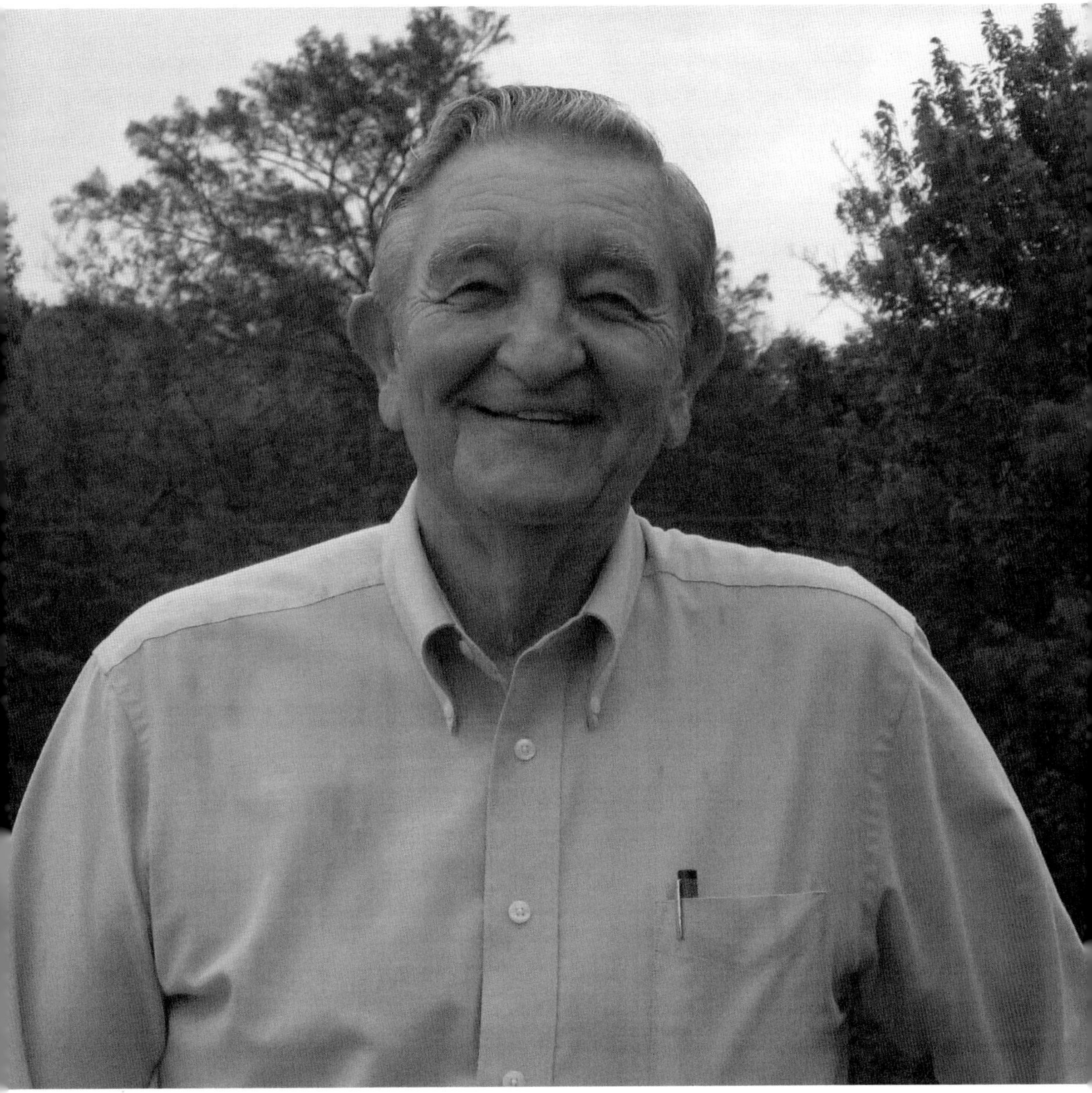

Bill Hammond
Lovers of Fort Myers' natural environment owe much to Bill Hammond. He has held leadership roles in almost every conservation-related organization in the area over the last five decades, including Audubon of Southwest Florida and the Conservancy of Southwest Florida. He retired in 2007 from Florida Gulf Coast University, where he was a founding faculty member and taught in the ecological and marine studies division. He was instrumental in saving what became Six Mile Cypress Slough Preserve, a jewel of the county's public lands, and worked to establish the Calusa Nature Center and Planetarium, serving as its first director. His honors include the Theodore Roosevelt Service to Conservation in the Nation Award and the National Wildlife Federation's National Conservation Educator for the Year. (Photograph by the author.)

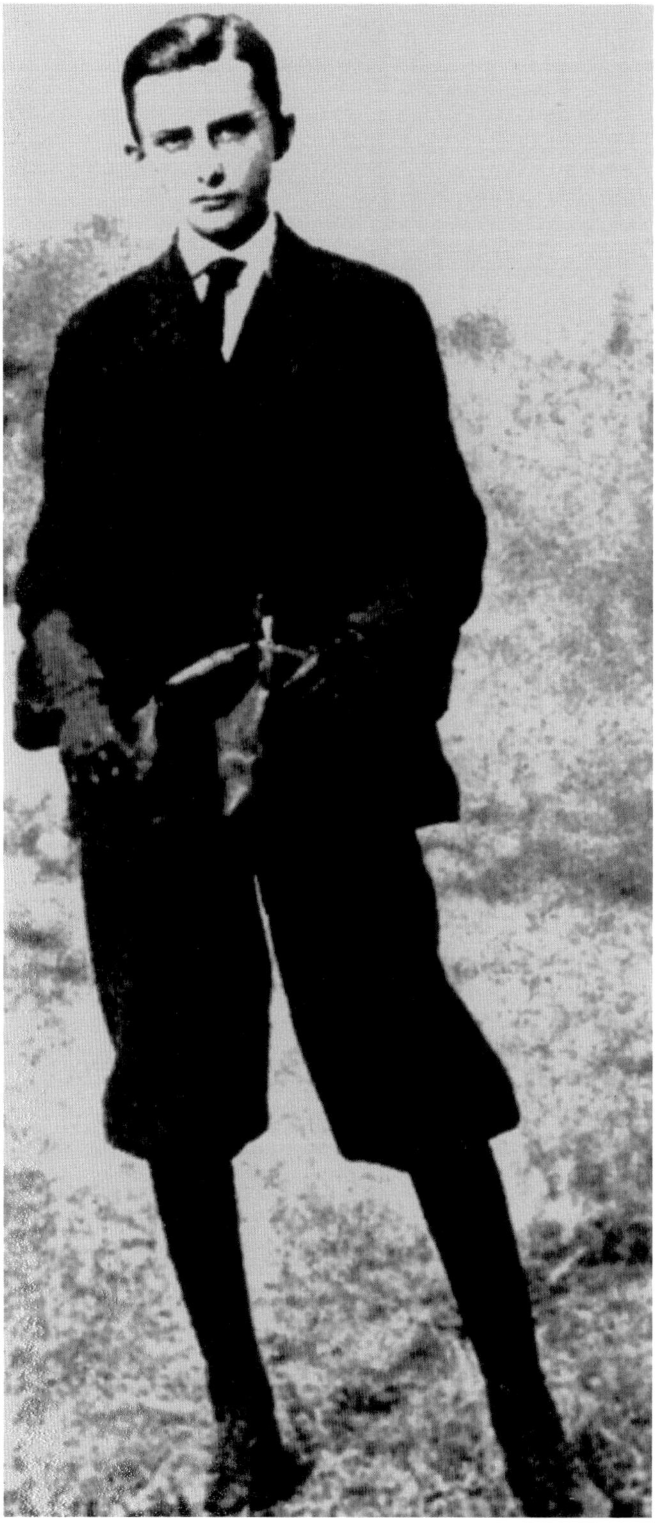

Laurence J. Lesh
The boy genius pictured here at about age 15 was fascinated with flight from an early age. While in his teens in Chicago, Lesh met Octave Chanute, an aviation theorist and mentor of the Wright brothers. His family moved to Montreal in 1907, where the 14-year-old made aviation history by becoming Canada's first glider pilot. As early as 1907, he published articles about his experiments with automatic stability devices in prestigious journals such as *Scientific American*. During World War I, he designed planes for the French Aeronatica while stationed in Paris as a civilian engineer with the US Army. He was a member of the Early Birds of Aviation, whose members must have flown an airship or airplane during the first 13 years of aviation. He held many patents in the radio field. Perhaps it was his work as an engineering consultant and the two nearby military bases that brought him to Fort Myers during World War II. He had a contract with Buckingham to develop a gun sight that would automatically set the correct "lead" for a moving target. People who were teenagers during World War II remember the inventor at the municipal swimming pool, where he tested models such as an underwater "airplane" propelled by gliding. During his days in Fort Myers, he preferred the simple life in a house he built himself on an acre of land. He died in Fort Myers in 1965 and is buried in the Fort Myers Cemetery. In 2008, he was inducted into the Quebec Air and Space Hall of Fame. (Courtesy of K.M. Molson Collection.)

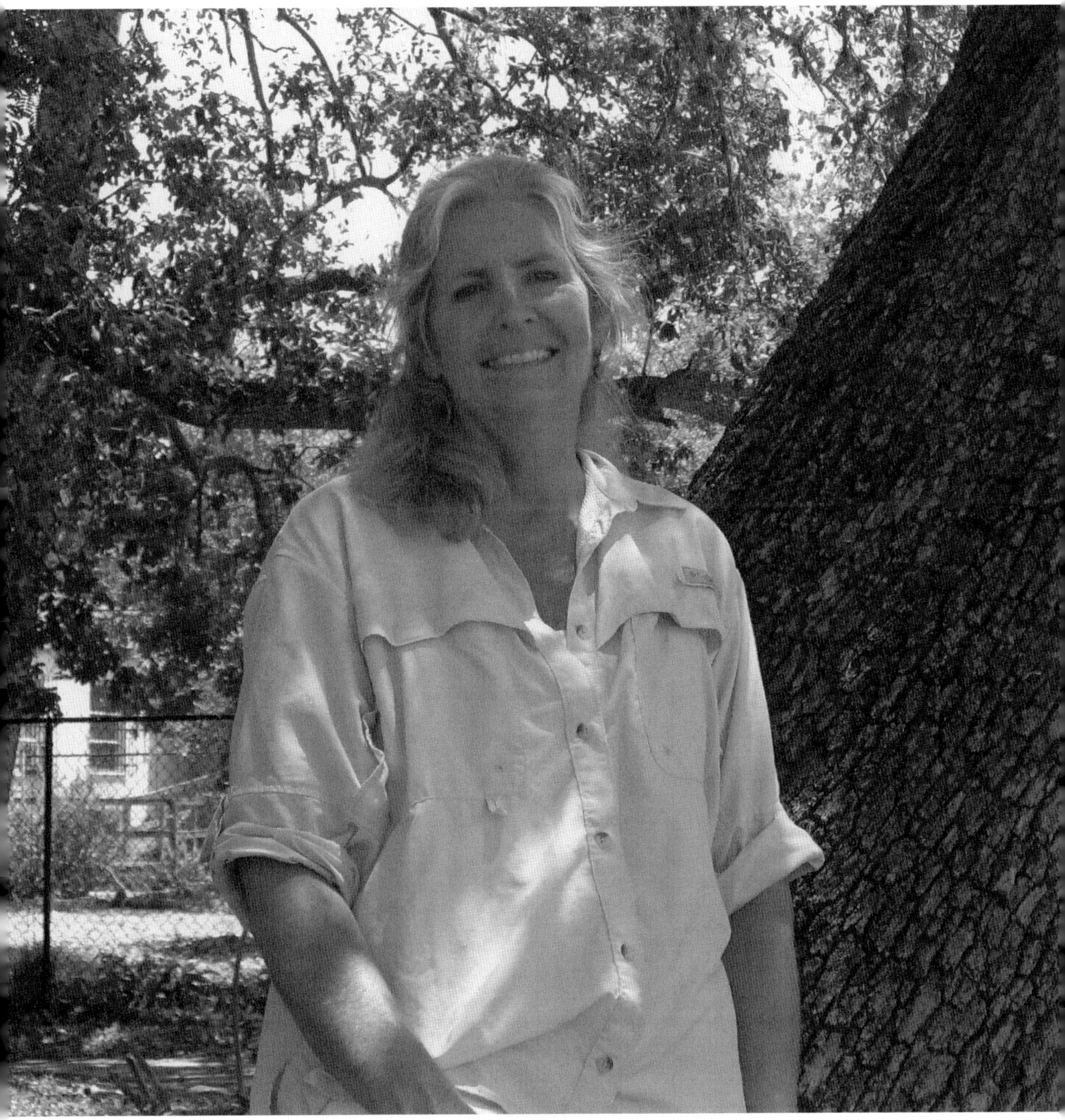

Carol Newcomb-Jones
A job as the Calusa Nature Center's first full-time naturalist brought Carol Newcomb-Jones to Fort Myers in 1979, and ever since, she has been an environmental educator and activist, serving on the boards of Keep Lee County Beautiful and Audubon of Southwest Florida, among others. Devotion to volunteer work enabled her to work toward environmental sustainability while raising children at home. She helped to design Florida Gulf Coast University's signature colloquium for a sustainable future, was a consultant for Babcock Ranch, a planned environmentally sustainable city, and cofounded a local branch of the nonprofit US Green Building Council. (Photograph by the author.)

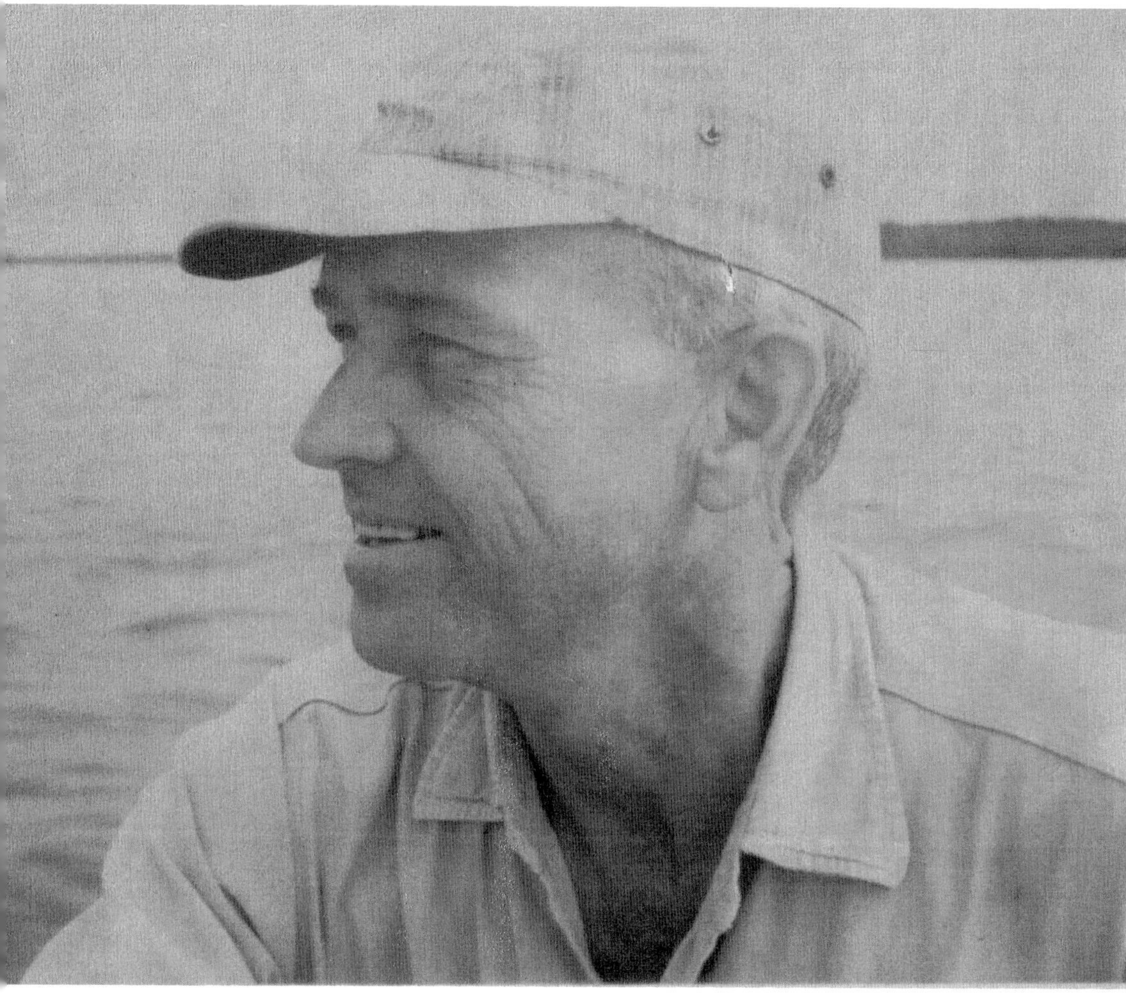

Charles Edgar Foster

When "the Caloosahatchee River Rat" died in 2005 at the age of 91, Foster was remembered by locals as a supreme educator who taught them about the land and water of their home ground. A member of the pioneer Hendry and Blount families, Foster's roots and passions ran deep in the region defined by the river that gave him his nickname. After serving in World War II and completing a master's degree at Columbia University, he taught in the Lee County schools. After retiring in 1975, he devoted himself to prodigious volunteer work, notably the Calusa Nature Center and Planetarium and the Alva Museum, which he helped to found. He wrote *The Benevolent Dane*, a biography of Capt. Peter Nelson, founder of Alva, Florida. He cofounded the Caloosahatchee River Citizens Association with Rae Ann Wessel, and delighted in leading river outings. (Courtesy of Rae Ann Wessel.)

CHAPTER SIX

Achievers and Doers

Some people are born to excel, doing the seemingly impossible or the very difficult tasks most people prefer to decline. Take Stafford Cleveland, who in 1884, set out for a subtropical wilderness with a printing press in tow and started a newspaper that is still in business today. Dr. Franklin Miles retired to Fort Myers for his health, but instead ended up inventing the area's modern agricultural industry. Nell Gould was hired as a teacher, but earned a raise when she took the initiative to save the school from fire. Jessie Bennett Sams did not let poverty and racism stop her from becoming a bestselling author, and football coach Charlie Bevis just kept breaking records. Nell Barden knew that a woman's place was at home—and in elected city office. It is the gumption of such legends that have built Fort Myers.

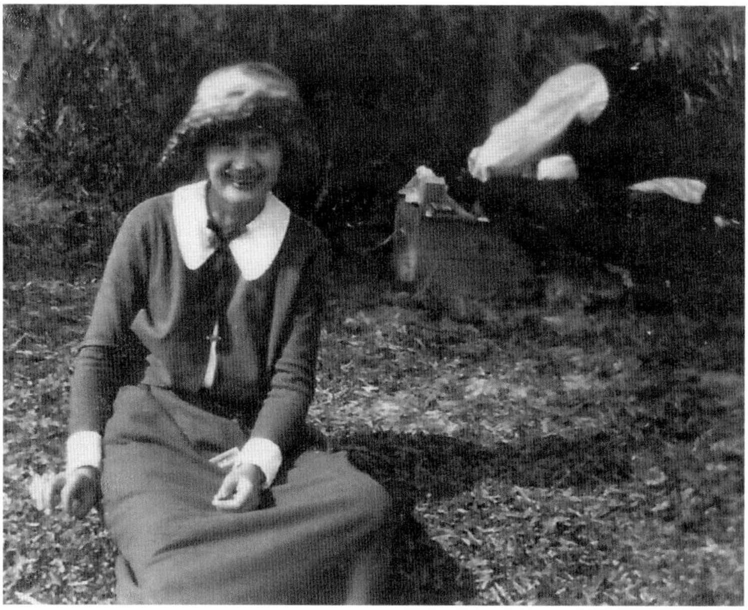

Nell Barden
Barden moved from South Carolina in the early 1900s. In 1929, she was elected city clerk, collector, and treasurer, an office she held until 1933, when she retired for health reasons. She was the first woman in Fort Myers to hold elective office. She died in 1985 at age 98. (Courtesy of Rebecca Kinzie Holmes.)

Carolyn (Barden) Smith
Carolyn Barden Smith was the only aviatrix at Buckingham Army Air Force Base's gunnery school in World War II. A member of the Civil Air Patrol, she was a test pilot and aircraft inspector. These photographs confirm the opinion of Smith's niece, Rebecca Kinzie Holmes, that her aunt could do anything, from playing golf like a pro and making clothing patterns, to building cabinetry, selling real estate, and demonstrating her skill as markswoman. She died in 2011 at 92. (Courtesy of Rebecca Kinzie Holmes.)

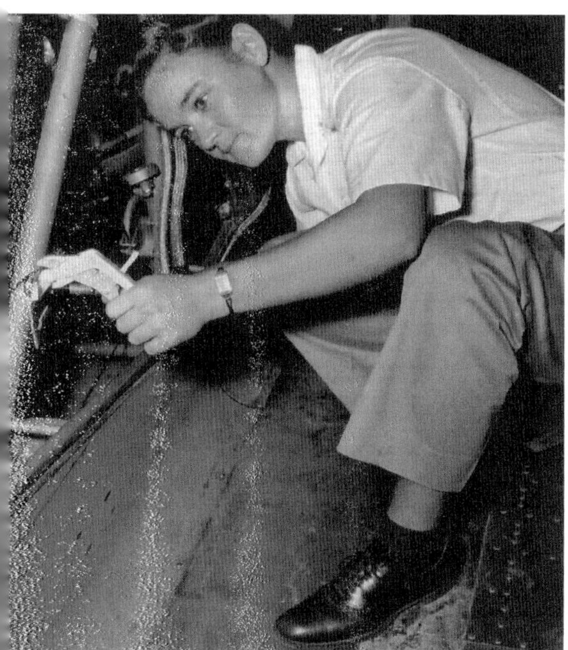

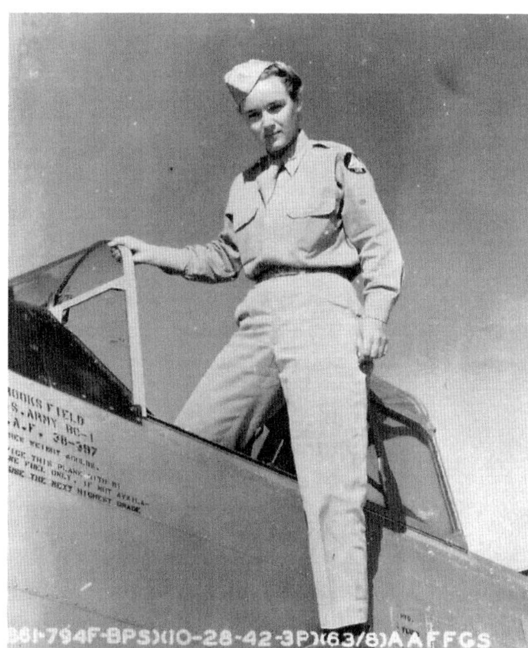

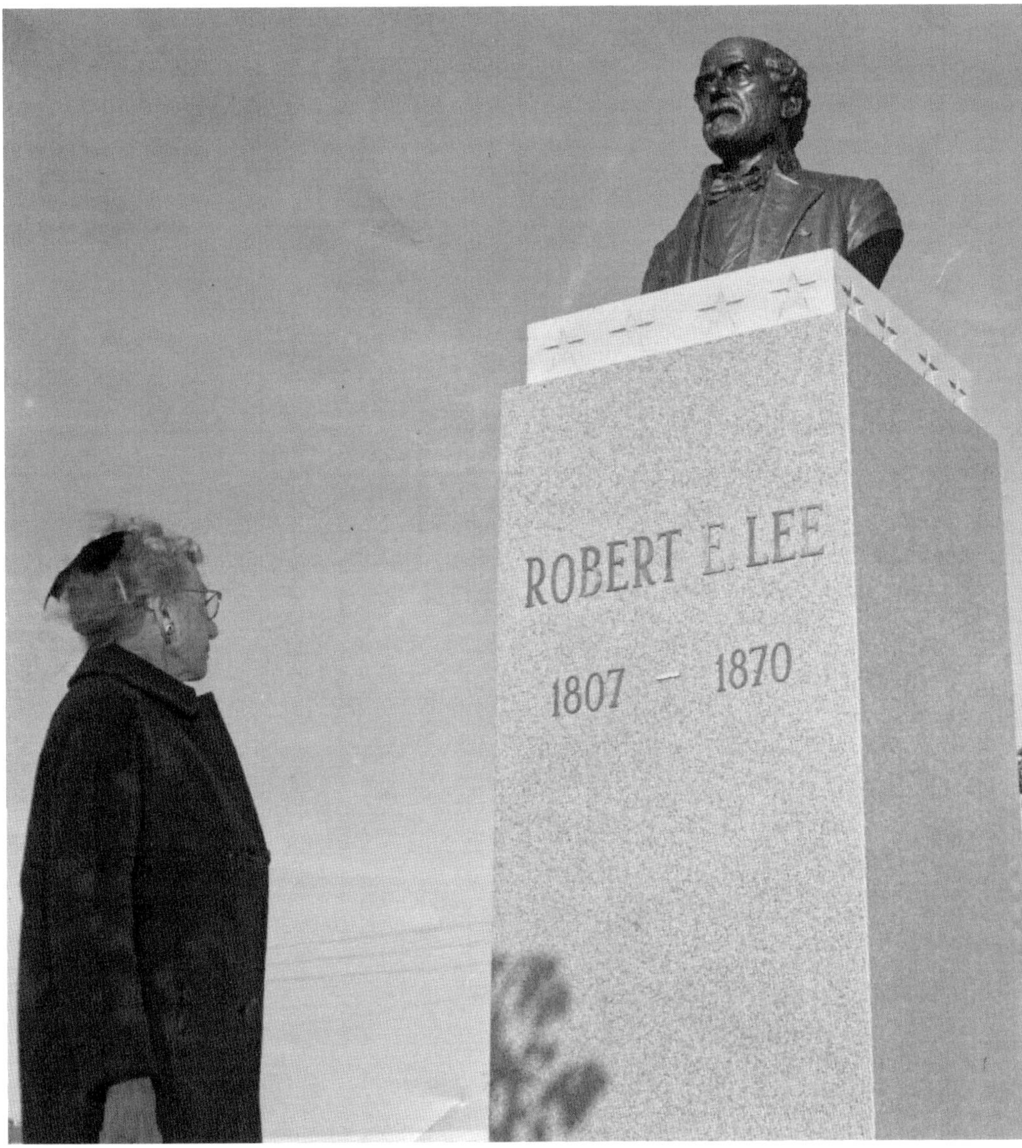

Edna F. Grady Roberts
On January 19, 1966, Roberts stood before a monument of Confederate general Robert E. Lee that took decades to realize. The fact that it was the 159th anniversary of the general's birth added even more significance to the day. Roberts had served as the chair of the monument fund committee of the Laetitia Ashmore Nutt Chapter of the United Daughters of the Confederacy, which upon forming in 1913, had initiated plans for a monument to honor the general. Decades later, she revived the plan and ran a successful campaign, culling the support of other organizations and local officials and offices. Thirteen days before the dedication on January 19, 1966, she and James Clifford placed battlefield artifacts into the concrete foundation of the monument. The $6,000 bronze bust atop a gray Georgia-granite base was the only one of its kind in a Southern state outside of Richmond, Virginia. Roberts was an active member of the First United Methodist Church and pursued mission work for more than 40 years. She died in 1984 at age 98. (Courtesy of SWFHS.)

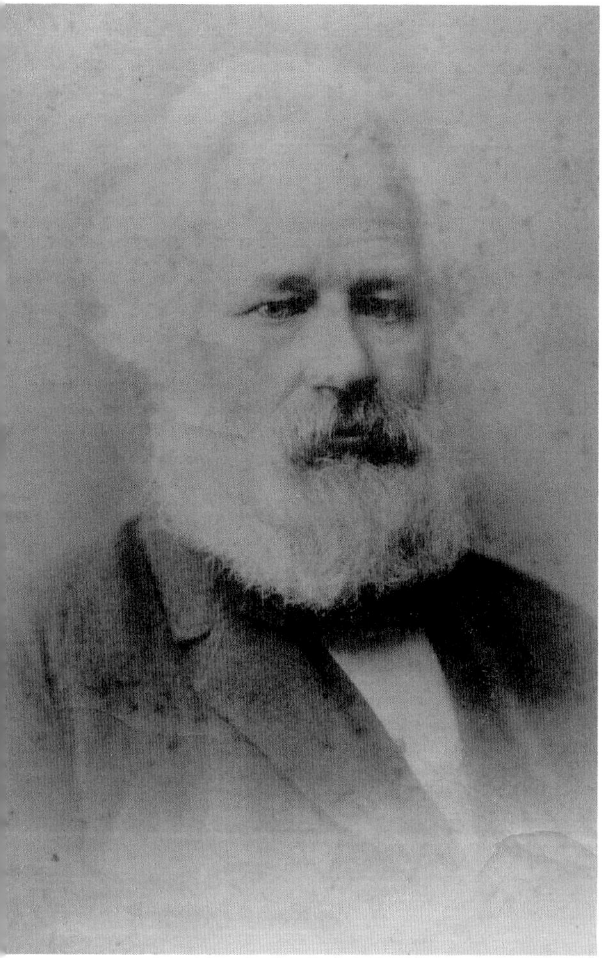

Stafford Cleveland

Fort Myers got its first newspaper, the *Fort Myers Press*, in 1884 because of a friendly shanghaiing. Advised to move south for his health, former postmaster and legislator Stafford Cleveland of Penn Yan, New York, put himself and his printing equipment on a schooner, intended destination Fort Ogden. Waylaid to Fort Myers by boat captain Henry Roan, Cleveland was convinced by citizens to start a newspaper in their town instead. (Courtesy of SWFHS.)

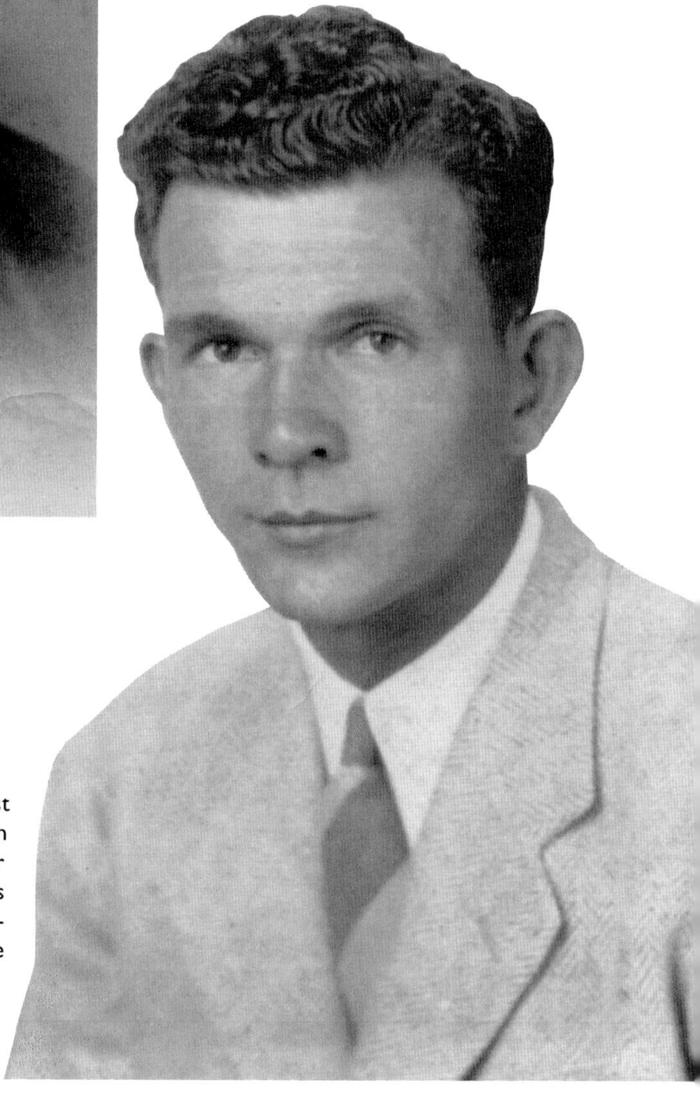

Charlie Bevis

Bevis is remembered as one of the best football coaches ever at Fort Myers High School. So appreciated was he that after one record-breaking season, the school's booster club gave him a brand-new two-toned blue Hudson automobile. He began coaching in 1942, and from 1948 to 1953, he served as the first elected school board superintendent. He died in 1971. (Courtesy of SWFHS.)

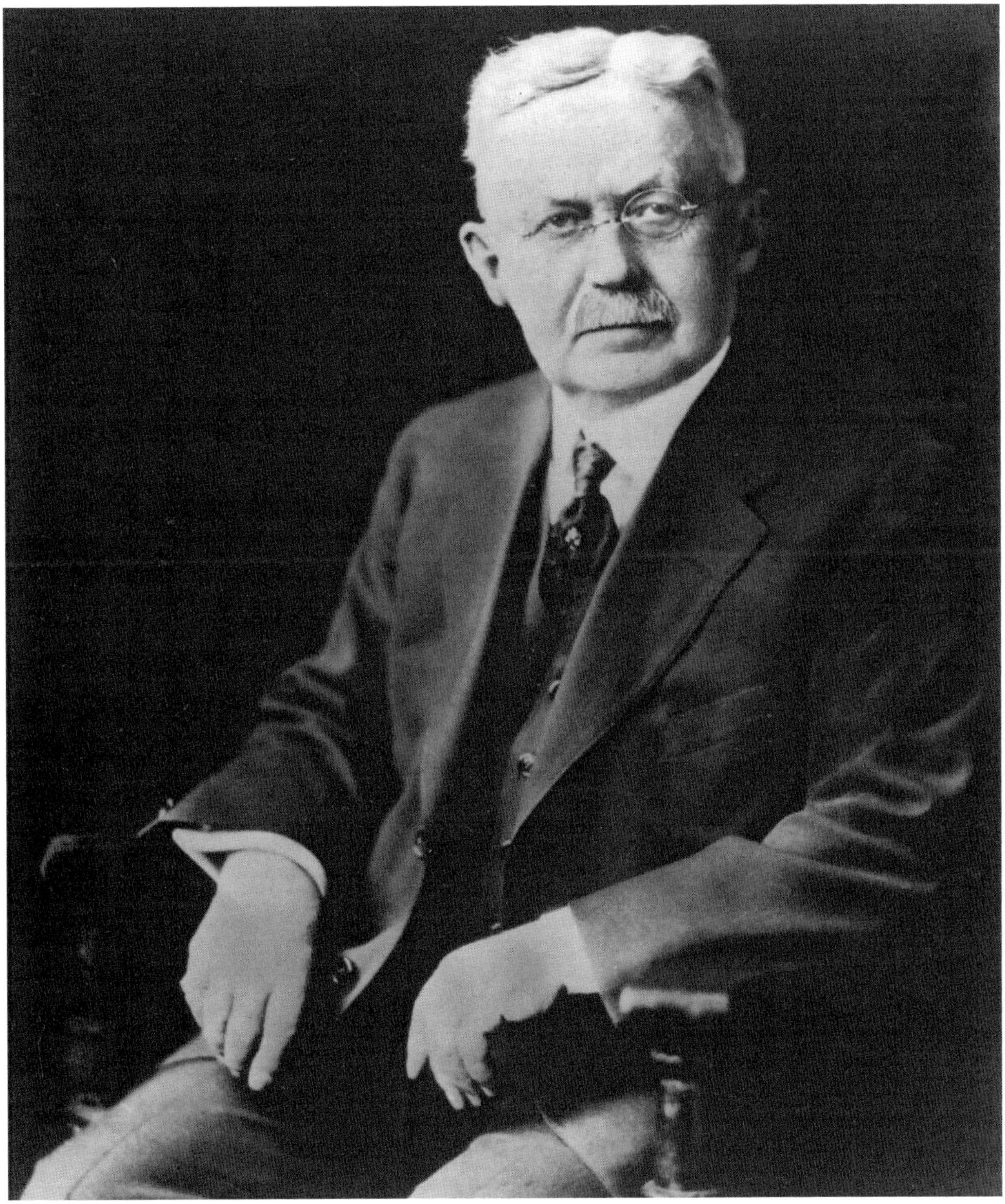

Dr. Franklin Miles
A heart specialist and inventor of patent medicines, such as Miles Nervine, Miles settled in Fort Myers in the winter of 1904–1905 for his health. Founder of Dr. Miles Laboratory, he was known as "the father of Alka Seltzer." Like Thomas Edison years before, he saw the southwest Florida landscape as a laboratory and subsequently greatly impacted the economic and agricultural history of the area with science-based methods on his 16,000 acres of land. He started a school for truck farmers and helped found the Lee County Packing Company, which packed and distributed crops via railroad from the downtown Fort Myers waterfront. He died in 1929, not long after completing the Miles Building, a Mediterranean Revivalist downtown architectural treasure. (Courtesy of SWFMH.)

Mary Laycock

Among this group of dynamic women community activists is Mary Laycock (seated right). They pose c. 1929 as honored creators of the Fort Myers Library. The institution began in 1903 with the opening of a small reading room sponsored by the Woman's Club and adjoining a drugstore at First and Hendry Streets. Generous club members and winter residents donated reading materials. Subscribers paid the librarian's salary of $1 per week and the rent, for a total of $12.71 per month. Tootie McGregor Terry was among the major donors. The revolving librarian position was held at one time or another by Julia Hanson, Olive Stout, and Mary Laycock, who earned the title the "Fairy Godmother of the Fort Myers Library," largely due to her tireless fundraising. The widow who had come to Fort Myers in 1903 with her son Harry was instrumental in the running of the reading room. She chaired the Woman's Club funds-solicitation committee for the library from 1905 to 1925 and served on the first library board appointed by the city. She collected money from subscribers, measuring progress by 10- to 25-cent contributions, including one enthusiastic subscriber who gave 50 cents. Another of Laycock's important causes was the Women's Christian Temperance Union. She died in 1931 at age 80. Other women who fought for and supported the reading room that evolved into today's extensive Lee County Public Library System are, from left to right, Mary Florence Hill, Minnie Gardner (standing), Julia Hanson, and Olive Stout. (Courtesy of SWFHS.)

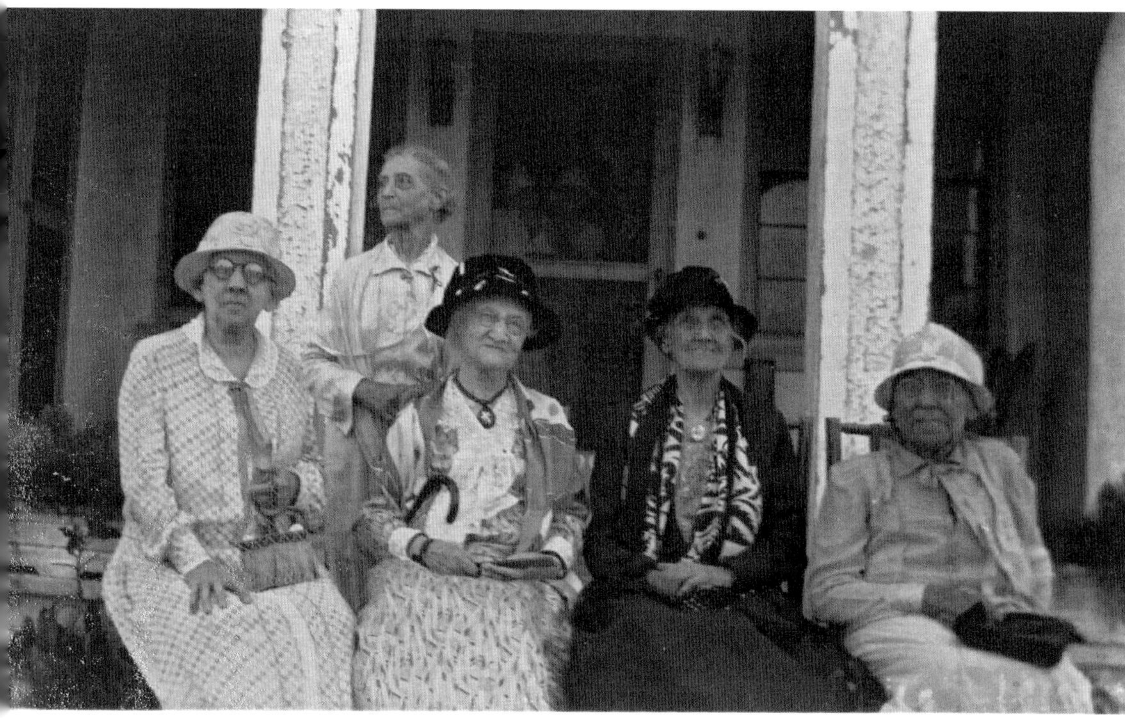

Col. William S. Harney (RIGHT)

During the Second Seminole War in July 1839, Harney escaped with his men on the Caloosahatchee near what is now called Harney's Point near the foot of the Cape Coral Bridge. He was to have established a trading post following agreements with the Seminoles about reservation lands. Realizing that the whites had no intention of honoring the oral agreements, 160 Seminoles led by Chief Chekaika of the Spanish Indians attacked in the early morning hours, killing 13 soldiers. Fourteen others, along with Harney, escaped via the river, the lieutenant colonel in his underwear. Harney had failed to post sentries that night. The event is known as the Harney Point Massacre. Harney retaliated against Chekaika a year later. (Courtesy of SAF.)

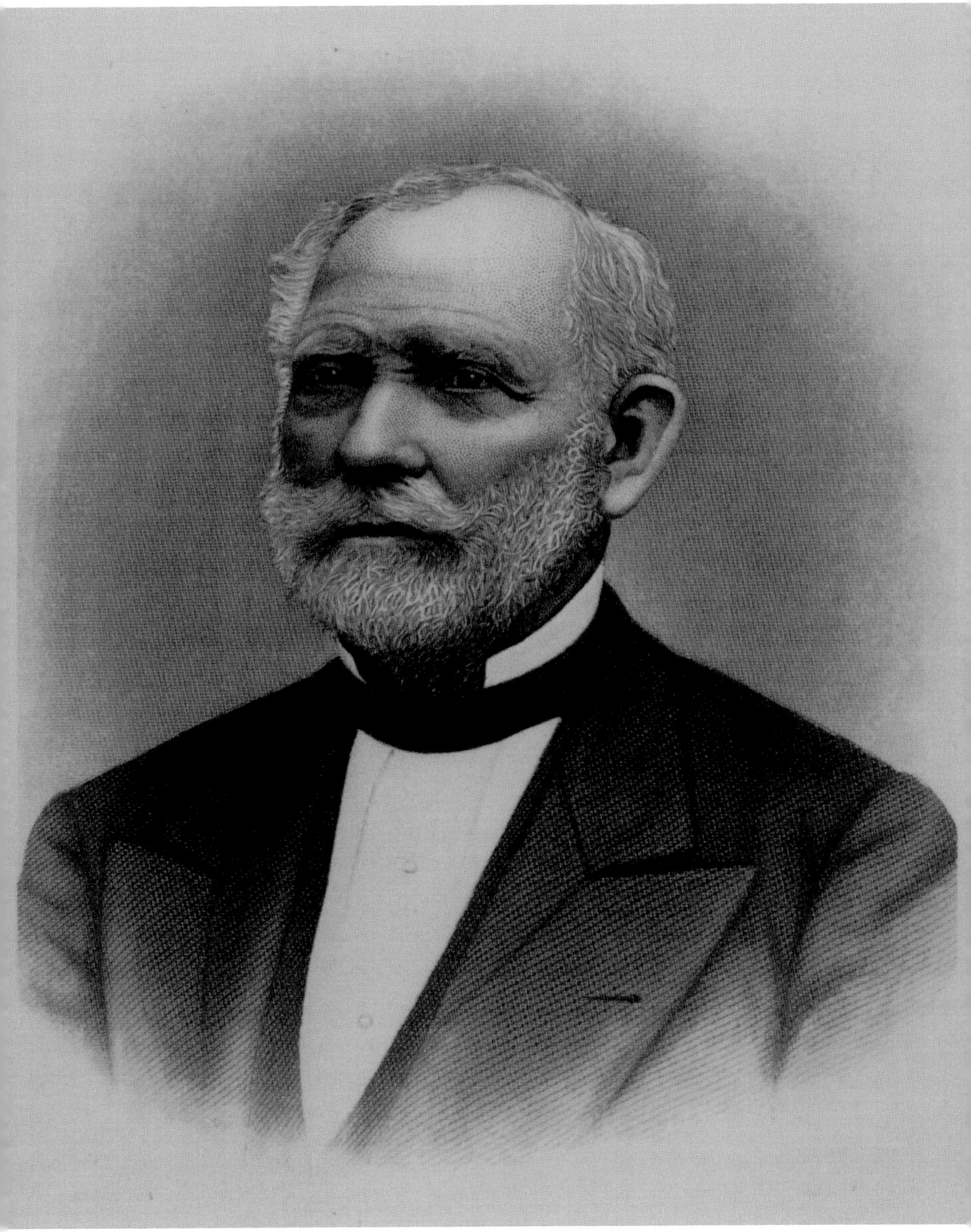

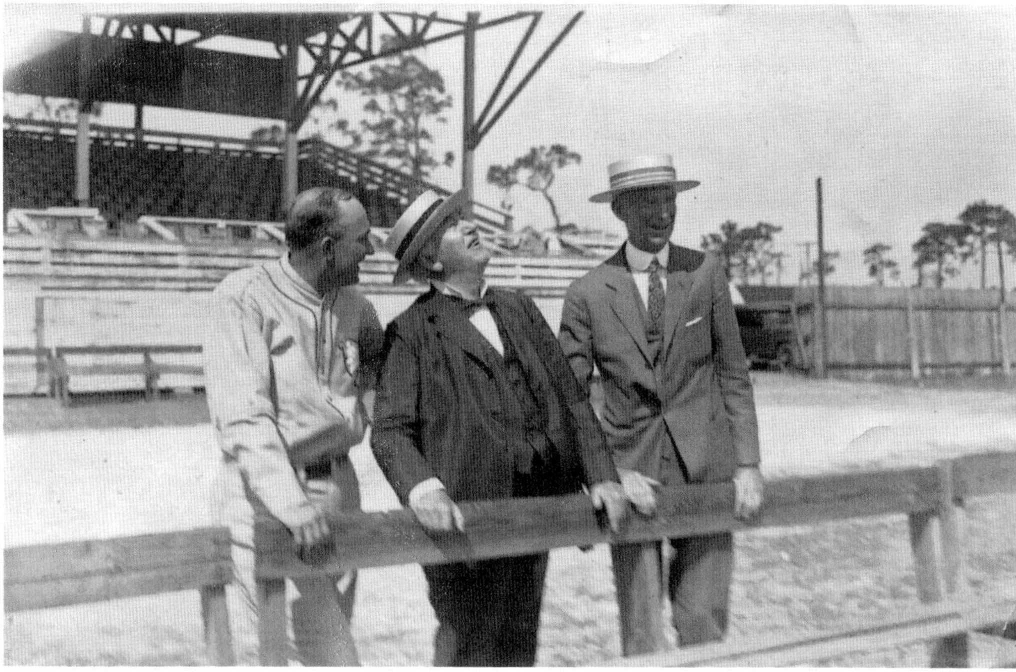

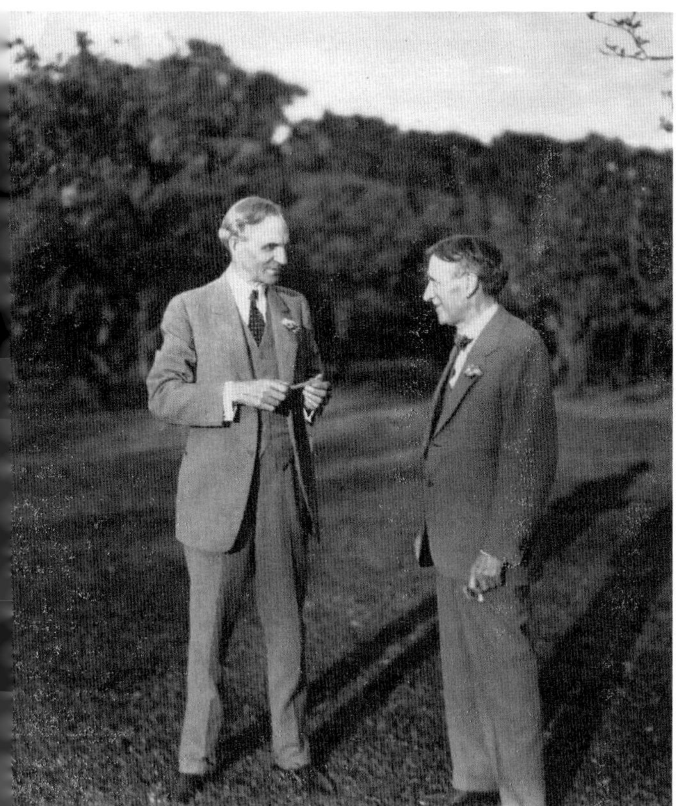

Thomas A. Edison

The famous inventor came to Fort Myers in 1885 and snapped up his estate. Construction on Seminole Lodge, a laboratory, and a wharf soon commenced, and the following year, he brought Mina on their honeymoon. On his last visit in 1931, several months before his death, he dedicated the Edison Bridge. He appears at Terry Park with Ty Cobb (left) and Connie Mack Sr. (right), owner and manager of the Philadelphia Athletics, who spring-trained in Fort Myers. (Courtesy of SWFHS.)

Henry Ford

In 1916, industrialist Henry Ford bought a winter estate adjacent to that of his good friend Thomas A. Edison and named it the Mangoes. The City of Fort Myers acquired the home in 1988 and today the combined Edison & Ford Winter Estates and Laboratory are Fort Myers' most famous attraction. In the photograph, Ford (left) speaks with Harvey Firestone. (Courtesy of SWFHS.)

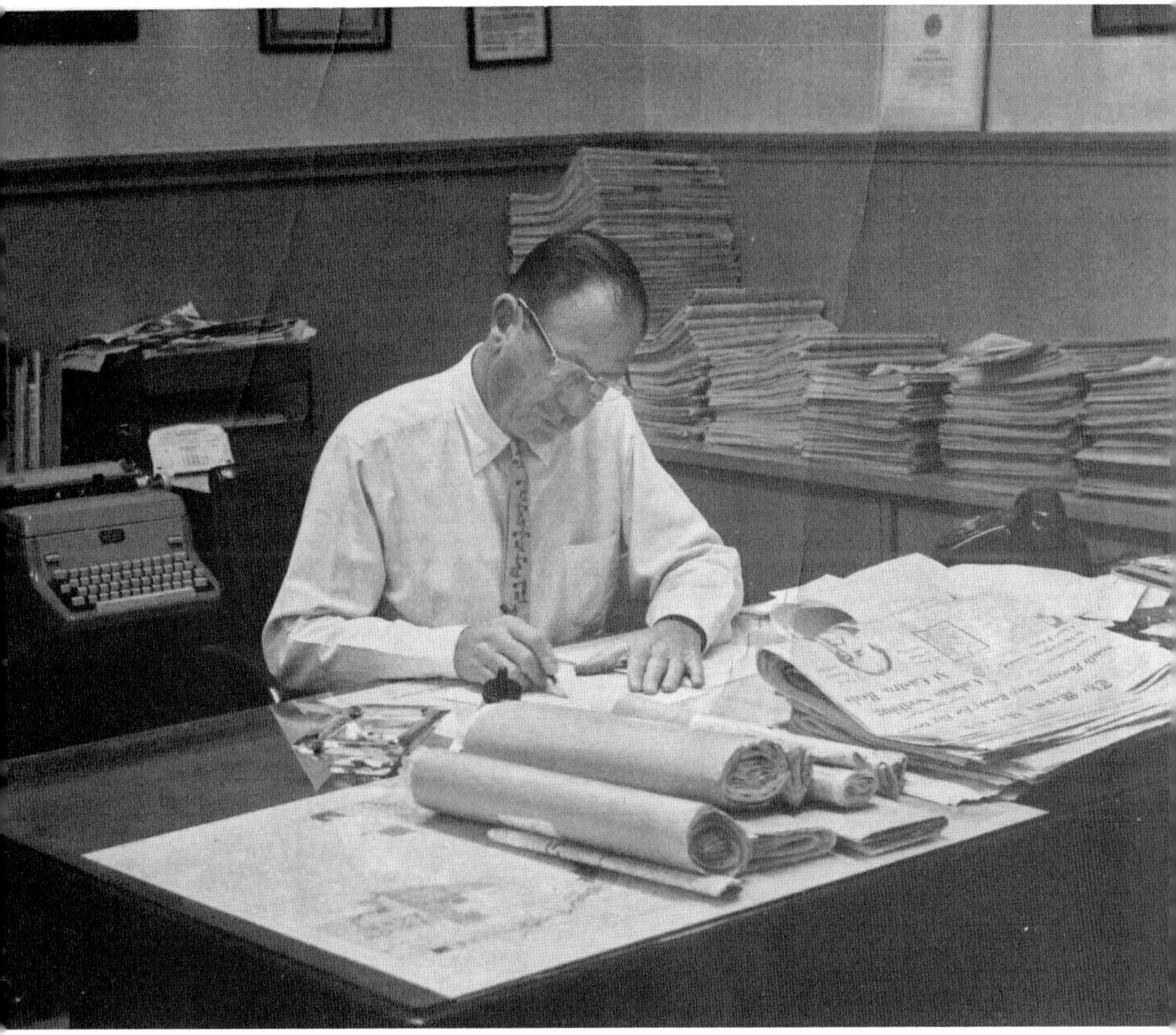

William R. Spear

Spear began a newspaper career of almost a half century as a teenager at the *Fort Myers Press* in 1926. He eventually worked for the Associated Press in major cities; was involved in the initial coverage of the Lindbergh baby kidnapping; and served in World War II, for which he was awarded the Bronze Star Medal for services in the European Theater. He returned to Fort Myers after covering the dedication of Everglades National Park in 1947 and renewing his acquaintance with President Truman and the Washington, DC, press corps. He was editor of the *Fort Myers News-Press* for 26 years, watching the city grow into a metropolitan area and endure the social upheaval of the 1950s and 1960s. Under his editorship, the paper's circulation increased tenfold. (Courtesy of SWFHS.)

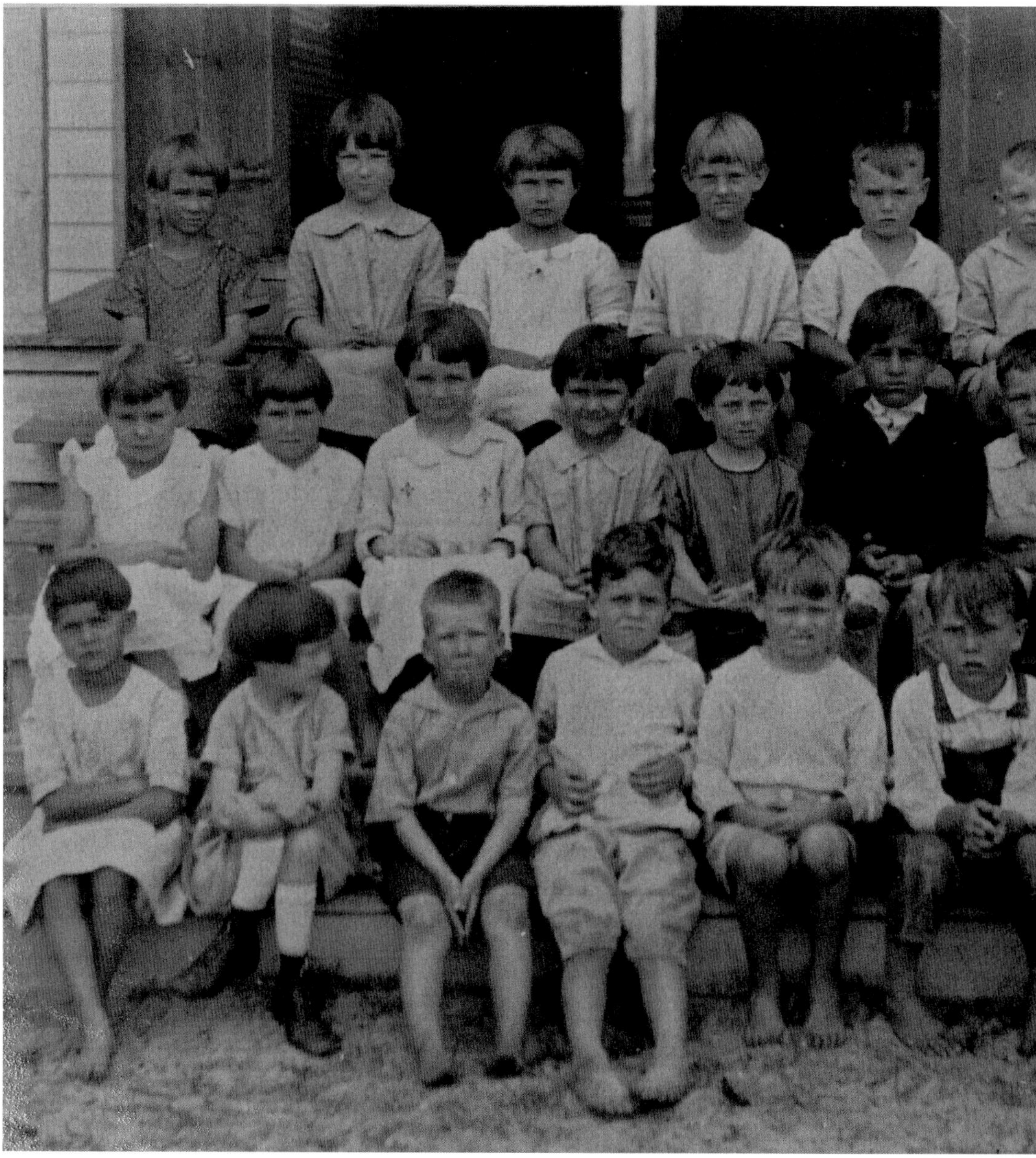

Nell Gould

Gould started her 47-year teaching career at age 18. Arriving in Fort Myers in 1910 from Clay, West Virginia, she was first assigned to the spartan one-room, seven-pupil schoolhouse that sat perched on stilts over the water at Punta Rassa. She and her students survived the 1910 hurricane by seeking refuge aboard the steamer *Mildred*. She further proved her worth and mettle at various schools scattered throughout largely unsettled southwest Florida. When she rallied students at Captiva and they saved the building from burning, the school board raised her salary to $50 per month. The much-loved teacher took her last teaching post at Edgewood Elementary in 1918, which lasted until she retired 39 years later. She died in 1984 at age 92. (Courtesy of SWFMH.)

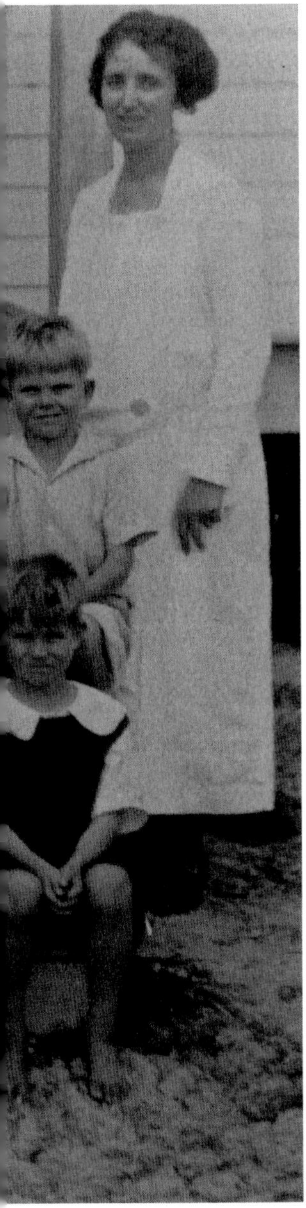

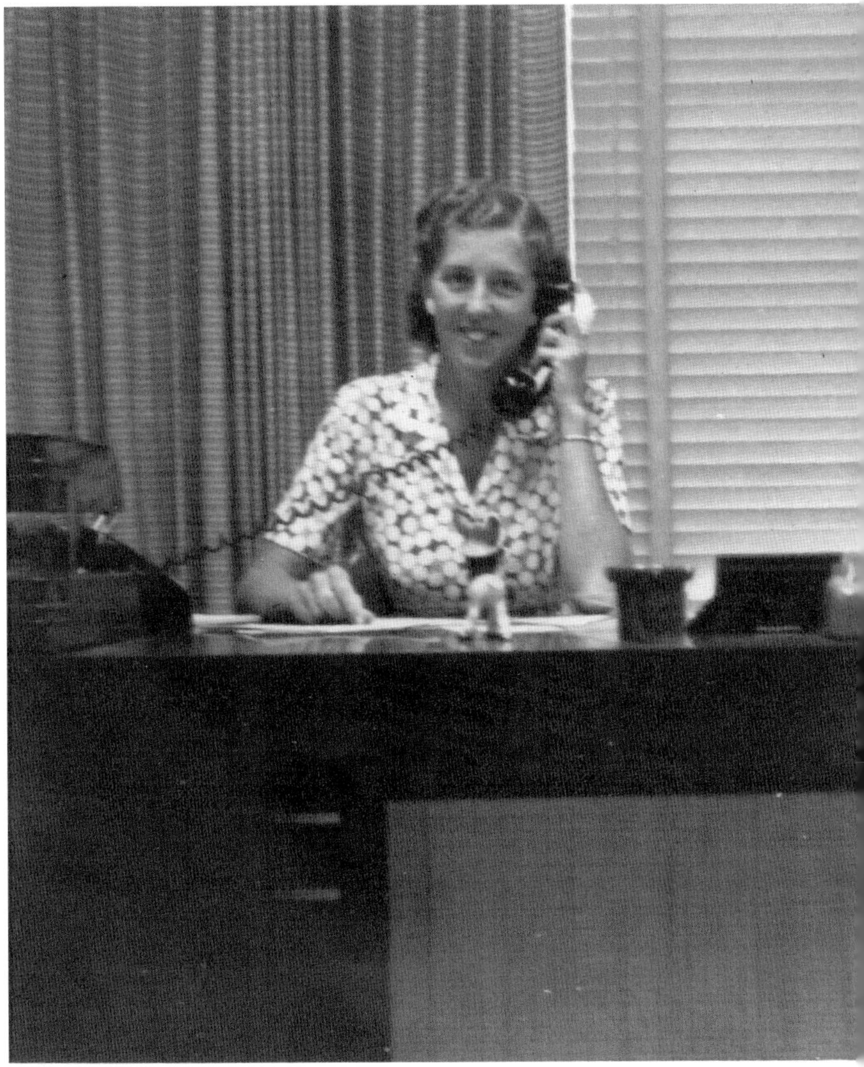

Sara Nell (Hendry) Gran

Sara Nell Gran is remembered for her reverence and enthusiasm for history and for her generosity. The great-granddaughter of the "Father of Fort Myers," Capt. Francis A. Hendry, she was considered Fort Myers' premier historian. Her 29-year career with the city included 19 as city clerk. After retiring in 1969, she led a busy volunteer life and served on many boards. Affiliations included the Southwest Florida Historical Society, the Daughters of the American Revolution, the Pioneer Club of Lee County, and history-related state organizations. She traveled extensively, globetrotting even to Antarctica. In 2008, the Board of Lee County Commissioners recognized her strong commitment to Lee County and her efforts to bring the region's history to life for new generations of Floridians. In 2010, the Southwest Florida Historical Society christened a research room in her honor. She died in 2011 at age 93. (Courtesy of SWFHS.)

Marion "Skeet" Durrence

In the 1920s, Skeet Durrence—who earned her nickname because the mosquitoes bothered her—discovered Fort Myers on her honeymoon. Starting her musical career as a substitute teacher, she went on to create one of the town's most loved holiday traditions, the Singing Christmas Tree. In 1945, she directed the first one with the combined glee clubs of Fort Myers Junior-Senior High Schools. Florida governor LeRoy Collins heard the tree in 1957 and invited her to perform at the governor's mansion. In 1960, the group sang for the opening of Pres. Dwight D. Eisenhower's Pageant of Peace at the White House. When Durrence retired in 1975, she had directed the glee club for 30 years. Until she died in 1991, the pianist played for civic groups and directed special events. (Courtesy of SWFHS.)

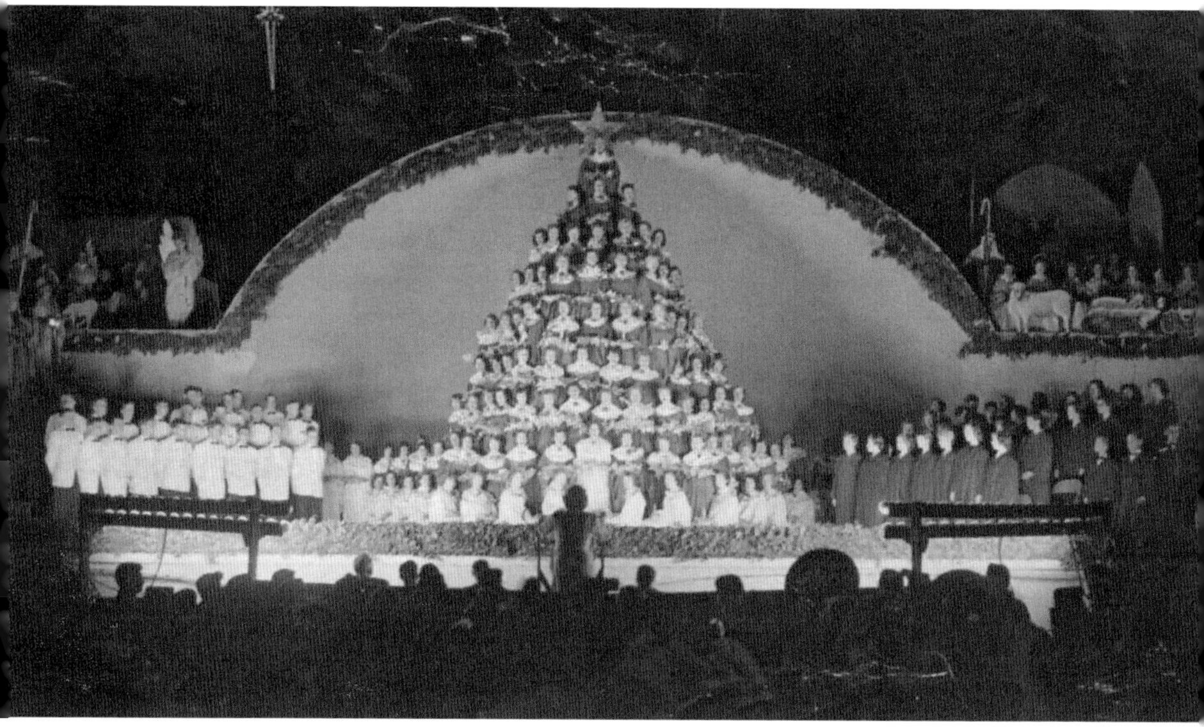

Jessie Bennett Sams (RIGHT)

Sams' bestselling autobiographical novel, *White Mother*, is a loving tribute to Rossie Bass Lee, a Fort Myers white woman who virtually adopted her and her twin sister. In 1923, Fort Myers was a racially segregated town, and only blacks who worked downtown were allowed there. The eight-year-old black twins showed up on the doorstep of Lee's mother looking for work so they could buy shoes. She introduced them to her daughter. Miss Rossie, as Lee became known to them, hired the girls as maids, fed them, got their paralyzed father medical care, and made sure they returned to school. Friendship and support continued over the years. Sams graduated from Dunbar High School in 1928 and later earned a degree from Florida A & M University, aided by the Lee family. She returned to Fort Myers to teach at her alma mater, but eventually moved permanently to Los Angeles where she continued teaching. In 1953, she returned to her hometown for the death of Miss Rossie in the house on Royal Palm Avenue, where the twins' lives had been transformed by simple kindness. (Courtesy of SWFHS.)

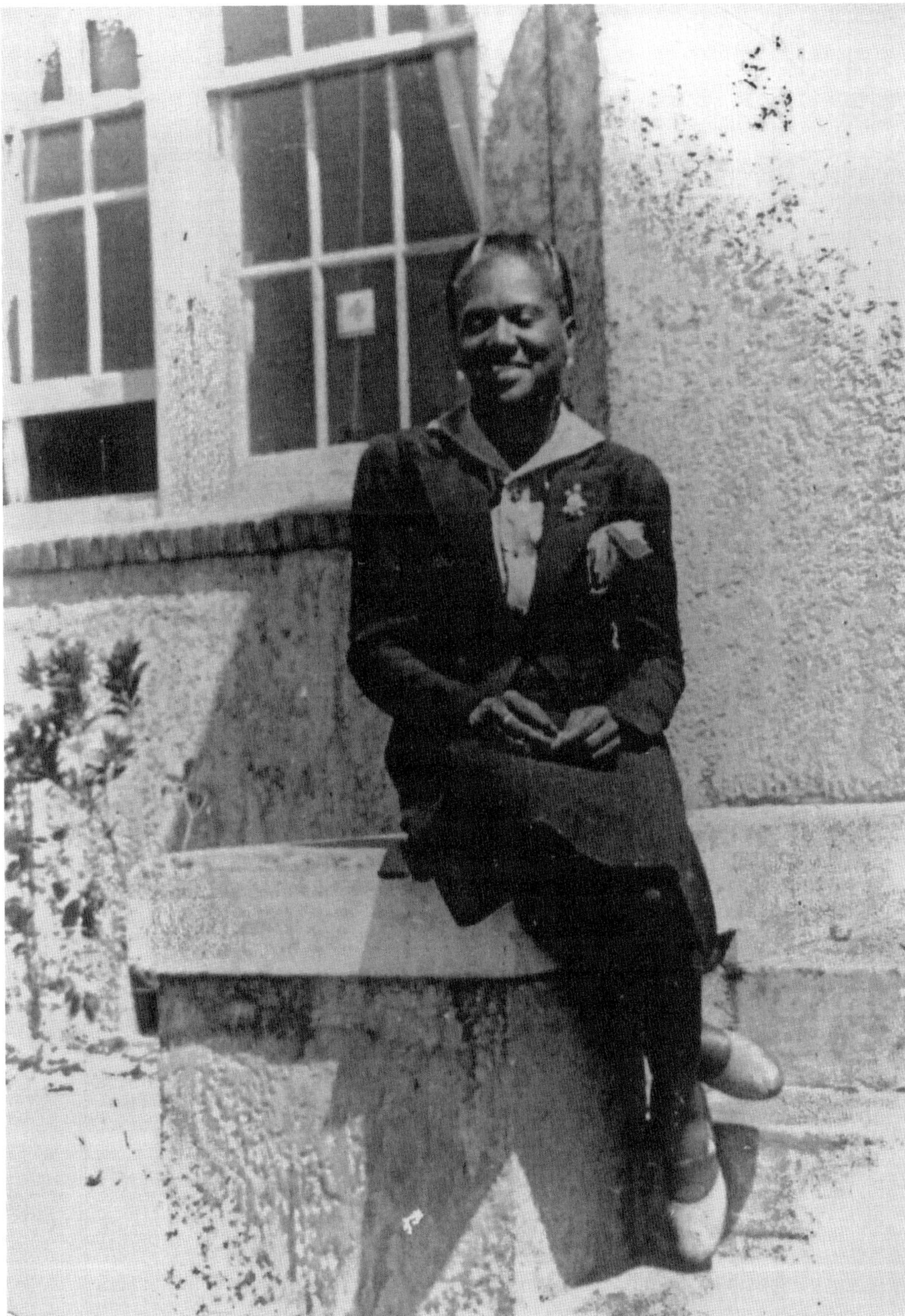

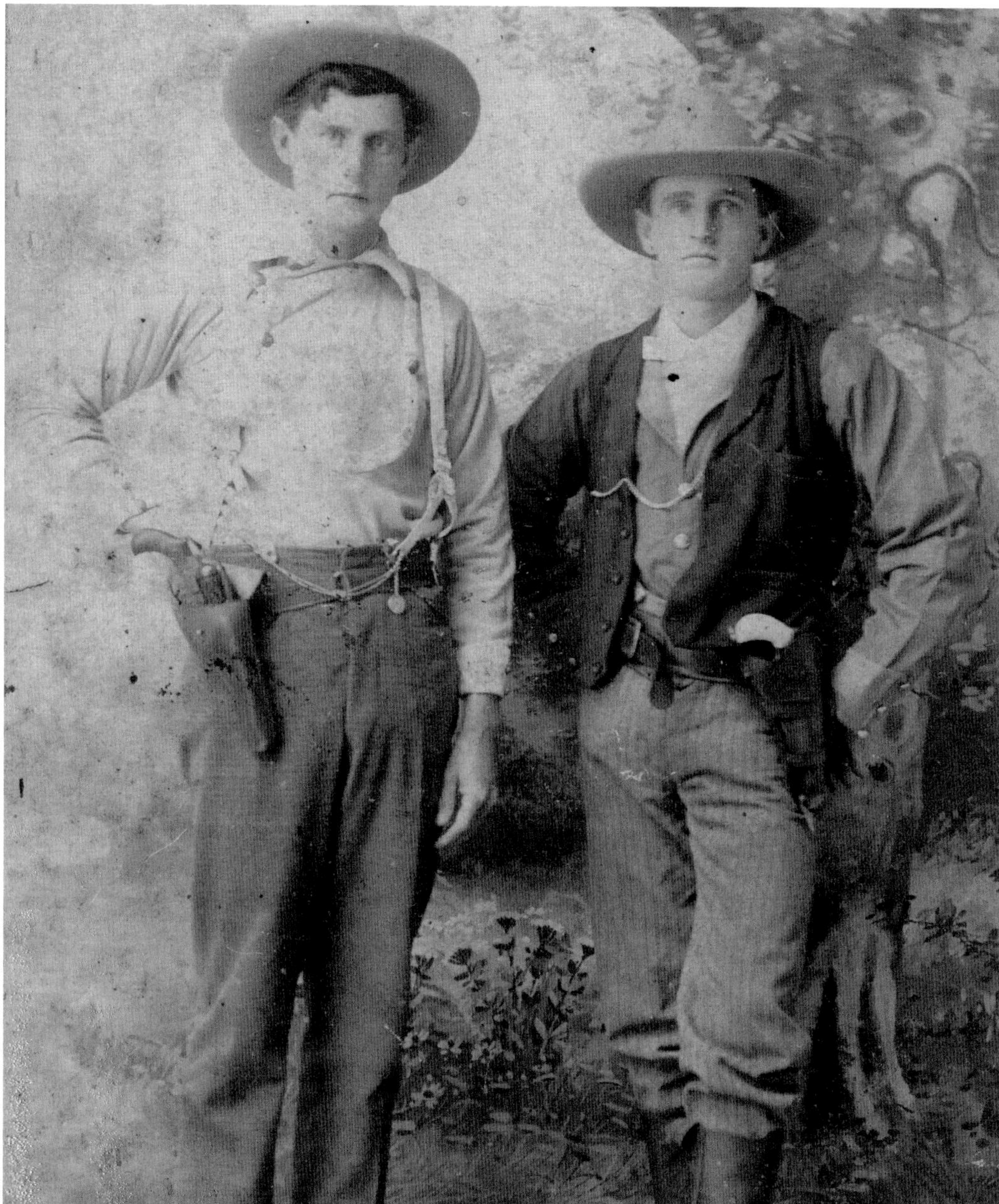

Walter G. Langford

In this photograph with Frank Carson, young Walter Langford (right) looks more like a cowboy than a banker. Langford inherited considerable business acumen from his cattleman father, Dr. Thomas E. Langford, for whom he worked for a time. In 1899, he married Carrie Watson, daughter of the infamous Edgar Watson, and settled down. He played an important role in convincing the Atlantic Coast Line Railroad to extend its route to Fort Myers and organized and served as the first president of the First National Bank, which had organized in 1907 as the Lee County Bank. He died in 1920 at the age of 47, less than a year after building one of Fort Myers' premier historic homes, now owned by the City of Fort Myers and headquarters for the Fort Myers Woman's Community Club. (Courtesy of SWFHS.)

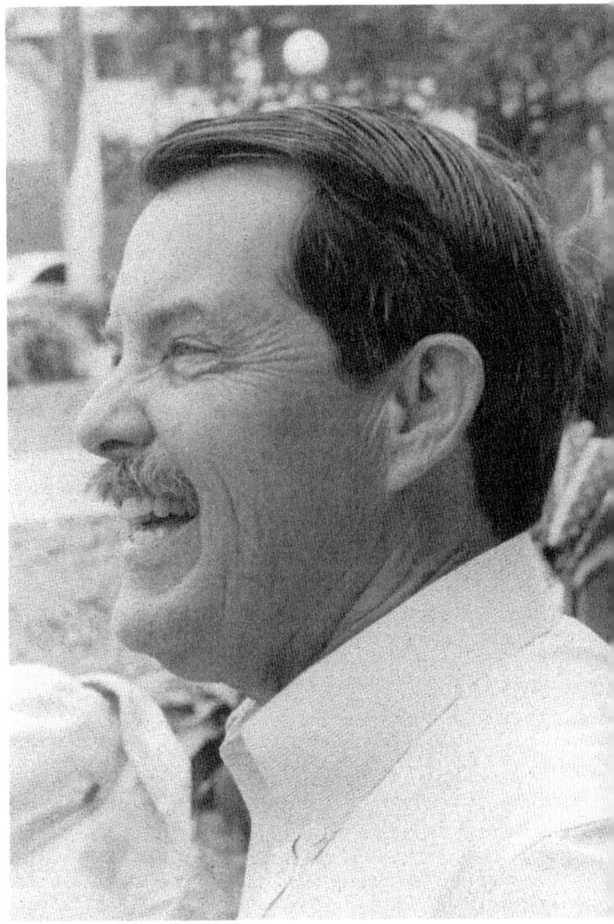

Ray Judah
As a marine biologist, Ray Judah, county commissioner since 1988, understands the need to champion conservation efforts, including the acquisition of critical water resource areas in the Corkscrew Regional Ecosystem Watershed (CREW), an organization he cofounded, and Conservation 20/20, a public fund for purchasing environmentally sensitive land. His awards include the Community Coordinating Council's Most Outstanding Public Official in 2001; and Conservationist of the Year from Florida Audubon (1984, 1996) and the Florida Wildlife Federation (2007). (Photograph by David Krupick, courtesy of Ray Judah.)

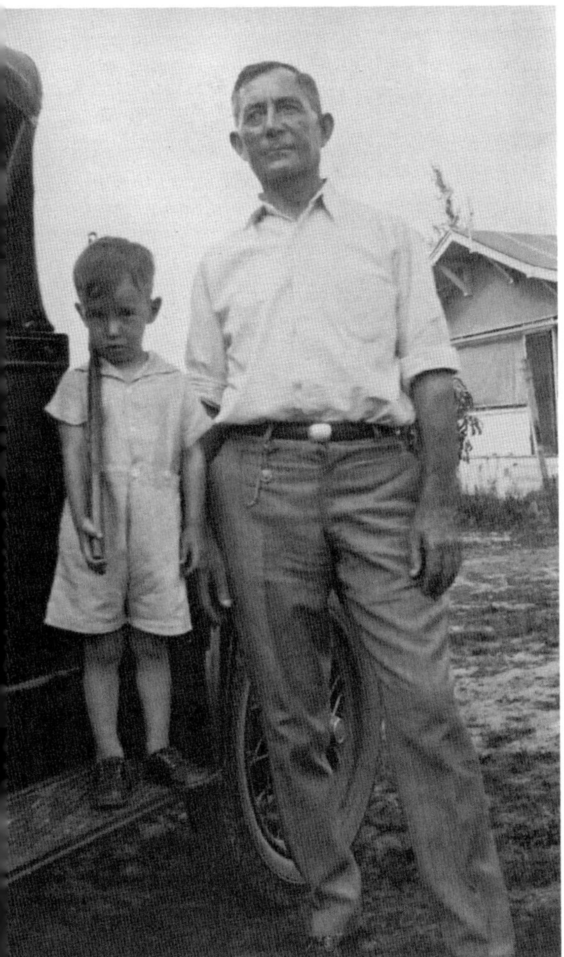

Charles N. "Kandy Kitchen" Smith
Smith's delectable secret recipes delighted schoolchildren and adults for decades. He opened the first of three shops in Tonnelier Court around 1912, when he arrived by boat from Key West, where he had served in the US Navy during the Spanish-American War. Smith's unrecorded recipes died with him in 1934. He is pictured with his grandson, Walter Kaune. (Courtesy of Genevieve Smith Bowen.)

Tamiami Trail Blazers

When the Fort Myers contingent of the Tamiami Trail Blazers left town on April 4, 1923, with great fanfare, they optimistically hoped to arrive in Miami within several days. These intrepid road builders who endured mud, water moccasins, mosquitoes, alligators, heat, hunger, and long stints of walking in razor-sharp sawgrass were, from left to right, (front row) L.J. Van Duyl, Alfred Christensen, Maurice Ayrer, George W. Dunham, Cyril B. Shawcross, and L.A. Whitney; (second row) Ora E. Chapin, Charles Hunt, George Prime, Alan Andrews, Seminole guide Assumhachee, Fred C. Garmon, Milton Thompson, J.P. Cosden, Clark Taylor, and W. Stanley Hanson. Seminole guide Billy Conapatchee is absent from the photograph. It was not until April 23 that their procession was greeted by cheers, newsreel cameras, and the silver-tongued William Jennings Bryan—politician turned land developer—on Miami's Flagler Street. Plans for the road linking Tampa and Miami, today's heavily traveled US 41, began in 1915 but weren't completed until 1928, partly because of World War I, but mainly because of the treacherous landscape of the Everglades. (Courtesy of SWFHS.)

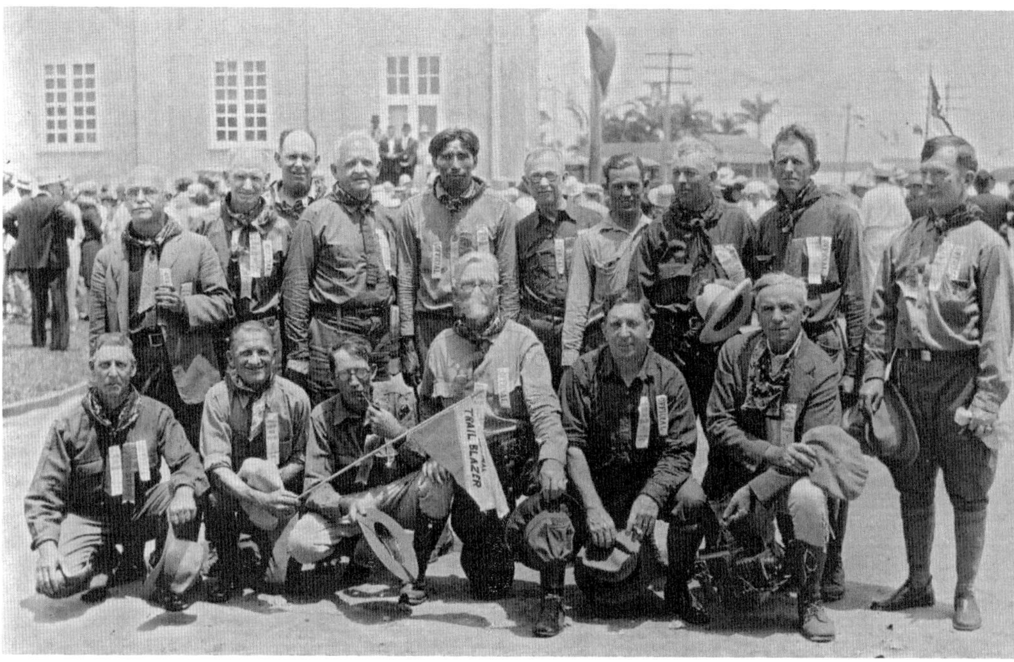

Theo (Ellis) McAfee (RIGHT)

In her 45-year nursing career, McAfee saw sweeping changes in sterilization techniques, hospital facilities, and racial policies. When she started in 1922, Lee Memorial Hospital had only 20 patient beds and no full-time physician. The nurses' quarters had five rooms with two beds per room. Her job description included cutting firewood for the stove to heat water for sterilizing surgical instruments. She was paid $75 per month and she was on call seven days a week, 24 hours a day. Almost nothing could faze her, including a man who arrived at the hospital with a knife wound to the belly, his small intestines spilling into a hat. She cleaned the debris from the intestines with saline solution and assisted the doctor in reinserting them and stitching the abdomen. On another occasion, she retrieved a surgeon's glass eye when it fell into a patient's abdominal cavity during an appendectomy. In 1943, she moved to the WPA-built modern hospital on Cleveland Avenue. However, in that age before prepackaged sterile disposable supplies, she still had to cut gauze from 100-yard bolts and cut sponges to size. She recalled that before Lee Memorial was integrated, she had to pack up surgical instruments and basic supplies when she was required at Jones-Walker Hospital, the hospital for blacks. (Courtesy of SWFMH.)

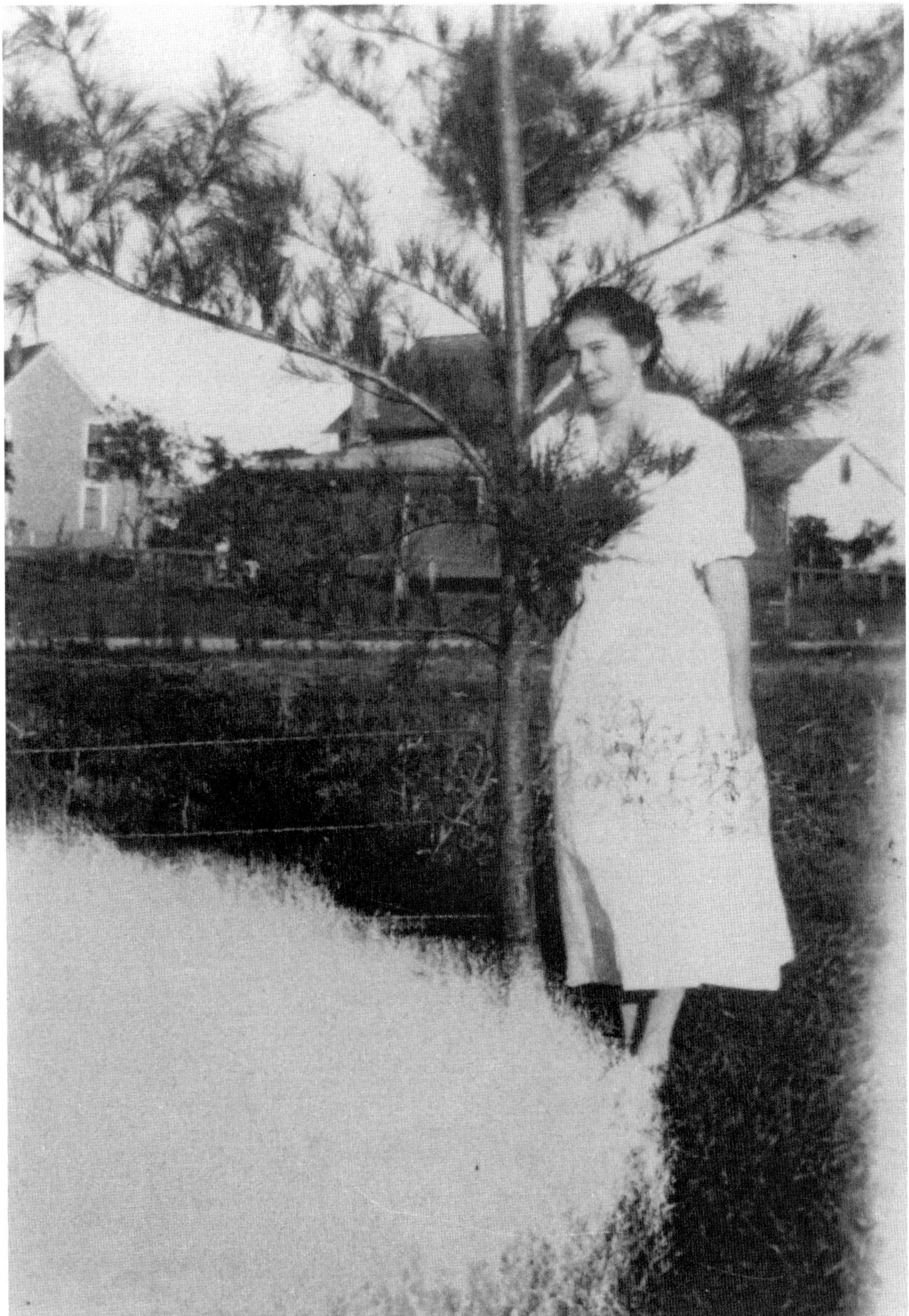

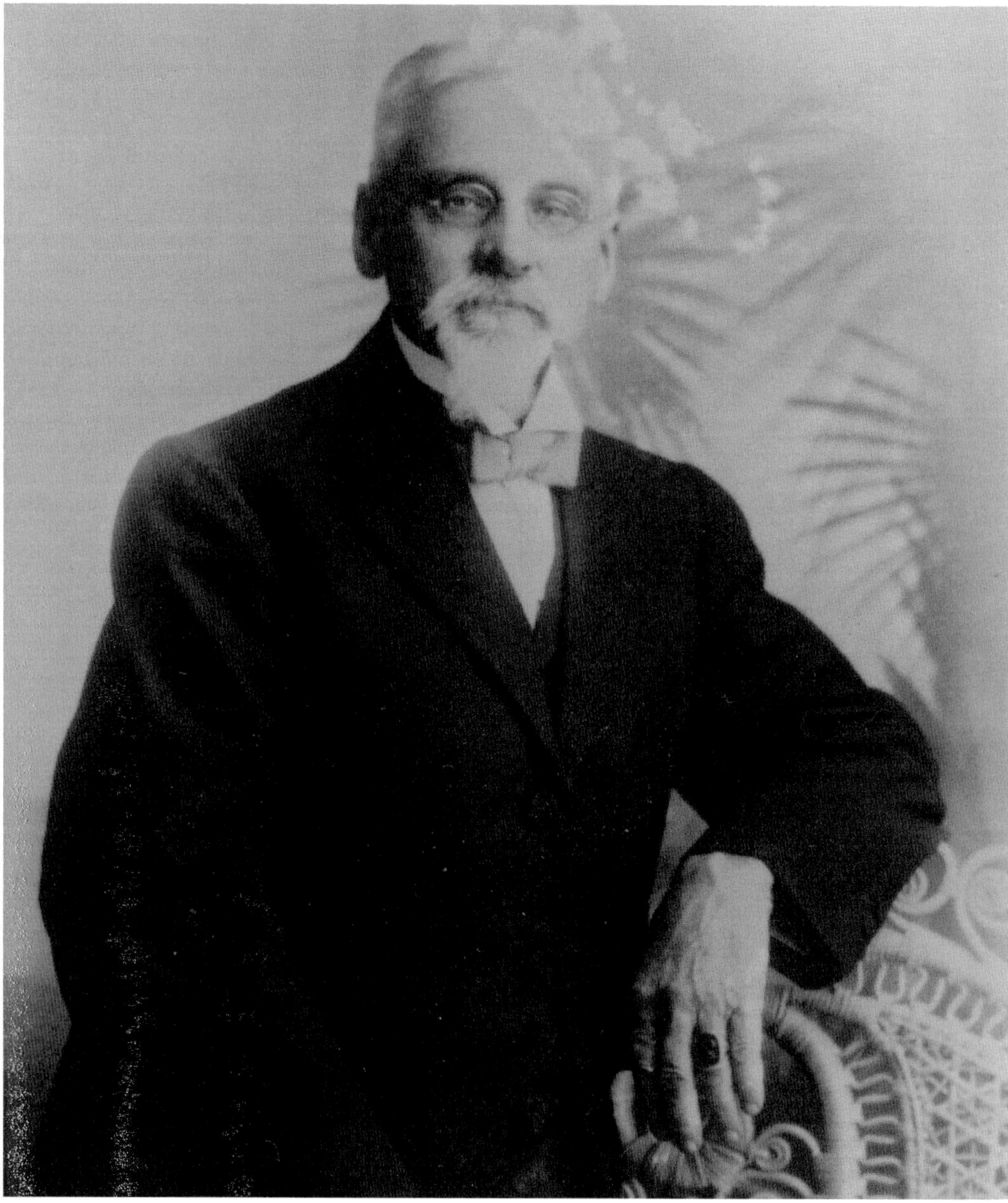

Dr. Jacob E. Brecht

When Brecht and his wife Clara came to Florida in the early 1880s, they became interested in the welfare of the Seminole Indians who remained in Florida after the Seminole Wars. In 1891, the Women's National Indian Association (WNIA) hired the Brechts to live on their reservation, the Old Allen Place. The physician worked as a medical missionary, special disbursing agent, and industrial teacher for the Office of Indian Affairs. After moving to Fort Myers in 1899, he continued to provide the Indians free medicine and legal defense funds. He built a respected practice in town and helped to build Lee Memorial Hospital. Brecht died in 1919. Even in his final moments, the welfare of others was primary. He told attending physician Dr. W.B. Winkler, "Doctor, it is a shame to get you out at this time of night." (Courtesy of SAF.)

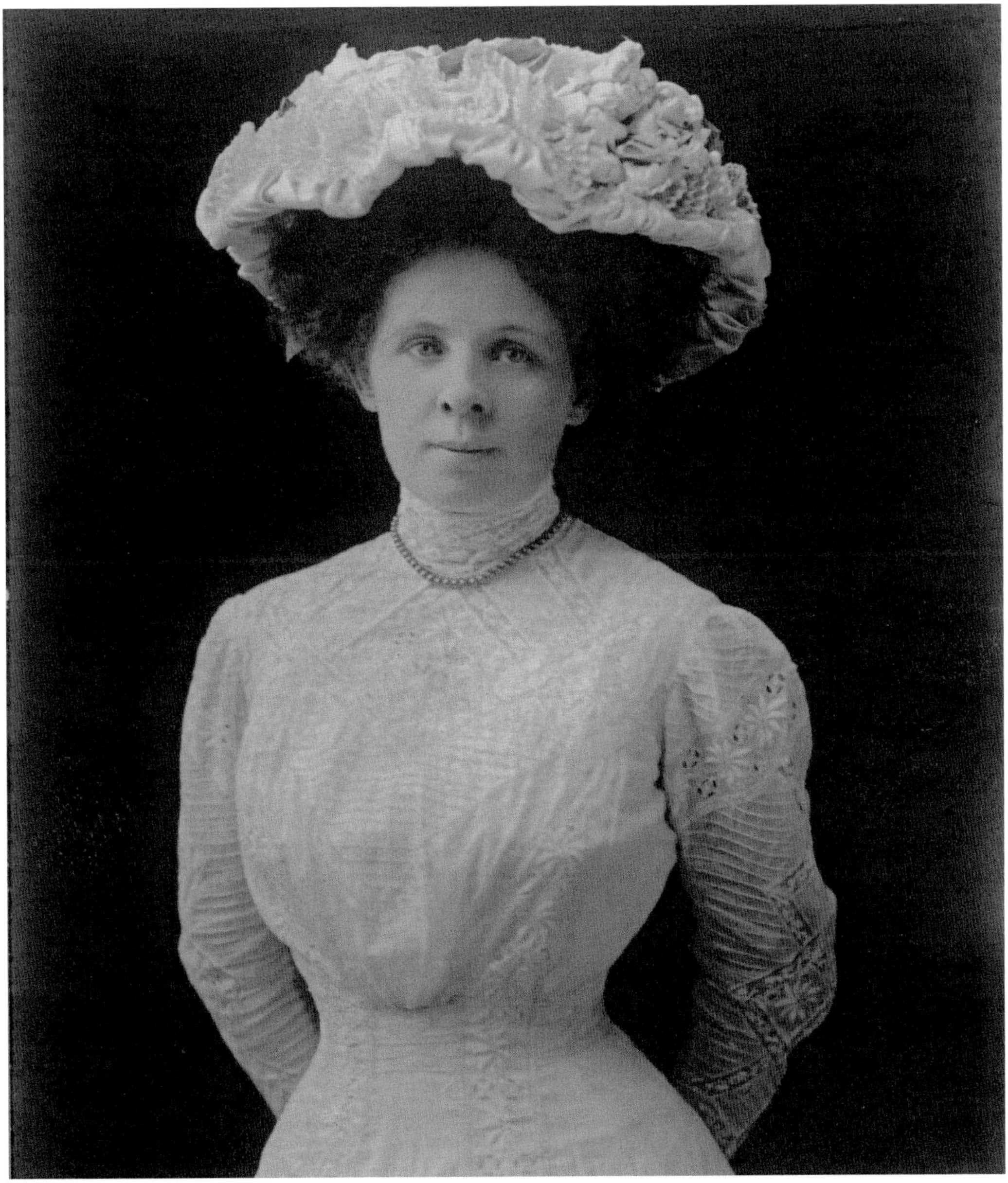

Flossie Hill
"Miss Flossie" opened a downtown women's clothing store in 1905, the year this photograph was taken, and ran it for over 50 years. She understood hard work and entrepreneurship, for she had helped her widowed mother, Mary Hill, run Hill House, founded in 1889. After deciding to start her own business, she lined up investors like Olive Stout, James E. Hendry Sr., and D.S. Borland, and went on a buying trip to New York City, launching the career of one of Fort Myers' most successful and respected businesswomen. She wasn't all business, however. She served on the library and hospital boards, held open houses for British soldiers training in the region, and volunteered at the First Presbyterian Church. She died in 1956 and left the store to her employees of 10 or more years. (Courtesy of SWFHS.)

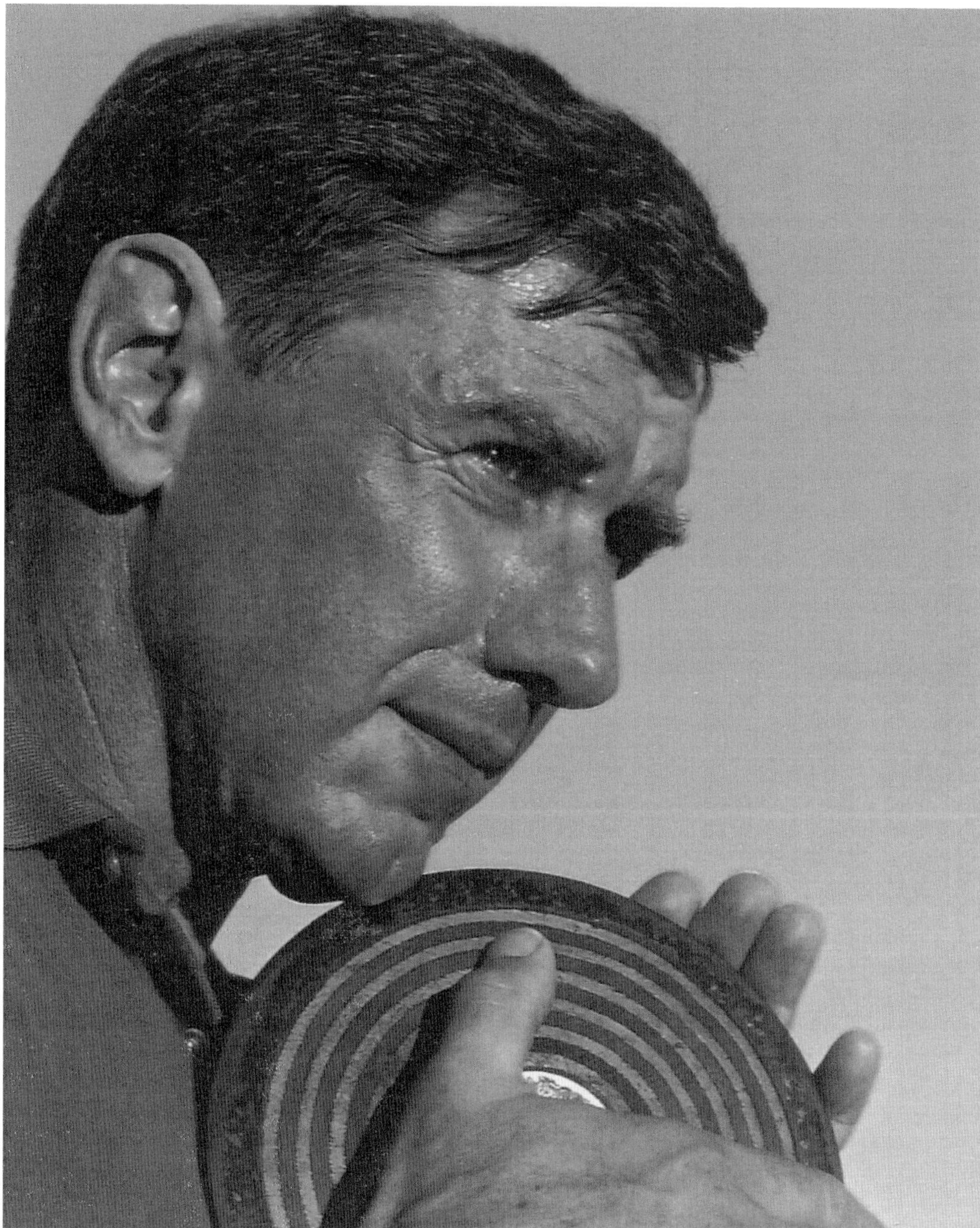

Al Oerter
A four-time gold-medalist, Olympian discus thrower Al Oerter participated in the games from 1956 to 1968. One of the greatest track and field athletes of the 20th century, Oerter also was an abstract painter and was instrumental in establishing Fort Myers' Art of the Olympians Museum. He died in 2007 at age 71. The museum's mission of demonstrating the very real relationship between art and sport to the general public honors the athlete's legacy. (Photograph by Michelle Tricca, courtesy of Cathy Oerter.)

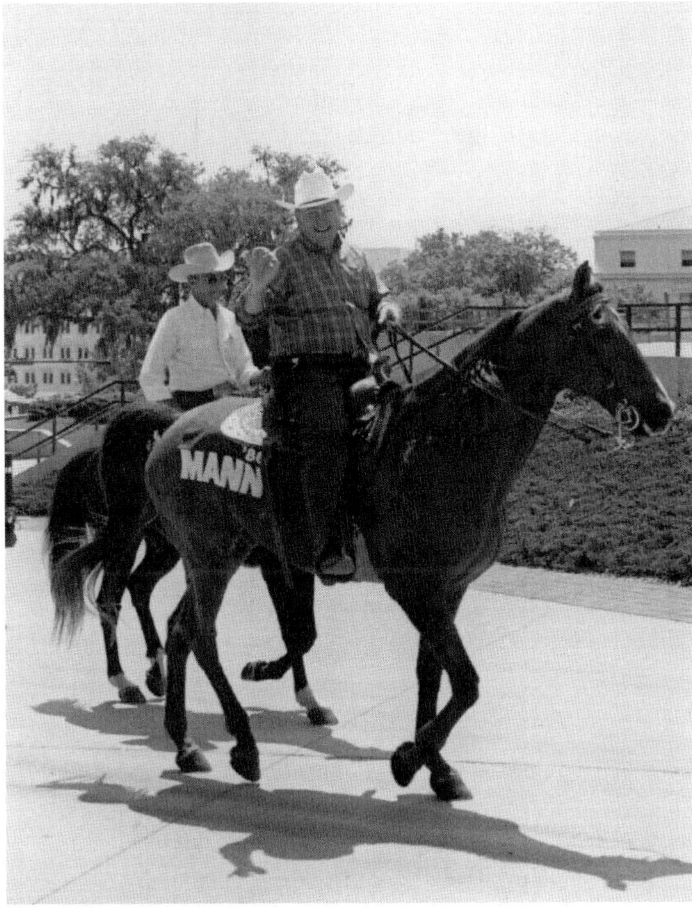

Frank Mann Sr.
When Mann announced his candidacy for governor of Florida in 1985, he literally and symbolically campaigned on a dark horse, which he later rode to Tallahassee. As a state legislator, he served eight years in the House and four in the Senate. In 10 years on the Natural Resources Committee, he championed land preservation. Post-legislature, he served 17 years as chief spokesman for the Association for Retarded Citizens of Florida. He is a Lee County commissioner. (Courtesy of SAF.)

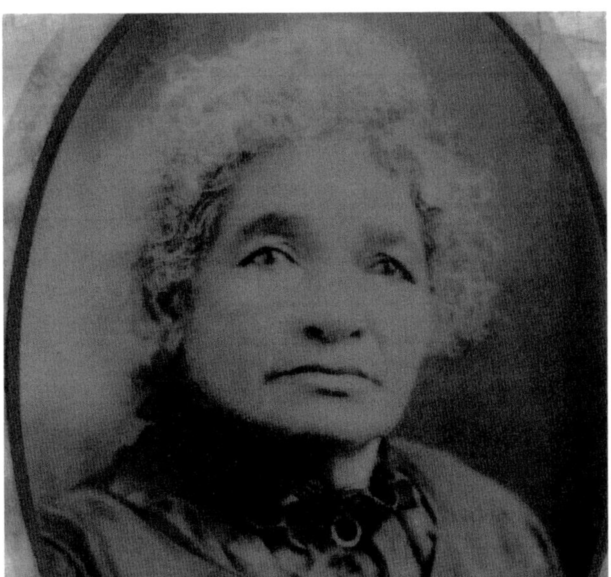

Melissa Jones
Community activist Melissa Jones, along with Candis Walker, spearheaded the effort to establish the first hospital in Fort Myers designated for blacks, Indians, and other nonwhites. Jones-Walker Hospital opened in the late 1920s in the heart of the Dunbar community and was named in their honor. Ivy Posey and Julia Barker also took part in raising matching funds at church and school functions. Once the hospital was built, surgery for blacks was conducted at Lee Memorial Hospital but the post-operative recuperation took place at Jones-Walker. Jones was also active in the black chapter of the Women's Christian Temperance Union. (Courtesy of LCBHS.)

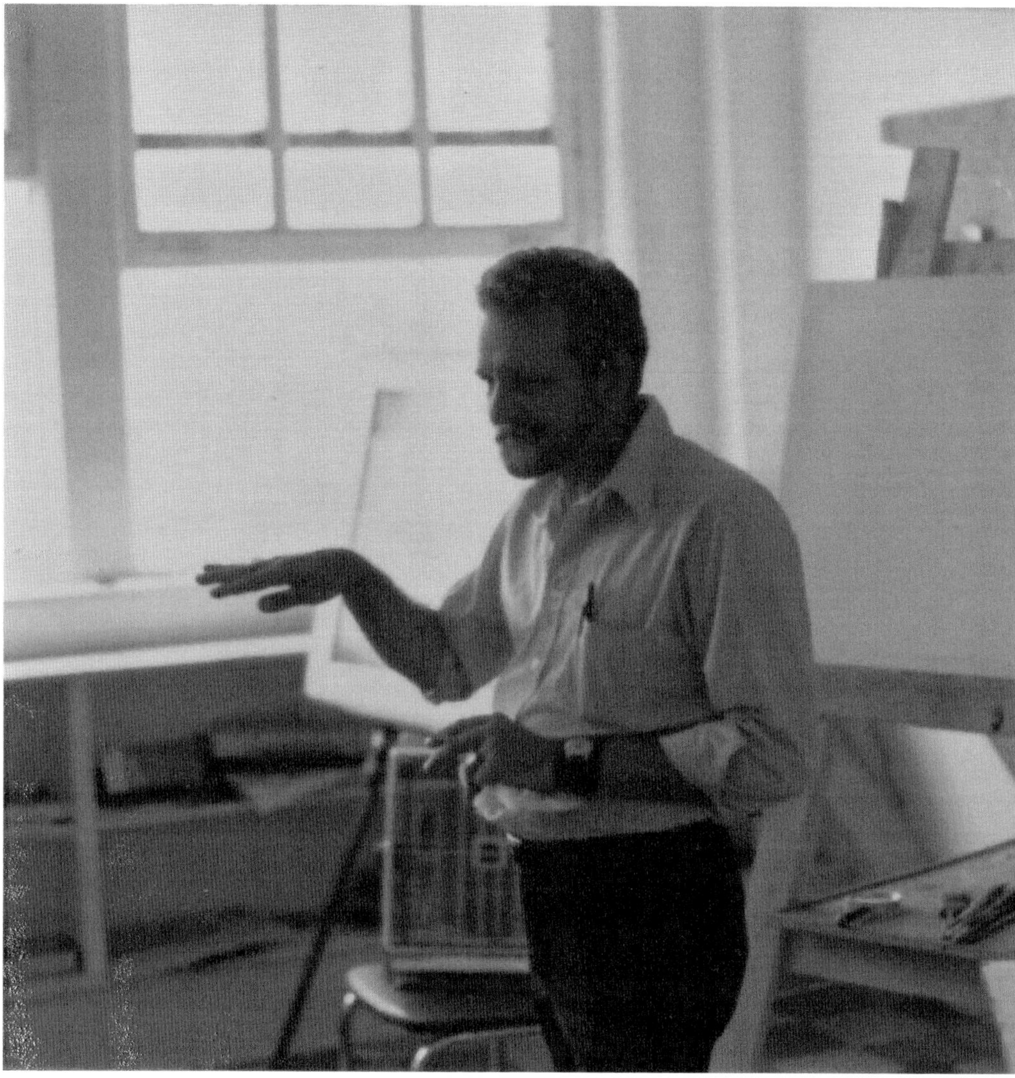

Gale Bennett

Artist, teacher, and music and art critic, Bennett is considered by many to have been Fort Myers' most influential art teacher. He founded the summer ArtStudy Giverny program in 1996 to enable artists to paint in Claude Monet's Garden near Paris, France. He received the Angels of the Arts Artist of the Year award in 2006 and the Lifetime Achievement award in 2008, the year he died at the age of 68. (Courtesy of Greg Biolchini.)

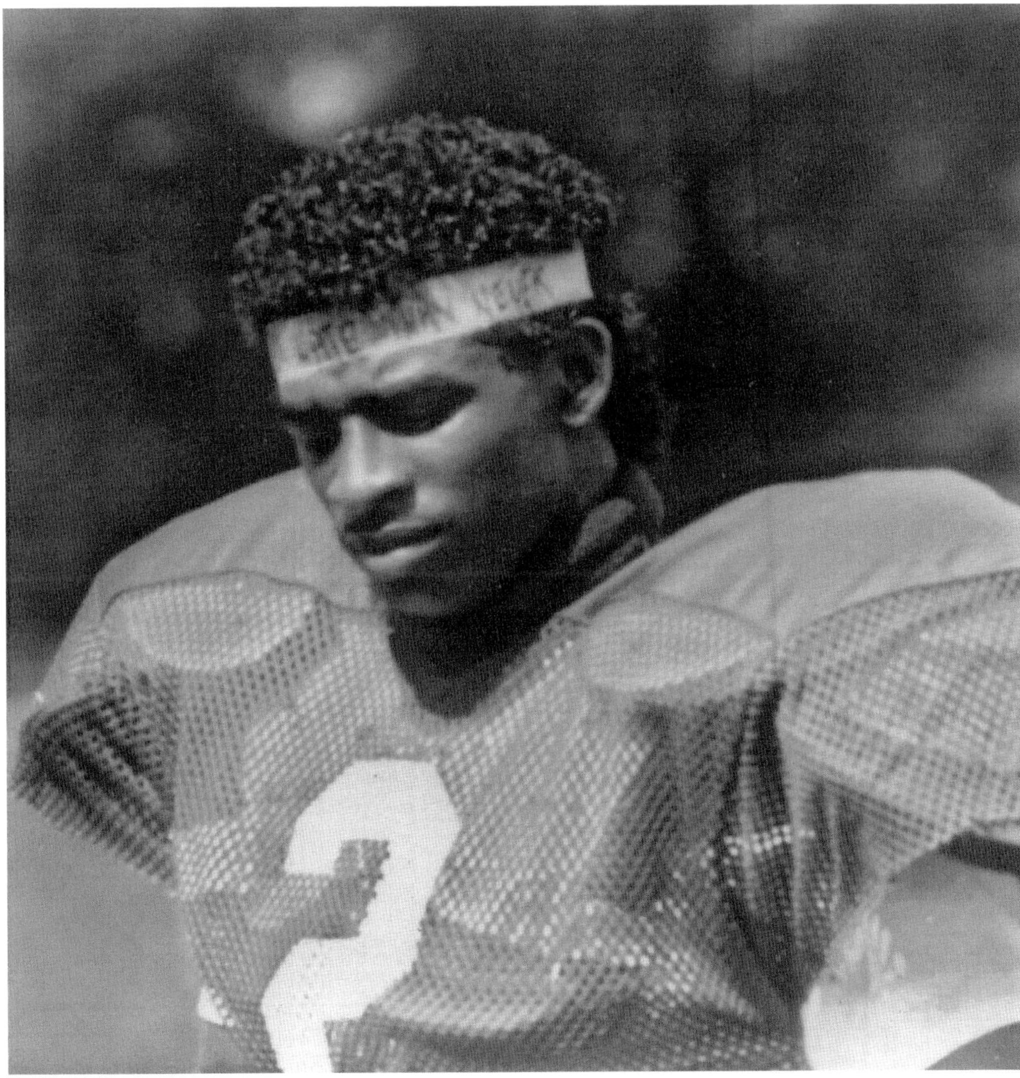

Deion Sanders
A 1985 graduate of North Fort Myers High School, Sanders won the Jim Thorpe Award as the nation's top college football defensive back while at Florida State University. He earned the name "Prime Time," playing professional football for the Atlanta Falcons, San Francisco 49ers, Dallas Cowboys, Washington Redskins, and Baltimore Ravens; and major league baseball for the New York Yankees, Cincinnati Reds, and San Francisco Giants. In 2011, he was inducted into the Pro Football Hall of Fame. (Courtesy of SAF.)

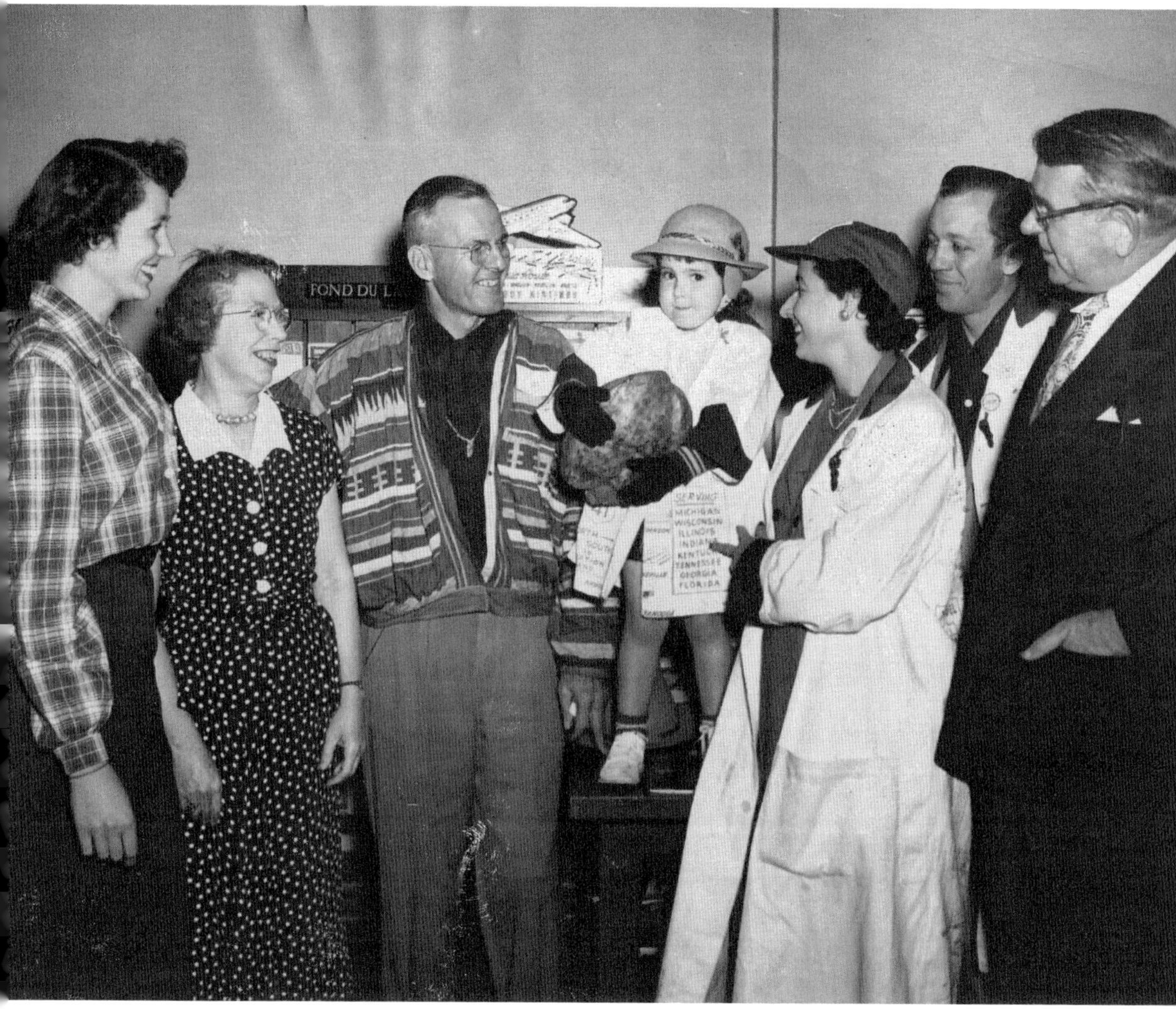

Bob Halgrim

Halgrim came to Fort Myers with his family in 1914. A friend of Thomas A. and Mina Edison, he worked summer vacations in the Edison gardens and laboratory. He left studies at Cornell University to return home and take a permanent job with the inventor. When Mina Edison gave the estate to the city in 1947, she stipulated that Halgrim be supervisor. He was the first curator of the Edison home and museum from 1948 until he retired in 1971. Wearing a Seminole Indian jacket in the photograph, he speaks with a group of unidentified people. In 2005, Cornell University awarded him an honorary certificate for his work at the Edison Winter Home. He died in 2005. (Courtesy of SWFHS.)

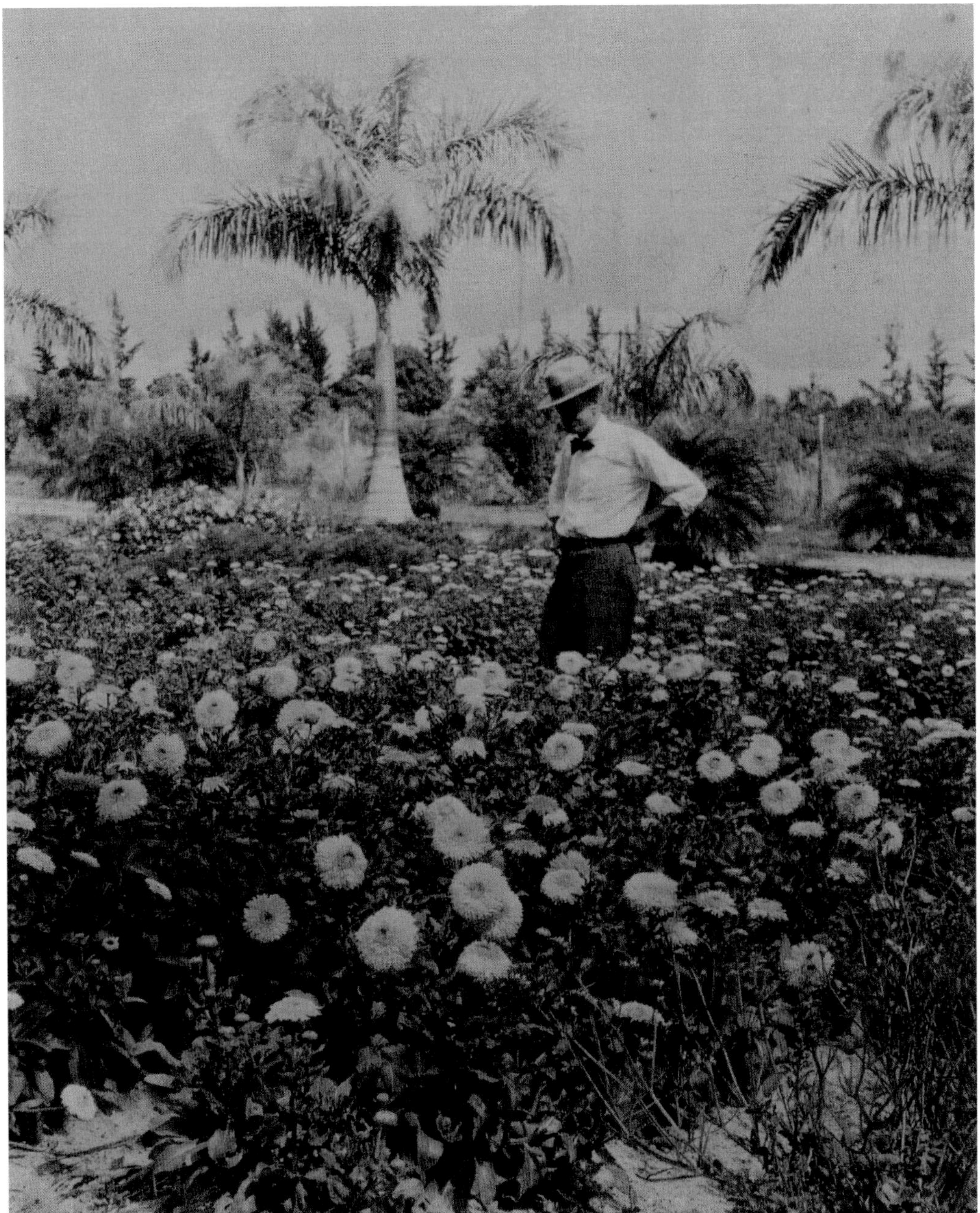

James E. Hendry Jr.
Grandson of Capt. Francis A. Hendry, James E. Hendry Jr. is known for his horticultural work and city-beautification efforts. Instrumental in making Fort Myers the "City of Palms," he founded the Everglades Nursery in 1908 and ran it until he died 47 years later. In 1915, Hendry was appointed to serve on the city's first park board. In that capacity, he oversaw the planting of many streets with the signature palms, only one of his many city-beautification efforts. He was largely responsible for bringing the Seaboard Airline Railway to East Fort Myers in 1927. (Courtesy of SWFHS.)

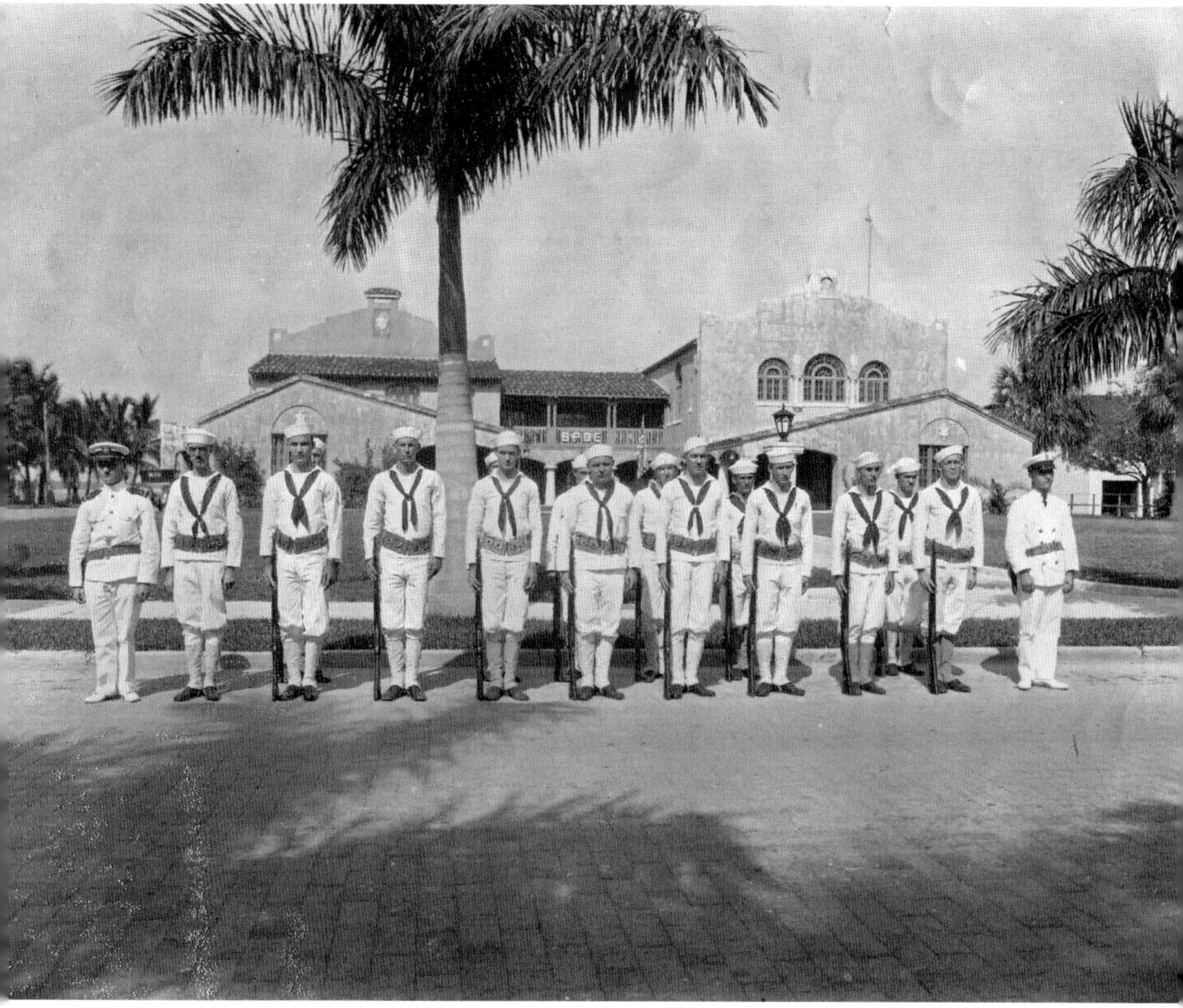

US Naval Reserve Radio Unit of Fort Myers

The US Naval Reserve Radio Unit of Fort Myers stands before the headquarters of the BPOE Lodge No. 1288 on First Street in November 1930. The unit did their part to keep the town secure in times of peace and war, including guarding President-Elect Herbert Hoover in February 1929 when he visited Thomas Edison on his 82nd birthday. From left to right are (first row) Lt. Edgar Sherouse, Carl Johnson, Gorden Perry, Bryan Moore, unidentified, Curtis Davison, Slim Roberts, Tavy Bryan, Joe Kepler, Whittaker (first name unknown), and Cmdr. Bill Grogan; (second row) unidentified, Claire Merchant, Frances Des Rocher, Ernest Hart, Durdin (first name unknown), and Ernest James. (Courtesy of AL.)

BIBLIOGRAPHY

Barnes, Alberta Colcord, and Nell Colcord Weidenbach. *Early Fort Myers: Tales of Two Sisters (Stories of Pioneer Days and Depression Times in a Once-Upon-a-Town Named Fort Myers)*. Punta Gorda, FL: Chris the Printer, Inc., 1993.

Board, Prudy Taylor, and Patricia Pope Bartlett. *Lee County: A Pictorial History.* Virginia Beach, VA: Donning Company/Publishers, 1985. Second printing 1990.

Board, Prudy Taylor, and Esther B. Colcord. *Pages from the Past: A Pictorial Retrospective of Lee County, Florida.* Virginia Beach, VA: Donning Company/Publishers, 1990.

Fort Myers News-Press. Fort Myers, FL.

Fort Myers Police Department: 125th Anniversary, 1885–2010. Evansville, IN: M. T. Publishing Company, Inc., 2009.

Godown, Marian Bailey, and Alberta Colcord Rawchuck. *Yesterday's Fort Myers.* Fort Myers, FL: Press Printing, 1975.

Grismer, Karl H. *The Story of Fort Myers: The History of the Land of the Caloosahatchee and Southwest Florida.* Fort Myers Beach, FL: Island Press Publishers, 1949/1982.

Lee County, Past to Present. 6 Nov. 2010. Southwest Florida Pioneers Historical Society. Accessed 30 Dec. 2011. www.rootsweb.ancestry.com/~flswphs.

Stone, Donald O. *The First 100 Years: Lee County Public Schools, 1887–1987.* Fort Myers, FL: Department of Printing Service, School Board of Lee County, 1987.

INDEX

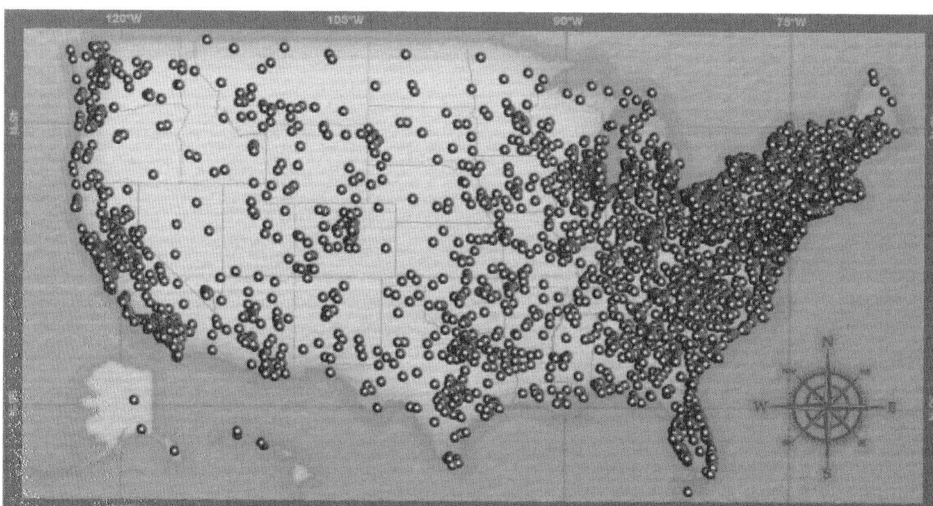

Consistent with our mission to preserve history on a local level, this book was printed in South Carolina on American-made paper and manufactured entirely in the United States. Products carrying the accredited Forest Stewardship Council (FSC) label are printed on 100 percent FSC-certified paper.

MADE IN THE USA